Japan and the North East of England

JAPAN AND THE NORTH EAST OF ENGLAND

From 1862 to the Present Day

Marie Conte-Helm

The Athlone Press   London and Atlantic Highlands, NJ

First published 1989 by the Althone Press Ltd
44 Bedford Row, London WC1R 4LY
and 171 First Avenue, Atlantic Highlands, NJ 07716

© Marie Conte-Helm 1989

British Library Cataloguing in Publication Data
Conte-Helm, Marie T. *1949*—
  Japan and the North East of England: from
1862 to the present day.
  1. North-east England. Japanese companies.
  2. Great Britain. Economic relations, 1862–
1988 with Japan. 3. Japan. Economic
relations, 1862–1988 with Great Britain.
  I. Title.
  338.7′4′09428
  ISBN 0–485–11367–8

Library of Congress Cataloguing-in-Publication Data
Conte-Helm, Marie. 1949–
    Japan and the north east of England: from 1862 to the present day
    Marie Conte-Helm.
        p.   cm.
    Bibliography: p.
    Includes index.
    ISBN 0–485–11367–8
    1. England, Northern——Civilization. 2. England——Civilization——
Japanese influences. 3. Japan——Civilization——English influences.
4. England, Northern——Foreign economic relations——Japan. 5. Japan——
Foreign economic relations——England, Northern. 6. Great Britain——
Foreign relations——Japan. 7. Japan——Foreign relations——Great
Britain. 8. Japanese——England, Northern——History. I. Title.
DA670.N73C66 1989
303.4′82428052——dc19

88–36615
CIP

Typeset by J&L Composition Ltd, 1 Mitford St, Filey, N. Yorks
Printed and bound in Great Britain by
Butler & Tanner Ltd, Frome and London

For Bill and Jessica

Contents

Note on Order and Spelling of Japanese Names

Japanese names are normally presented in the usual order of surname first and given name second throughout the text. The spelling of Japanese names is sometimes reliant on newspapers and other recorded references which may account for unusual romanizations.

Acknowledgements

In tracing the links between Japan and the North East of England, it has been necessary to delve into many fields and into many periods of history. I am very grateful to a great number of people, both in Japan and in the UK, who have assisted me in this process.

To the Great Britain-Sasakawa Foundation and to Donald Warren-Knott, its UK administrator, particular thanks for enabling me to pursue my research in Japan. To Professor Kita Masami, I extend my thanks for the many contacts which he provided during my stay. Professor Nakagawa Keiichiro and Professor Yui Tsunehiko were most helpful as were the staff of Shiryo Chosa Kai in Tokyo and the *Mikasa* Preservation Society. My thanks to Mr Kanamori Tadashi for sharing his enthusiasm for Japan's naval history and to Mr Shinohara Hiroshi for his generosity and assistance in locating sources and photographs. In researching NYK's links with the North East, I was assisted, in the UK, by Mr A. Sugawara and Mr Leslie and, in Japan, by Mr M. Yonesato who kindly provided photographs and other materials which have been invaluable to me in my research.

Of the many people in the UK who have provided assistance of various kinds, I must extend a special thank you to Mr Oba Sadao for the generous help he has given me over the last few years. My thanks also to Joe Clarke for his advice on North East shipping, to Olive Checkland for access to material on Thomas Glover, and to Suzuko Neary for help with last-minute translations. I am grateful to Frank Manders and Trish Sheldon of the Local History Department of Newcastle Central Library for access to photographs; to the Chief Archivist of the Tyne and Wear Archives Service and his staff for their assistance; and to the Science Museum (Newcastle), Sunderland Museum and Art Gallery, Newcastle Literary and Philosophical Society, Middlesbrough Central Library, and HMS *Calliope* for further favours. My thanks to Mrs Laila Spence for access to Amie Noble's *Memoirs* and to Rosemary Rendel for permission to quote from the *Rendel Papers*. A further acknowledgement is due to Vickers Defence Systems for permission to quote from the *Armstrong Papers* and especially to Peter McKenzie for help with photographs. I would also like to thank the following organizations/ individuals who have similarly provided photographic material for this book: the National Trust; Middlesbrough *Evening Gazette*; *Sunderland Echo*; Newcastle *Journal* and *Chronicle*; Japanese Saturday School at Washington; David Hughes (Furness Museum); Ian Neary; and Mrs Sanderson. A particular thank you to the Washington Arts Centre for photographs and material relating to the 1986 Japanese Festival.

One of the most fascinating dimensions of my research has been tracing the history of Middlesbrough's early Japanese community. This would not have been possible without the tremendous interest and help of Tommy Doi who introduced me to this chapter of Middlesbrough's Anglo-Japanese past and enabled me to meet Akiyama Taichi before his death in 1986. Tommy has given me access to family photographs and papers as have other descendants of Japanese seamen including Roy Betsho, Diane Furihata, Robert Ikeshita and Tamako Akiyama. My thanks to them all.

I am grateful to the Japanese Embassy (London) and to former Ambassador Yamazaki for allowing me to photograph the Oguiss paintings in the Ambassador's residence. Thanks are also due to Nissan Motor Manufacturing (UK) Ltd, Komatsu UK Ltd and Tabuchi Electric UK Ltd for assistance with photographs and to all of the other Japanese companies in the North East for allowing me access to information in researching the latter chapters of this book.

My thanks to the Northern Development Company for access to data on Japanese companies and to Chris Fraser, especially, for information and guidance on inward investment from Japan. I am similarly indebted to Ed Robson of Sunderland Borough Council for his advice on the text and provision of photographs and other materials. To Sunderland Polytechnic, I must register my particular thanks for their continued support of my research and for providing me, through the Japanese Studies Division, with the vehicle to do that which I most enjoy doing.

A very warm and special thank you to Mrs Caroline Pennington, a former student, who has been of such great assistance in tracing newspaper sources and following up so many small details on my behalf. I am similarly grateful to my secretary, Elaine Obee, for her help and cheerful support throughout the writing of this book.

There are two further individuals to whom particular thanks are due. Professor Norman McCord has read the text in its entirety and I am grateful to have had the benefit of his advice and access to his considerable knowledge of North East history. Richard Tames has, as a historian and a friend, also read the full text and has generously and helpfully contributed something of the clarity of his own teaching and writing style in his comments and suggestions.

My final and most complete thanks are to my husband, Bill, whose guidance, encouragement and support have been constant from the first stages of research to the writing of the last lines. I am very certain that this book would not have been written without his steady influence and good cheer.

The author and publisher gratefully acknowledge the support of the Midland Group in the publication of this book.

Foreword

By the Rt. Hon. the Lord Jenkin of Roding,
Chairman of the UK-Japan 2000 Group

There is always a risk when one comes fresh to a subject of which one knows little, that one's 'discoveries' are not equally new to everyone else. My involvement with UK-Japan relationships goes back only a few years, so that I am for ever 'discovering' what others, much better versed than I am in the subject, have known for many years.

Marie Conte-Helm's book, however, recounts a story which will be new to almost everybody. Of course, even the most superficial student of Japanese history knows that Admiral Togo beat the Russians at sea in 1905 with a fleet largely built on the Tyne. And, of course, anyone who has followed the progress of inward investment into Britain by Japanese companies knows that Nissan is not only the largest Japanese investment in Britain; it is the largest Japanese investment in Europe. Yet, how many people know significantly more than that about the Japanese involvement in the North East? Yet, by recounting in fascinating detail the dramatic ups and downs of Japanese involvement in the North East, she has not only produced a most interesting piece of local history; she has succeeded in shedding a flood of light on the entire process which brought Japan from the feudal isolation of the Tokugawa Shogunate to the influential role she plays on today's world stage.

It is not, of course, the whole story, for that would fill many volumes. But it is a very revealing succession of events, episodes and personalities; because she has set them in the particular context of the North East of England, she has succeeded in illustrating the wider theme with great vividness. Her detailed accounts, for instance, of the Japanese determination to catch up with the West in defence, in the advancement of her manufacturing industry, and in the development of an indigenous capacity to make what they could only import, were for me a revelation.

It is not easy for the observer today, acutely conscious of Japan's successes in beating us at our own game, to understand why our forebears were so liberal with their technology, so ready to demonstrate their skills, so willing to pass on their expertise to their enquiring Japanese visitors. Here and there, there is evidence of a contractual provision intended to protect the intellectual property of the British firm; but the general picture is of British shipbuilders, engineers and manufacturers, supremely confident in the superiority of their technologies, only too pleased and proud to demonstrate that superiority to the Japanese. What else might they have done, offered as they were a glittering prospect of an endless succession of lucrative orders, generating thousands upon thousands of jobs and millions of pounds of profits? Today, when the boot seems to be so firmly on the other foot, those who wish to learn from the successes of the Japanese in conquering one international market after another, expect to pay full value for any information and technology transferred.

Marie Conte-Helm's story falls naturally into three distinct phases. The first covers the sixty years from 1860 to 1920, the heyday of the British pre-eminence in shipbuilding, coal-mining and heavy engineering. This co-incided with the determined search by a Japanese nation, bent on rapid modernization, for the best of Western experience on which to model themselves. Perhaps the apogee of this phase of British-Japanese relations was the 1902 Alliance which placed Britain firmly at the forefront of Japan's trading partners.

The second phase saw the collapse of this relationship in the rising militarism of Japan in the 1920s and 30s, culminating in Pearl Harbor, perhaps one of the darkest moments of World War II.

The third period covers the 35 years from the Coronation of Queen Elizabeth II, the first official event of consequence, after the war, to which the Japanese were invited to send a Royal personage, and the present day when each year sees more and more Japanese firms, keen to establish factories in the European Community, choosing Britain as their base.

Marie Conte-Helm entitles her concluding chapter 'A Relationship Reversed?' – and I have to say that I believe that the question-mark is wise. There are, in fact, few parallels between the Japanese search for rapid modernization in the first of those three phases and the Japanese response to the world trading scene in the third. Not only are the technologies vastly different; so are the motivations both of the British and of the Japanese; and so is the impact upon the local populace in Britain. Nevertheless, it is striking that when the Japanese Ambassador, attending a Japanese cultural festival in the North East in 1986, recalled the warmth of that nineteenth century relationship between the people of Newcastle and Sunderland and their Japanese customers and apprentices, he struck deep and responsive chords. History is *not* bunk and it is to the author's great credit that, by unfolding such a detailed tapestry depicting, in a local context, an important and eventful period in British-Japanese relations, she sees this as a continuum; the past has undoubtedly influenced the present and will influence the future.

To the modern student of international relations it is the more recent history which catches the attention. Writing after a TUC Conference which saw the Electricians' Union expelled for insisting on the right to enter into Single Union Agreements, I find it instructive to learn that it was the Amalgamated Engineering Union which signed a Single Union Agreement with the Japanese bearings manufacturer, NSK, as long ago as 1976. Or again, it is worth being reminded that it was the combination of opposition by the UK television industry and its Trade Unions which persuaded a very luke-warm Labour Government to discourage the Hitachi Company from establishing a Colour Television Factory at Washington a year or two later. A Granada Television documentary on this subject started with a sequence showing the image 'of a Japanese industrialist swinging a golf club fading into a samurai warrior wielding a sword'. If that attitude had prevailed, many thousands now in work in the North East would still be unemployed!

Perhaps I may be forgiven for expressing a particular interest in the events which led to the establishment of Nissan's factory at Washington. When I was appointed Secretary for Industry in September, 1981, although the fact that Nissan was examining a proposal that it should site a European car factory in the UK had already been made public, the Company had not yet reached a decision. I met the representatives of Nissan on many occasions both in London and in Tokyo. I became deeply impressed by the thoroughness with which they were looking at all the options and by the efforts they were making to resolve the differences within the Company about the wisdom of the project.

Initially, my negotiations were with Mr Okuma Masataka, Executive Vice President of Nissan, Mr Kawai Isamu, a Nissan Managing Director, and Mr Goto Mitsuya, their Senior United Kingdom Representative. There were many issues to be resolved, but two of the most important centred around the terms of any Government support by way of Special Financial Assistance and the level of local content which the factory would reach as it progressed through the various stages of expansion. It became apparent to me that while the team led by Mr Okuma were becoming more and more enthusiastic, and that they enjoyed the support of his immediate superior, Mr Ishihara, there were still serious doubts in Tokyo, where the Company's

Chairman Mr Kawamata and the head of the principal Trade Union, Mr Shoiji, still believed that expansion would be best at home and not overseas.

I well remember a particular evening when Mr Okuma had come to London with the unwelcome news that, contrary to his hopes, he was not yet able to announce any progress towards a decision. Though this was disappointing, I nevertheless hosted a Dinner at Brown's Hotel for him and his team at which I expressed to him our complete understanding of the difficulties he faced, our readiness to await the Company's decision and our confidence that in the end his own vision and enthusiasm would be vindicated. To my surprise and consternation, Mr Okuma was so overcome by emotion that he found it difficult to respond. It would have been tempting to have played a much rougher game and to have capitalized on their difficulties. Nevertheless, I am convinced that patient understanding was much the best tactic and this was vindicated by the extremely positive and friendly meeting I had a month or two later with Mr Kawamata in Tokyo.

I did not lose touch with the venture when I moved to the Department of the Environment. In Britain, we have a Secretary of State for Scotland and a Secretary of State for Wales, but there are no regional Secretaries of State in England. For better or for worse, this role falls to the Secretary of State for the Environment. The Company had not yet decided precisely where it would locate its factory and the final choice fell between two Special Development Areas, one at Shotton in North Wales and the other on the site of the old Sunderland Airport at Washington, Tyne and Wear. In Wales, there is the Welsh Development Agency with a range of special powers; in the North East of England there was the North of England Development Council, the Washington Development Corporation, and the local authorities, notably Tyne and Wear County Council. For central government, however, in contrast to Wales there are only the Industry Act Powers. At a very critical moment in the decision making process, it came to my ears that, contrary to undertakings given to the Treasury, there was evidence that Wales was concocting an additional incentive to entice Nissan to Shotton. The North East made a fuss, I made a fuss, and we were supported by the Prime Minister (who has always had a soft spot for the North East). The Welsh Secretary of State, Nicholas Edwards MP (now Lord Crickhowell) agreed that the extra incentive should be withdrawn, so that Nissan could make its choice on the basis that the incentives would be the same at both locations.

This proved crucial and in the event Nissan chose the North East, a triumphant conclusion to a very hard fought campaign on the part of all the local agencies. I have no doubt that the management of Nissan regards the choice they made as the right one and they have certainly backed their decision with formidable amounts of investment in buildings, plant and human resources. Given the long Japanese involvement with the North East, it was in my view entirely right that that region, which had not yet succeeded in attracting its fair share of inward investment, should get the Nissan plant.

There is one other footnote to add. When the time came for the official opening of the Nissan Plant, it became public knowledge that the Prime Minister had been invited to perform the ceremony. There was some attempt in the House of Commons on the part of Northern Labour MPs to say that she would not be welcome and that it was an impertinence for her to take credit for the jobs that Nissan would bring when, since 1979, there had been so many jobs in heavy industry lost. Outside the Chamber, I drew the attention of the principal objector to the very substantial efforts Mrs Thatcher had made to persuade the Nissan Company to invest in Britain, and to the support she had given me when I insisted that Wales should not be allowed to offer more than the North-East. I am happy to say we heard no more of that rather foolish piece of politics!

Marie Conte-Helm's book throws light on a number of other matters which are of concern to the UK-Japan 2000 Group of which I have the honour to be Chairman. There is the question of education and whether it is right to expect the children of Japanese staff simply to attend the local schools in the area where the family is based. Some of the difficulties are well described in the book, as well as some of the solutions. The problem of re-entry when the family returns to Japan is a very real one and although the Japanese education system is currently undergoing a substantial reform, it will be some years before children who spend several critical years abroad are not placed at a disadvantage when they compete for University places at home.

The 2000 Group has expressed general support for the concept of establishing special schools in the host country for the children of families from the other country. There are now several such Japanese schools in Britain and steps are being taken to establish a British school in Tokyo.

There is the problem of language teaching. It has already been recognized that there is substantially too little teaching of the Japanese language and of Japanese studies in British Universities and some increases are already being made and more are being demanded. No less important is the case for extending the availability of Japanese language teaching at other higher and further education establishments. Marie Conte-Helm teaches at Sunderland Polytechnic, but I have no doubt that the advantage to Britain would be significant if more higher and further education students could be taught basic Japanese so that when they go to Japan they could quickly extend their ability to speak and understand the language and so help to cement relations between the countries.

This is a valuable book, the product of a great deal of painstaking research, and with a wealth of fascinating illustrations. I am very happy to commend it to all those who are concerned to strengthen the ties between our two countries and to promote wider contacts. It will be of particular interest to all who are or will become involved with Japanese investment in Britain. An understanding of the past is almost always helpful in trying to understand the present and predict the future. Marie Conte-Helm's book is a worthy addition to the range of books on Japan which the Athlone Press has published in recent years.

Introduction

Much has been written of the relationship between Japan and Britain over the last hundred years. Japan's reopening to trade in the 1850s brought her into the sphere of British interests in the East and it was with British assistance and technology that the rapid metamorphosis from feudal empire to modern state took place.

Comparisons were early drawn between the two island nations who each relied so heavily on the sea for protection, commerce and trade. As the relationship intensified in the latter years of the nineteenth century, Japan was hailed the 'Britain of the East' and Britain's image was set in the mould of Victorian achievement and success.

The role played by different regions of Britain in this larger process has not yet been fully assessed. Japan, the eager pupil looking for guidance to the West, chose her models carefully and well; among them, the North East of England with its reputation for coal-mining, shipbuilding and heavy engineering attracted her attention and respect. The goal of military modernization, so important to the nation's 'coming of age', led a steady stream of Japanese ministers and naval officials to the region that would become identified with the 'making of the Imperial Japanese Navy'.

Ships and the sea formed a constant backdrop to Japan's relationship with the North East over these years. Each of the region's rivers contributed to its growth: the warships built on the Tyne carried Japan to victory in the Russo-Japanese War of 1904–5; the merchant ships built on the Wear aided in the development of her trade and commerce; and the lengthy association of NYK's European Line with Teesside fostered international trade and social intercourse.

If the story of Japan's relationship with the North East of England began with trade and the transfer of technology, it has today come full circle. The twenty-three Japanese companies currently in the region are building a new reputation for the North East as one of Europe's most important centres for inward investment from Japan. NSK Bearings Europe Ltd was the first such company to establish a manufacturing base in the area in 1976. The arrival of Nissan Motor Manufacturing (UK) Ltd in Sunderland in 1984 has played an important part in reorientating interests to Japan. Representing the largest single investment by a Japanese company in Europe, Nissan's car plant has contributed to regional revival and to the attraction of other companies from the East. It is estimated that by 1992 Japanese investment will total almost £728 million and will have created 7300 jobs. In local parlance, the launching of ships has given way to the launching of Japanese companies, with Nissan seen as the 'flagship' of Japanese investment in the North East.

Today's economic partnership provides yet another reflection of the earlier relationship with Japan in the interplay of societies and cultures to which it is giving rise. The presence of Japanese workers and families in the North East is, like Japan's erstwhile presence in the region, serving to challenge mutual images and adjust perspectives. While the consequences of such interaction cannot be so finely measured or foreseen as the material impact of inward investment, the growth of knowledge and awareness is an accumulative process which must be valued in an increasingly interdependent world.

My own path to the North East has been almost as circuitous as that of Middlesbrough's early residents from Japan. As a post-graduate student at the East-West Center of the University of Hawaii in the 1970s, I was introduced to the 'lifestyle' rather than the concept of intercultural exchange. I left the Japanese Embassy in London for a teaching post at Sunderland Polytechnic in 1979, thinking my involvements with Japan were to be geographically severed. Since that time, I have been fortunate to have the opportunity of participating in another phase of East-West exchange in a region which shares so many historic associations with Japan.

This book has been written in an attempt to record the history of a relationship which is of growing significance to Japan and the North East of England. Its audience should extend well beyond the region, however, to those parts of Britain and other countries which have particular involvements with Japan. For the Japanese, it raises issues which are central to the internationalization debate and the common interests of two island nations. For students of Japan, it illustrates – through the experience of the North East – wider facets of Anglo-Japanese relations in the last century. It is, finally, a tribute to the echoes of the past in the present and to the reciprocal ties which continue to link this region of Britain with Japan.

1 Victorian Britain and Meiji Japan: The North East Dimension

On 26 May 1862, a reception committee gathered at Newcastle upon Tyne's Central Station to greet Britain's first official envoys from Japan. The party of twelve Japanese 'ambassadors' who alighted from the London train had travelled north to the heartland of British industry. How appropriate, then, that the Mayor and other civic dignitaries should be there to meet them. The dark, sombre morning suits of the city fathers contrasted with the 'silk tunics' and 'Chinese straw hats' of the eastern visitors and served to highlight sartorially the very different worlds that these men usually inhabited. Represented by each group was a culture distinct from the other and a history and traditions which knew no common ground.

Japan in 1862 was a nation on the brink of change. For over 200 years, one government (that of the Tokugawa Shogunate) had held the reins of power, controlling the lives of its citizens through a policy of seclusion that had been strictly enforced since 1639. A feudal state, Tokugawa Japan was divided into some 250 domains or *han*, each headed by its own lord or *daimyo* who owed allegiance to the Shogun. The Shogun was the supreme military ruler of Japan and the Bakufu was the central government over which he presided at Edo (modern-day Tokyo).

Japan's warrior class, the samurai, adhered to a code of honour (*bushido*) which has been likened by many writers to the conduct and chivalry of Europe's medieval knights. From the twelfth century, this military élite wielded great influence and commanded loyalty and respect from both retainers and commoners. The long and short sword of the samurai came to symbolize the power and the martial values which were central to the tiered society that was Tokugawa Japan. While Japan's samurai class represented a military élite at the core of government, their soldiering function, through two centuries of peace, became somewhat eroded in the light of their growing bureaucratic responsibilities. They aided in imposing the Shogun's authority through many forms of censorship and state control.

Travel was strictly regulated in Tokugawa Japan; indeed, ships larger than fifty registered tons were not allowed to be built – a material restriction on contact with the outside world. This, like so many other facets of life, would change as western nations, looking for another trading partner in the East, turned their eyes towards Japan.

While seclusion had bred a stable society, it quickly became clear that Japan in the 1850s was an antique culture which could not compete technologically or militarily with the West. Like Rip Van Winkle, Japan had slept peacefully through a century of industrialization in the West. Her sleep was broken by the arrival of the American Naval Commander, Matthew Perry, and his squadron in Uraga Harbour on 8 July 1853. America, a new Pacific power, wanted a coaling station on the route to China and, eventually, trade with Japan. The Japanese procrastinated. Perry underlined his message by returning with a larger force in February 1854. In the face of western military might, Japan, that proud samurai nation, was persuaded to yield. A subsequent British mission headed by Lord Elgin in 1858 was also successful and treaties were concluded with the major European powers to regulate the opening of Japan's ports to foreign trade.

These were fascinating years in Japan. The first British diplomats and traders to settle in the 'treaty ports' were provided with a 'through-the-looking-glass' experience. For many, Japan was not only different and exotic but a pre-industrial society that fuelled the national penchant for nostalgic reflection. When J. W. Murray described Japan's Tokaido highway in the 1860s, he wistfully focused on the lack of modernity, seeing in Japan a reflection of England as she once was. Murray wrote:

> There is no traffic on the roads of a nature likely to cut them into ruts, or necessitate their frequent repair.
> There are no carriages, public or private of any sort in Japan – no rattling teams of fast horses with heavy 'Busses' behind them – no coaches with emulative whips trotting along at an exhilarating pace – such a profession as a Post-boy is unknown! The echoes of the lovely dells, of which there are many on the Tokaido, are never roused by the cheering sound of the Guards horn, the remembrance of which still suggests to ancient lovers of the days of posting in England the wish, that stage coaches in their glory had not been superseded by the

rapid whirl of the railway engine – foot passengers and horses, shod alike with shoes made of straw, or coolies carrying goods and norimans or native chairs are the only traffic taking any wear and tear out of any road.[1]

Japan in the 1860s, however, was also a decidedly dangerous place for British and other foreign residents to be. Witness poor Mr Richardson, in Yokohama on leave from China in 1862, and out with a riding party. Their failure to give way to a passing *daimyo* and party of samurai from the Satsuma clan led to Richardson's bloody demise. The diplomatic crisis and the bombardment of Kagoshima in August 1863 by the British fleet that followed this assault on a civilian symbolized once and for all the values old and new, East and West, which were coming into direct conflict as Japan opened her doors to the West. One year later, a further naval attack was mounted against the Choshu clan for their hostility to foreign ships passing through the Straits of Shimonoseki. Eight British ships supported by French and Dutch corvettes and an American steamer resorted once again to force to keep the Straits open to trade.

There were many different views as to how Japan should deal with the unwelcome but unavoidable foreign presence from the late 1850s. Sakuma Shozan, a samurai of Matsushiro in Shinano, whose lord was placed in charge of coastal defence, coined the slogan, 'eastern ethics, western science'. He did not favour foreign contact but, as early as 1842, argued that only the purchase and production of western-type armaments could ensure Japan's successful self-defence.[2] The Bakufu was slow to heed the warnings of men like Sakuma but particular *daimyo*, as with the leaders of Satsuma and Choshu, responded in kind to the threat posed by British and other foreign warships. Such pragmatism would be witnessed in various fields before the end of the century as Japan took up the challenge of catching up with the West.

In January 1862, a British ship left Japan carrying a Bakufu mission of some forty men to Europe – its purpose, to persuade the European treaty powers to postpone temporarily the opening of further treaty ports until the unrest caused by the existing foreign settlements had subsided. Britain signed the agreement on 6 June 1862 (postponing the opening of further ports until 1 January 1868) and Russia, France and Holland followed later in the year. The party's stay in Britain coincided with the opening of the International Exhibition (1 May 1862) in South Kensington which they attended. Featured among the exhibits was Sir Rutherford Alcock's collection of Japanese art, amassed during his time as the first representative of the British government at Edo. The artefacts exhibited at South Kensington

The Japanese Ambassadors at the International Exhibition (1862).
These 'dark-haired sons of the mysterious East' travelled to
Newcastle upon Tyne on 26 May 1862 to observe North East
coal-mining technology (*ILN*, 24 May 1862).

made up the first public display of Japanese art to appear in Britain. They
served too as a reminder of the land and the traditions from which these
visitors stemmed. On 26 May, part of the Bakufu group boarded a train for
Newcastle upon Tyne on a very different kind of mission. They were set on
observing those aspects of North East industry that had a relevance to the
future of the new Japan.

The North East of England in 1862 was on the threshold of its great age of
prosperity and industrial importance. The region's reputation rested on coal-
mining, and it was coal that proved to be the crucial ingredient in the development of new industries in the second half of the nineteenth century.
Output from the Great Northern Coalfield had risen from some 4.5 million
tons to around 10.5 million in the first half of the century while jobs within
the industry increased from approximately 12,000 to 40,000. These
increases had a necessary impact on commercial facilities for the sale and
shipping of coal, port and dock facilities, and the expansion of the wooden
sailing collier fleet, an important segment of Britain's merchant marine.[3]
North East coal had a ready market in London but the high output of the
coalfield also contributed to the growth of heavy coal-using industries in the
region. Hence, through the expansion of coal production, the North East
gave rise to engineering works and shipbuilding concerns which would, in
the second half of the nineteenth century, greatly widen its industrial base.

In 1852, the Palmer's Shipbuilding & Iron Company on the south bank of the Tyne at Jarrow launched the first iron screw-steamer, the *John Bowes*, which was to transform the coal carriage trade overnight and inaugurate the age of iron shipbuilding. Within ten years, the Jarrow yard was turning out 22,000 tons of shipping per year.[4] Other firms followed Palmer's lead and the North East rapidly rose to shipbuilding pre-eminence.

The city of Newcastle upon Tyne was and remains the region's capital. A city with Roman and medieval roots, Newcastle underwent many physical changes in the nineteenth century. Factories sprang up along the River Tyne, parts of which were widened to handle the larger flow of traffic and commercial activity. From 1850, the Tyne Improvement Commission set a series of major port improvements of this order in motion. The medieval bridge crossing the Tyne gave way to an iron road-and-railway-bridge and, most dramatically, in 1876, a hydraulically-operated swing-bridge.

The North East played a crucial role in the evolution of railway transport in the first half of the nineteenth century. Wagon ways extending from collieries to shipping points had been developed to facilitate the movement of coal. In themselves, they represented a prototype for the more sophisticated railway networking that would evolve later in the century. Such early pioneers as the Stockton & Darlington Railway (1825) and the Stanhope & Tyne Railway (1834) certainly drew on the experience and technology of these colliery wagon ways. The development of railways in the North East brought about a great reduction in coal transport costs. Passenger-carrying, it should be remembered, was a later and unforeseen development.

By 1850, Newcastle had become the nexus of the regional passenger service with Newcastle Central Station serving London-bound and other

The Central Station, Newcastle upon Tyne, designed by John Dobson, has been described as 'one of the best in England'. This engraving shows it at about the time of the Bakufu mission's visit to the city in 1862.

extra-regional travellers. That the railway line cut right through the bailey of the medieval castle from which the city took its name is perhaps a comment on the relentless march of progress in the early-Victorian period. John Dobson, the leading local architect, was responsible for the railway station (1846–50), described by Nikolaus Pevsner as 'one of the best in England'[5] and certainly among the largest nineteenth-century buildings in Newcastle. Its sweeping arches and majestic facade would come to symbolize to newcomers the supreme self-confidence of the Victorian age and the proud prosperity of Newcastle upon Tyne, an eminently Victorian city.

The group which alighted from the 4.40 p.m. London train on 26 May 1862 were not the sort of travellers that the people of Newcastle had come to expect in these early years of railway transport. The party of twelve Japanese, accompanied by the Edo legation officer, John MacDonald, and several others, was beginning a two-day visit of historic import. It was to mark the start of Japan's relationship with the North East of England, a relationship that would grow and prosper in the coming years. The Japanese ambassadors had come to the North East specifically to observe coal-mining in the region and, consequently, the second day of their visit was spent at the recently opened North Seaton Colliery. The chief ambassador and five of his party went down the mine, showing great interest in the various operations observed. While there were sources of coal in Japan, mining activity was at a very basic stage in the 1860s. If the Japanese had come to the North East because of the region's reputation in this field, the Newcastle press was not over-modest in surveying the wider strengths of the locality. The *Newcastle Daily Journal* (27 May 1862) posed the question:

> And to what part of the country which is better
> calculated to show them these [industrial sensations]
> could they go than to our own neighborhood? Here in
> the cradle of the locomotive and the railway system; in
> the home of the High-Level Bridge; in the birthplace of
> the hydraulic engine and the Armstrong gun; and in the
> great centre of the coal trade, where works for the
> manufacture of lead, iron, and glass rise up on every
> hand – where, with one exception, the largest ships in
> the world have been built, and where alone, in England
> the beauties of Continental Street architecture are
> worthily rivalled, the illustrious party whom we
> entertain today will find the real secret of England's
> greatness among nations. They may not find much of the
> picturesque or the beautiful about it; but they will, at

least, see that it is noble and useful and, with their
Eastern acuteness, they will not be slow in learning the
great fact, of which we may all be proud, that it has only
been by dint of hard work of hand and head that our
country has attained to her present pre-eminence; and
that those who seek to rival or excel her must do so, not
by launching ships of war or building forts, but by
treading in her own footsteps, and legitimately trying to
outvie her in the paths of peace and industry.

The sentiments were proud, moralistic, and, with hindsight, prophetic.
The Japanese emissaries had entered a world in which 'eastern ethics,
western science' was no match for the full sway of Victorian values.

That Japan was so little known in the 1860s certainly accounts for the
curiosity with which the Bakufu visitors were received. Culture shock was
no doubt experienced on both sides as Japanese and Novacastrians crossed
paths for the first time. Informal aspects of the stay in Newcastle included
an expedition to the Theatre Royal where the melodrama *Peep O'Day* and
the farce *Nursery Chickweed* were viewed, though not necessarily understood.
The Japanese visitors nevertheless responded eagerly to 'the enthusiastic
cheers which greeted their appearance from all parts of the house'.[6] For a
nation just recently emerged from over 200 years of isolation, such forays
into not just western culture but idiosyncratic Victorian theatrical forms
must have produced extreme bewilderment. The social implications of
technical transfer cannot always be assessed with any accuracy but there are
hints and resonances in various accounts of the worlds that were blending.

Despite the anti-foreign feelings in Japan at this time and the average
Briton's almost total lack of knowledge of that distant land, the Bakufu
mission seems to have been a diplomatic success in both its official and
unofficial capacities. In the course of their stay in England, various centres
of industry were visited. The Japanese, it can be safely said, when not
arguing for the postponement of the opening of the 'treaty ports', focused
their attention on coal, ships and guns. These three elements would form
the basis of their continuing dialogue with the North East of England.

The itinerary for the Bakufu party included several excursions to the
Royal Arsenal at Woolwich to observe the casting and fitting of Armstrong
guns. The intense interest manifested by the group in the sophisticated
weaponry was such that they reportedly, 'lingered over the operations in the
gun-factory as if under some spell, wholly regardless of the fierce heat from
the furnaces to which they were often exposed, and they left the place with
evident reluctance'.[7] Indeed, John MacDonald, the legation officer who
accompanied them, noted the surprised reaction of observers at Woolwich

Choshu interference with foreign vessels led to the bombardment of
their gun batteries in the Shimonoseki Straits in September 1864.
The British ships, with their Armstrong guns, drove home to the
Japanese the full implications of modern naval armament
(*ILN*, 19 November 1864).

to their total absorption in the production process: 'No visitors among our
own countrymen, or foreigners, had displayed such earnest and untiring
interest, even in the most minute detail connected with the manufacture of
the Armstrong gun, as the Japanese.'[8] The Bakufu visitors were also given
the opportunity to witness the effectiveness of the Armstrong 100-pounder
and of other guns of a smaller bore at a target practice at Portsmouth
Dockyard.

The agreement postponing the opening of Edo, Osaka, Hyogo and
Niigata until 1 January 1868 was signed in London on 6 June 1862. Their
business concluded, the envoys returned to a Japan beset with internal
conflict. An attack on the British legation in Edo that same month was
followed in September by the Richardson incident and the bombardment of
Kagoshima. In September 1864, Choshu interference with foreign vessels
led to the bombardment of their gun batteries in the Shimonoseki Straits.
This was to provide a more dramatic demonstration of Armstrong guns in
action. In reporting the battle, the *Illustrated London News* (19 November
1864) pointed to the impact made by the superior armament of the British
ships:

> The first shots were fired by the corvettes and instantly
> returned. For about twenty minutes, the Japanese fire
> was very lively; but when the light squadron took part in
> the conflict, and the two frigates, presenting their
> broadsides, opened with their great guns, most of the
> guns on shore were soon silenced.

According to Ernest Satow, the young British diplomat who was present
during the action, the Japanese guns were dated 1854 and had been cast in
Edo.[9] The allied squadron moved on to the forts at Hakusima on 6 September.

It was suggested, however, that 'the successes of the previous day and the play of the Armstrong guns induced the occupants of these forts to retire'.[10]

The Choshu, like the Satsuma clan, had early realized the importance of acquiring modern ships and up-to-date weaponry. After conceding defeat, the Choshu leaders turned their full attention to the British ships that had fired on them, all of which were fitted with Armstrong guns. The 100-pounder breech-loading gun on the *Euryalus* was particularly advanced compared with Japanese armament. In his account of the peace settlement, Satow was to remark upon the delight of the bumboatmen 'with the novel and wonderful sight' as they were shown over the ship.[11] The conflict at Shimonoseki drove home to the Japanese the full implications of modern naval gunnery. As for the Choshu leaders, they showed a willingness to learn from defeat that stood them in good stead in the pro-Imperial and anti-Bakufu troubles that were brewing in Japan.

Two Choshu samurai, Ito Hirobumi and Inoue Kaoru, had been smuggled out of Japan to study in London in 1863, returning before the Shimonoseki incident. Ito, in particular, would play a key role in the new government formed after the fall of the Tokugawa Shogunate and the restoration of Imperial rule in 1868. As the powerful Choshu and Satsuma clans joined forces in the 1860s, the Bakufu government was steadily weakened by its failure to deal satisfactorily with the foreign presence.

The 3rd of January 1868 witnessed the anti-Bakufu coup led by Choshu and Satsuma forces which ended the long rule of the Tokugawa and

'Inside the Lower Battery at Simonosaki (sic) after the Conflict'. According to Ernest Satow, the young British diplomat who was present during the action, the Japanese guns were dated 1854 and had been cast in Edo (*ILN*, 24 December 1864).

launched the fruitful years of the Meiji era (1868–1912). When the new government was formed, leading Choshu and Satsuma clansmen took on the responsibility of bringing Japan into the modern age. The victors' slogan – *fukoku kyohei* ('enrich the country, strengthen the army') – had earlier been put into practice in their own territories but, from 1868, the former samurai would be applying this ideology to the country as a whole.

It is perhaps one of the most striking ironies of Japan's modern history that the anti-foreign movement of the 1860s which brought about the downfall of the Shogunate should give rise to a new form of government in 1868 that embraced all things western in the years that followed. Many reforms were instituted. Most significantly, in August 1871, the Emperor announced the abolition of the feudal domains and the disbanding of domain armies. In one fell swoop, the central government took on the full responsibility of military leadership. The war department of the executive council formed in 1869 was, in 1872, divided into separate army and navy departments. As the domains had been broken up in 1871, the position of the samurai, Japan's traditional military élite, was likewise affected. Samurai lost the right to use their swords 'on the lower orders with impunity' and, indeed, were 'permitted not to wear a sword at all'.[12] By 1876, new legislation banned the wearing of swords entirely, a more than subtle change in policy. Japan was fast becoming a modern state and at the heart of this lay a new-style military establishment which took its impetus from western models.

The samurai monopoly on bearing arms and the privilege this entailed were finally abolished with the adoption of a policy of military conscription in 1872. The pride associated with the military life became, as in the West, a national pride as opposed to the regional and dynastic loyalties engendered by the old feudal system. Education played an important part in this democratization of society. A compulsory system of primary education, replacing the *terakoya* of the commoners and the *han* schools, was instituted in 1872, ensuring a basic educational standard for all Japanese citizens.

Crucial to the changes taking place in Japan in the 1870s was the impact made by the visit of the Iwakura mission to Europe and America in 1871. Feelings ran high in Japan over the 'unequal treaties' signed with America, Britain and various European nations in the 1850s. The extraterritoriality clause dictating that foreigners committing crimes in Japan could not be tried in Japanese courts was a particular bone of contention, especially as Japanese abroad were subject to the jurisdiction of foreign courts. The political motivation behind the Iwakura mission was, therefore, the revision of the 'unequal treaties'. A further motivation was the acquisition of more knowledge about western institutions, industries and culture. The

The fact-finding Iwakura Mission to America and Europe left Japan in 1871. The new-style ambassadors from Meiji Japan travelled to the North East of England in October 1872 (International Society for Educational Information, Tokyo).

party of nearly one hundred men which left Yokohama in November 1871 included some of the future architects of Japan's modernization programme. Among them were Iwakura Tomomi, Minister of Foreign Affairs, and Ito Hirobumi, Vice-Minister of Industry. Students, secretaries and interpreters accompanied the envoys and facilitated the close observation and recording of information that made the visit such a success. The delegation returned to Japan in September 1873 but, in the eighteen months spent touring the major cities of Europe and America, a great deal of information was accumulated which would be directly applied to the remodelling of Japan. The mission did not achieve its political goal (the 'unequal treaties' would not be revised until 1894) but, in its fact-finding capacity, it was to prove invaluable to the nation's progress.

The Iwakura mission arrived in London in August 1872. Division into smaller groups enabled the party to cover sufficient points of interest across the country. In this way, the cities of Liverpool, Manchester, Glasgow and Edinburgh were visited before the eastern visitors, accompanied by Sir Harry Parkes, Britain's Minister to Japan, arrived in Newcastle upon Tyne on the evening of 21 October 1872. The Royal Station Hotel provided accommodation for the Iwakura ambassadors and it was there that they were met the following morning by Sir William Armstrong, owner of the Elswick Engine and Ordnance Works. It had been ten years since the Bakufu mission came to Newcastle to observe local industry and here, once again, was a delegation from Japan eager to learn from the West.

During their stay in the North East, members of the Iwakura Mission visited Gosforth Colliery where 'the plans and the workings were minutely examined' (Newcastle City Libraries).

In the intervening decade, Japan had undergone a dramatic change of government. The appearance of the Iwakura ambassadors served to underline the transformation of society that had been set in motion. According to the *Newcastle Daily Chronicle* (23 October 1872), 'The gentlemen were attired in ordinary morning costume and except for their complexion and the oriental cast of their features, they could scarcely be distinguished from their English companions.' These new-style envoys were to be guided through Tyneside by Sir William Armstrong, inventor of the Armstrong gun and one of the most famous industrialists ever to have emerged from the North East of England.

Armstrong was a lawyer-turned-industrialist who also made his mark as an inventor. Perhaps the combination of a legal mind, business sense and imagination accounted for his tremendous ingenuity and success in so many endeavours. His reputation was early established for his work in the field of hydraulic engineering. In 1847, W.G. Armstrong & Company was established some one-and-a-half miles west of Newcastle on the Elswick Estate. The manufacture of hydraulic cranes, accumulators, mining machinery, together with other general engineering work was undertaken in the firm's early years. It was, however, his development and improvement of the breech-loading gun during the Crimean War (1853–6) which set the course of his future career. When Armstrong guns were adopted for service in the field in 1858, Armstrong generously released all his patents to the government and was rewarded in 1859 with an appointment as Engineer of Rifled Ordnance to the War Department. He also received a knighthood and, nine months later, was appointed superintendent of the Royal Gun Factory at Woolwich, a post which he still held at the time of the Bakufu visit of 1862. Meanwhile, Armstrong guns continued to be manufactured at Elswick but under the auspices of a newly formed company, the Elswick Ordnance Works, in which he had no financial interests. From the period of its formation, the Elswick Ordnance Works was pledged not to supply guns to any other government though, after Armstrong's resignation from his government appointments in February 1863, this situation altered. In 1867, an agreement was signed between Armstrong and Charles Mitchell who owned the Low Walker shipyard, a few miles down the Tyne from Elswick. Through their collaboration, new ships would be built at the Walker yard and armed at Elswick.

This, then, was the state of Armstrong's 'empire' and his career when the Iwakura mission made its tour of the North East. Armstrong guns were certainly known of in Japan from the early 1860s. In 1865, Armstrong's factory on the Tyne received an initial order for guns and ammunition from Thomas Glover, the British merchant acting as agent for Jardine Matheson & Company in Nagasaki. Thirty-five muzzle-loading and breech-loading guns and 700 tons of ammunition were ordered on behalf of the Bakufu with the possibility of considerable future business from Japan held out to the firm.[13] As Glover showed no particular preferences in dealing with the Bakufu or pro-Imperial domains in his pursuit of trade, he may also have supplied Armstrong guns to the Satsuma and other *han* during this same period.[14] In meeting the man behind the Armstrong gun in 1872, Japan's new government leaders established a more personal link with the sphere of North East industry which could best aid in her military modernization.

The five-volume journal of the Iwakura mission, kept by their chief secretary Kume Kunitake, was filled with detailed observations on the state of western industry. Kume was particularly well suited to recording the mission's impressions of the Elswick Engine and Ordnance Works for he

On 22 October 1872, the Iwakura party toured Sir William Armstrong's Engine & Ordnance Works on the Tyne. Their interest in the manufacture of Armstrong, Gatling, and various other types of guns was considerable (The *Journal* and *Chronicle* Photo Library).

hailed from Saga, one of the more progressive Japanese *han* that was early committed to experiments in industry, armaments and shipbuilding.[15] Thus, in his account, the Armstrong factory is minutely and eagerly described, in terms of both its products and its methods of manufacture.

At Elswick, the Japanese party was joined by Captain Andrew Noble and George Rendel, joint managers of the company. Noble was a gunnery expert and Rendel was responsible for the shipbuilding and armaments side of the business. The morning was spent inspecting hydraulic engines, the erecting and fitting departments, bridge shop, turning and boring shops, and the various stages of manufacture of the Armstrong, Gatling and other types of guns. This visit began a dialogue which would result in many future orders from Japan.

Coal-mining was another area of North East industry which the Iwakura ambassadors, like the 1862 Bakufu representatives before them, wished to observe. Mining technology was of increasing importance to Japan in her own industrialization and the developing coastal trade with China. The Japanese visitors were, therefore, escorted to the Gosforth Colliery where several of the party, supplied with woollen jackets and leather skull caps, descended into the mine. According to the *Newcastle Daily Chronicle* (23 October 1872), 'The plans and the workings were minutely examined, and a large amount of information was conveyed to the Japanese, who seemed most desirous to learn all the details connected with mining operations.'

Later in the visit, Ito Hirobumi, accompanied by R. Henry Brunton, Engineer to the Japanese government, toured the Bolckow & Vaughan Iron Works at Middlesbrough (on Tees) and the Cleveland iron-ore mines. The prospering iron industry on Teesside provided yet another model for the Japanese to follow.

The Newcastle and Gateshead Chamber of Commerce arranged for a full exploration of the river Tyne and its facilities. The Japanese were conducted on a river tour which included the inspection of the New Tyne Bridge and 'several of the most interesting manufactories'[16] on the banks of the Tyne including the Tharsis Sulphur and Copper Company near Hebburn and the Jarrow Chemical Works. At Hebburn, they visited a lead-manufacturing firm where, according to Kume's account, they 'asked various questions but could only receive satisfactory replies from those persons actually in charge of a particular operation'. Kume went on to comment about the division of labour in European factories, concluding that, 'One man cannot master everything as with chemistry, science, the theoretical, and the practical. So, therefore, it is better to apply the division of labour. That is why European industry is so advanced.'[17]

It may seem surprising that this tour did not incorporate visits to any of Tyneside's important shipyards. The Palmer Shipbuilding and Iron Company then owned large shipyards on both banks of the Tyne. There were, in addition, Andrew Leslie's yard at Hebburn and the Armstrong-Mitchell yard at Wallsend, among others. In the early 1870s, however, the Japanese still looked to the North East for coal and increasingly guns but associated the South of England with ships and naval training. Excursions had already been made by the Iwakura party to Southampton, Portsmouth and Greenwich, prior to their arrival in Newcastle. The North East coalfield and Armstrong guns brought them to the region but the role played by Armstrong and his managers must have been important in attracting future Japanese naval and merchant shipping orders away from the South.

Armstrong himself clearly impressed the Japanese visitors. He was sixty-two years old in 1872 and was described by Kume as 'taller than seven "shaku" [approximately one foot per "shaku"] and of mild demeanor'. He spent a great deal of time with the ambassadors, accompanying them on their tours of factories and other sites during the days and entertaining them well in the evenings. They dined with him at his house in Jesmond and also visited a private planetarium in Newcastle in his company after the day's business was accomplished. One imagines that a man with the intellectual curiosity and inventiveness of Armstrong would have struck a particular chord with the members of the Iwakura mission, all of whom were avidly in pursuit of knowledge. They showed their appreciation by subsequently sending a gift, described by him as 'two large and remarkably fine Japanese porcelain vases – the finest by far that I have ever seen'.[18] As the ambassadors returned to Japan, Armstrong was already developing new ideas and contemplating the further expansion of his 'empire'.

Makino Nobuaki, a student-member of the Iwakura mission who went on to become a statesman, wrote in his memoirs that 'Together with the abolition of the *han*, dispatching the Iwakura Mission to America and Europe must be cited as the most important of the events that built the foundation of our state after the Restoration'.[19] Certainly, from 1873, Japan's new leaders who shared in the experience of the mission embarked upon a policy of modernization and liberal reform that was built upon a foundation of western knowledge. The implicit realization that, if the 'unequal treaties' were to be revised, Japan must first prove herself a 'civilized' nation, capable of competing on an equal footing with the West, prompted a race towards progress which made Britain's Industrial Revolution seem, in comparison, a very long and drawn-out process indeed.

How did Meiji Japan modernize so rapidly? The process has fascinated many historians. Among them, the significance of the Iwakura mission as an impetus to change is readily acknowledged. While the representatives from Japan returned home in 1873 with a great deal of factual information about the nature of western industry, manufacturing processes and the acquisition of skills, they had also tapped into the history of western institutions and the philosophical, ideological and cultural underpinnings of Victorian economic success. This deeper layer of social values was more difficult to penetrate and, some felt, was not transplantable to Japan. The issues surrounding westernization were many and complex.

While the debate continued, Japan launched into the serious business of effecting economic and social change. The judicial system underwent a lengthy process of redesign under the influence of French and German law. In education, a western-style curriculum was blended with an eastern-style moral education. New technology was applied to agriculture. Manufacturing industry was developed along western lines with silk-reeling and cotton-spinning plants started in the 1870s. By 1880, the government owned fifty-two factories, three shipyards, ten mines and five munitions works.[20] Such was the level of direct government involvement in the modernization process, which was further aided by the development of railways, cable links and a new postal service.

The visible manifestations of progress and westernization multiplied as European-style buildings and western dress became the necessary adjuncts to economic reform. The changing face of Japan was matched by an increasing interest in all things western from the 1870s. Samuel Smiles's *Self-Help* (1859), published in translation as early as 1871, remained a best-seller for years. By 1880, translations of other western authors from Defoe to Rousseau were available. The culture which underlined western economic success was embraced and applied to the Japanese context.

The rapid modernization of Japan after 1868 would not have been possible without the involvement of the *yatoi* or 'government foreign employees'. In the Meiji period as a whole, the Japanese government employed more than 3000 foreigners as advisers, instructors and technicians in a number of different government ministries.[21] Even before the Meiji Restoration, in the period from 1854 to 1868, some 200 foreign technological and language instructors were hired by the Bakufu and regional *han*. The Dutch were responsible in these early years for building docks and factories, naval training in Nagasaki, and a naval school in Kobe. In the mid-1860s, the French helped to train Japanese in ship construction and repair through their dock-yard and workshop projects at Yokohama and Yokosuka. Some thirty British technicians were employed by the *han* from the mid-1860s to contribute their skills to various burgeoning industries such as mining and textiles.

With the Meiji Restoration, more co-ordinated schemes evolved for developing technology and industry, and the *yatoi*, employed by the central government, became a crucial ingredient in the training of Japanese to new roles. The British engineer, R. Henry Brunton, who accompanied Ito Hirobumi to Middlesbrough in 1872, served as chief of lighthouse construction in Japan from 1868 to 1879. He was an employee of the Public Works Ministry under Vice-Minister Ito and one of the many Britons hired by the Japanese government. The British represented one-half of all foreign nationals employed and two-thirds of those allocated to the Public Works Ministry which sponsored 'major technological projects and model industries'.[22]

Along with the hiring of *yatoi*, the Meiji government adopted a policy of encouraging Japanese to study overseas with the same goal in mind, that of expediting the modernization process. Overseas students from Japan had ventured into Europe and America in the pre-Meiji period (some supported by their *han*) but almost all of these travelled surreptitiously and without government approval. In 1868, there were six Japanese students in Britain while, in 1871, the number had risen to seventy-one.[23] After that, the numbers declined as the system of overseas study at government expense was abolished due to reforms in the Japanese education system and the employing of *yatoi* at home. From 1875, however, a loan system was instituted which increased opportunities for overseas study and raised the calibre of students.

Shipbuilding and naval training were areas, both at home and abroad, to which the Japanese turned their attention as a modern Japanese navy evolved from the coastal defence forces of the *han*. In the period from 1876–7, 42,133,774 yen was expended on overseas students by the Navy Ministry, more than was allocated for this purpose by any other ministry over the same years.[24] Naval architecture was taught by British instructors in Japan. In fact, it was the last subject to be taught in English at university level.

Fukoku kyohei – 'enrich the country, strengthen the army' – was an apt slogan for early Meiji Japan. Each confrontation with the West, from the arrival of Commodore Perry in 1853 to the bombardment of Shimonoseki over ten years later, spoke of an unequal relationship which the Iwakura mission hoped to resolve through close study of the opposition. Western military might had compromised the Bakufu leadership. Only in some of the more far-sighted domains had the importance of a military build-up been acknowledged. With the establishment of separate army and navy ministries in 1872, individuals from some of these same domains found themselves officially responsible for military modernization, a task which they relished and assumed with the full support of the Meiji government. When the Navy Ministry was formed, it had seventeen ships in its possession (totalling almost 14,000 tons), of which only two were ironclads. By 1894, the fleet consisted of twenty-eight modern ships (totalling 57,000 tons) and twenty-four torpedo boats.[25] The twenty-two years in between marked a period of intensive technology transfer in which Britain was to become a primary source for Japanese naval development.

Sir Harry Parkes, the British Minister to Japan who accompanied the Iwakura mission on their tour of Britain in 1872, had earlier attempted to undermine the influence of the Dutch and the French over Japanese naval matters. He insisted, for example, that a military mission instigated by the French Minister Leon Roches in 1866 be counterbalanced by a British naval mission that same year. Admiral Tracy was sent from Britain but the mission, arriving on the eve of civil war, had little impact. In the internal conflict that led to the fall of the Shogunate, the British sided with the pro-Imperial forces while the French aligned themselves with the Bakufu. Cancellation of all military and naval missions followed the Meiji Restoration of 1868 but, in 1870, the Japanese decided to adopt a British model for their new navy and a French model for their new army. Between 1871 and 1873, a programme gradually evolved for the employment of foreign instructors which led to British officers taking full charge of all training within the newly formed Navy Ministry. The British naval uniform was copied with some small differences, the ranking system of the Royal Navy made its way into the Imperial Japanese Navy, and the concept of the 'officer and gentleman' readily merged with the spirit of *bushido*. Britain, then, at the time of the Iwakura mission's stay in Europe, had already become the sole model for Japan's new navy.

In 1873, Commander Archibald L. Douglas arrived in Japan to head the British naval mission. He stayed for only two years and the mission, as such, was dissolved in 1876. British instructors, however, continued to be employed in large numbers through 1878–9. Out of a total of 215 foreign workers employed by the Navy Ministry between 1868 and 1900, 118 were British.

While Japan was spending massive sums on training and dockyard developments during these years, it was not until approximately 1914 that she would take on the full burden of naval construction. In the last decades of the nineteenth century and into the twentieth, most larger vessels for the Imperial Japanese Navy and merchant marine were built in foreign shipyards, and Britain, the source of Japan's naval practice, was to attract the lion's share of orders for new ships.

Ships and guns could be said to sum up and symbolize the shifting relationship between Japan and Britain in the second half of the nineteenth century. This relationship began with the Elgin mission in 1858. Lord Elgin had presnted the Japanese Shogun with a 400-ton steam-powered yacht, the *Emperor*, on behalf of Queen Victoria. The nature of the offering was, on the one hand, ironic given the restraints on travel and the construction of ships in the Tokugawa period. It was, on the other hand, prophetic of the technological co-operation that would tie the two nations in the not-too-distant future. The Bakufu visitors who came to Europe in 1862 travelled on a British ship, the *Odin*. They inspected British shipyards and arsenals, signifying the growing awareness in Japan of the importance of military advancement. The naval confrontations at Kagoshima and Shimonoseki in 1863 and 1864 saw Japan and Britain in direct conflict, both incidents reflecting the strength of anti-foreign feeling in Japan at the time. But the British fleet and the new technology of the Armstrong guns impressed the Choshu leaders. When they joined in the coup that finally toppled the Shogunate in 1868, they committed themselves to 'enrich the country, strengthen the army' by drawing on foreign expertise. This process was officially set in motion with the Iwakura mission's visit to Europe and America in 1871.

Coal and guns first brought the representatives of the new Meiji government to the North East of England where a particular link with Sir William Armstrong's Elswick Engine and Ordnance Works was forged. Ships and guns, however, would be the key determinants of the ongoing relationship between Japan and the North East as Armstrong, with great foresight, devoted his considerable energies to building up the naval side of his business over the next ten years.

2 Warships for Japan: Armstrong's and the Making of the Imperial Japanese Navy

When Armstrong resigned his government posts in 1863, he returned to the North East set on applying his expertise in the area of armaments to the building of warships. While superintendent of the Royal Gun Factory at Woolwich and Engineer of Rifled Ordnance to the War Department, it was incumbent upon him not to supply foreign governments with arms. However, after 1863, Armstrong could broaden his business interests and look to the international arena. His collaboration with Charles Mitchell's Low Walker shipyard from 1867 in the building and arming of ships was the first step along the way. The two firms amalgamated in 1883 to form Sir W.G. Armstrong, Mitchell & Company Ltd. With the opening of the new Elswick shipyard in 1884, orders for warships were handled at Elswick while the Walker yard concentrated on merchant shipping. Among their many international customers, the Japanese were prominent.

The new shipyard augmented Armstrong's 'empire' at Elswick which already consisted of a hydraulics factory and ordnance works. To make possible its construction, the river was dredged to a depth of twenty-six feet and an entire island, the King's Meadow, was removed opposite the Elswick Works. Newcastle's hydraulically operated swing-bridge which replaced the old stone Tyne Bridge in 1876 provided access for large ships to this part of the river, west of the city centre. In a decade, the face of the river had dramatically altered as had its facility for catering to the demands of warship production.

Elswick shipyard was built on the Elswick Estate along with a steel works which made Armstrong's 'the only factory in the world – nationally-owned or private – that could build a man-of-war and arm it completely'.[1] In armaments manufacture, Elswick was rivalled only by the Krupp's firm in Germany which, by comparison, was heavily subsidized by the German

View of the Elswick shipyard from the river, c 1880s. Ships were built at Elswick for many foreign navies including those of Argentina, Australia, Austria, Brazil, Chile, China, India, Italy, Japan, Norway, Portugal, Rumania, Spain, Turkey, and the United States (Newcastle City Libaries).

government. The Iwakura ambassadors had visited Krupp's during their fact-finding tour of Europe and America from 1871 to 1873 so the Japanese were well briefed on the capabilities of the leading arms manufacturers of the day even before they directed their attention to naval expansion.

In addition to Royal Navy commissions, Armstrong's company built ships for many foreign navies including those of Argentina, Australia, Austria, Brazil, Chile, China, India, Italy, Japan, Norway, Portugal, Rumania, Spain, Turkey and the United States. The interests of the firm became complex and diverse as foreign subsidiaries and joint ventures were established. Meanwhile, the active pursuit of foreign orders led to the internationalization of the company's assets and a new role for company managers, engineers and salesmen as Newcastle welcomed an interesting range of nationalities seeking to acquire ships, guns and machinery from Elswick. Armstrong's managers and agents travelled abroad to reap the harvest of increasing military expenditure in the East and elsewhere.

In 1875, the Japanese government authorized a naval construction programme following the success of an expedition sent to Formosa the previous year to retaliate against attacks on Japanese seamen. Orders for

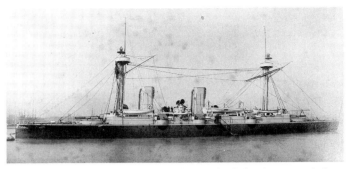

The fast protected cruiser, *Esmeralda*, was built by Armstrong's for the Chilean Navy in 1884 but was sold to the Japanese in 1894 and re-named *Idzumi* (Newcastle City Libraries).

three armoured cruisers, *Fuso*, *Hiei* and *Kongo*, were placed with various British yards while smaller, less sophisticated ships were built at Yokosuka with armaments supplied by Krupp's.[2] The suppression of the Saigo Rebellion, led by a leading Satsuma statesman against the Meiji government in 1877, gave an additional boost to the military ambitions of Japan's leaders.

It was not until the 1880s that Armstrong's began to receive serious enquiries from Japan regarding warships and guns. In July of 1882, Major S.T. Bridgford, acting on behalf of the firm, reported his assessment of the Japanese market potential in a letter to the ordnance department during a visit to the East: 'In Japan there is nothing doing at present. There is no money and the present court party will not allow the party holding the reins of government to pledge the credit of the country, by another foreign loan.'[3] He went on to describe Admiral Hawamura, the Japanese Minister of Marine, as 'pro-Reed and Krupp' and referred to a 'recent leaderette' on rifled guns in the *Japan Weekly Mail* by the editor, Captain Brinkley, which strongly advocated Armstrong weapons over Krupp's, recommending a trial of the guns 'in open court'. Brinkley was of the opinion that Hawamura was probably 'pledged to Krupp' and, in any case, lacked funds. This latter obstacle would be overcome in the course of the same year as the first Navy Expansion Bill was passed in Japan, providing for an expenditure of some 26,670,000 yen for the purchase and building of ships, development of shipyards and training.[4]

The North East was to benefit directly from this dramatic increase in naval spending. In April 1883, Captain Andrew Noble advised the Armstrong Board of Directors of a conversation with the ex-Chief Naval Constructor, Sir Edward Reed, regarding an enquiry for a cruiser received from the Japanese government.[5] As negotiations proceeded, interest was expressed in the fast protected cruiser – a practical type of armed high-speed cruiser – being built for Chile, the *Esmeralda*. Designed as a high-speed auxiliary to the heavy battleship, this vessel represented an important advance in warship construction. She was described by Armstrong as 'the swiftest and most powerfully armed cruiser in the world'[6] which, not surprisingly, made the Japanese especially eager to adopt her into their growing navy. While the Chilean government refused Japan's request to take over their order for the *Esmeralda* in 1883, she was eventually sold to the Japanese in 1894 and re-named *Idzumi*.

Major Bridgford played a significant role in Armstrong-Mitchell's early dealings with the Japanese. He accompanied Admiral Ito, who headed a Japanese naval mission, to Elswick in November 1883. A letter written to Stuart Rendel by Bridgford during Ito's visit suggests that rules of confidentiality could sometimes be breached where substantial orders were at stake. Bridgford requested information on 'the *intended* Compliment [sic] for the "Collingwood" on ships of the Admiral class. We know that the gross is to be 340 about. I should much like the distribution. I want it for the Japanese Mission for their private information and only if they decide on that type of ship and to get it from us'.[7] Details of the latest design of British Admiralty vessel were thus made available to the visiting naval mission from Japan.

By November of the following year, the Japanese had committed

Launch of the *Naniwa-kan* on 18 March 1885 at Walker shipyard, Wallsend. This was the first warship ordered by the Japanese from W.G. Armstrong, Mitchell & Company and was designed as an enlarged *Esmeralda* (The Science Museum, Newcastle).

Cragside, near Rothbury, was the country home of the first Lord
Armstrong. Many Japanese naval officers and ministers were guests
here from the 1880s (The National Trust).

themselves to orders for two protected cruisers, at a cost of £546,980.[8] The
first of these, the *Naniwa-kan*, was launched at the Walker yard on
18 March 1885. Its sister ship, the *Takachiho-kan*, was launched on 16 May
1885. Also in 1885, the unprotected cruiser *Arturo Prat*, completed for
Chile in 1883, was purchased by Japan and renamed *Tsukushi*.

The *Naniwa-kan* and *Takachiho-kan* were designed as enlarged versions of
the *Esmeralda* and, like the earlier ship, were constructed so as to combine
great speed with great offensive power. When delivered to the Japanese
government, they were to be the swiftest and most heavily armed cruisers
afloat. They represented, too, the type of protected vessel which Armstrong
had long advocated in preference to the costly and cumbersome armour-
clads.

In toasting the Emperor of Japan at the County Hotel dinner following
the launch of the *Naniwa-kan*, Sir William Armstrong alluded to the
changing relationship with Japan signified by such orders. A later account
written by Admiral Seki, who had helped to supervise the construction of
the hull and engines of the *Naniwa*, quoted from Armstrong's speech on
this occasion:

> He well recollected, when he was a boy, looking upon
> Japan as a strange and mysterious state, inhabited by an
> unknown people who might as well be the inhabitants of
> another planet. In those days he little thought how
> much he should ultimately have to do with the Japanese.
> The result of his intercourse with them, and it had now

been considerable, was that he had learned to regard them as one of the most interesting nations on the face of the world.

In referring directly to the launch of the *Naniwa-kan*, Armstrong prophesied that 'the ship was destined to the service of a country which was likely never to come into collision with our own peace-loving country'.[9] The dinner, attended by Prince Yamashine, Mr J. Hayi (a senior naval constructor), Mr Miyabara (a senior engineer) and several other Japanese naval engineers, marked the start of serious business with Japan.

With the completion of the Elswick shipyard in 1884, attention was increasingly paid to Japan as a potential market for warships built on the Tyne. Jardine, Matheson & Company, acting on behalf of Armstrong-Mitchell in the East, stressed the desirability of Armstrong's having their own agent in Japan.[10] Major Bridgford, who had received a £4000 commission on the sale of the two cruisers to Japan, was offered the position and, in 1885, assumed his new role.[11]

Under Japan's first Navy Expansion Bill, forty-six vessels were constructed,

Photograph of Lord Armstrong taken at the entrance to *Cragside* in 1900, shortly before his death. His extensive business involvements with Japan had earned him the 'Order of the Sacred Treasure of the Rising Sun' in 1895 (Newcastle City Libraries).

The *Yoshino* was considered to be the swiftest cruiser in the world in its day and enhanced the reputation of the Elswick shipyard in Japan through its performance in the Sino-Japanese War of 1894–95 (Newcastle City Libraries).

fourteen of these in Japanese yards, and the remaining thirty-two from British and French yards.[12] By the 1890s, Japan could boast a well-balanced fleet of cruisers, gunboats and torpedo boats, and the Elswick shipyard had played a part in its formation.

After Armstrong-Mitchell became a limited company in 1883, Armstrong increasingly left the day-to-day running of the business to Andrew Noble and retired to his country house near Rothbury, Cragside. Between 1869 and 1884, Cragside was redesigned and extended by the architect Norman Shaw to suit the lifestyle of his patron. The more-than-100-room country house which evolved from the original twelve-room mansion purchased by Armstrong in 1864 was a testament to the skill of the architect and the technical genius of Armstrong himself. While Armstrong retired from the daily management of the Elswick Works, he never relinquished his interest in or control over the firm's overall direction. Hence, in the 1880s and 1890s, as foreign orders were pouring in, Cragside became the venue for gatherings of Japanese, Chinese and other foreign naval officials whose business Armstrong was hoping to secure. A contemporary journal, the *Onlooker*, described the atmosphere at Cragside in those days:

> At one time Lord Armstrong, who was always a most
> hospitable host, had no smoking room; and it was
> curious to see a row of Japanese or other foreign naval
> officers, in charge of some war vessel building at the

The protected cruiser, *Tatsuta*, was launched from the Elswick shipyard on 6 April 1894 (Newcastle City Libraries).

famous Elswick works, sitting in a row on the low wall outside the front door, puffing away for all they were worth.[13] This was before the addition of the billiard room and gun room in the 1880s which deprived future observers of a similar view!

Andrew Noble became managing director of the Elswick Works and, as such, was its leading ambassador in the heyday of foreign sales. His Newcastle home, Jesmond Dene House, was the scene of many international soirées as the business entertainment side of the armaments trade was lavishly carried out. Noble's sons, Saxton and John, were early initiated into this side of the firm's activities and eventually, like their father, travelled to Japan and other countries on the company's behalf.

The Nobles were fastidious and imaginative in their pursuit of Japanese orders. The autobiography of Yamanouchi Masuji (1914) records the favourable impression that their efforts made upon visiting Japanese naval missions. Yamanouchi had been introduced to Andrew Noble by Captain Idzuke, the naval attaché in London in the late-1880s. He later wrote of how the Japanese had initially looked to France and Germany for guns but found the English more 'kindly'. Noble once organized a deer-shooting expedition in Redesdale in Northumberland in order to demonstrate to Yamanouchi the underlying principles of the quick-firing breech-loading gun. As a result of this experience, Yamanouchi pledged himself to twelve-inch Armstrong guns for the Japanese Navy. The first use of this type of gun was on the cruiser, *Chiyoda*, built for Japan at Clydebank in 1890.[14]

The Japanese battleship, *Yashima*, launched from Elswick on 28
February 1896, is pictured here, along the Quayside at Newcastle in
1898 (Newcastle City Libraries).

In 1890, the protected cruiser *Yoshino* was contracted for at Elswick and,
in May 1891, Yamanouchi's signature appeared in the Cragside visitors'
book. As the *Yoshino* neared completion, it was recorded at a directors'
meeting at Elswick that 'A Japanese commission to advise on the construction of new ships for the Japanese Navy had arrived in England and Mr Yaman
Ouchi one of its most important members was now at Elswick.'[15] The
Yoshino was considered to be the swiftest cruiser in the world in its day and
certainly enhanced the reputation of the Elswick shipyard in Japan through
its outstanding performance in the Sino-Japanese War of 1894–5. Another
Japanese vessel of this period, the gunboat *Tatsuta*, launched on the Tyne
in April 1894, was hastily completed and sailed for Yokohama on 31 July,
just before the declaration of war between Japan and China. The *Tatsuta*
was held up at Aden until January 1895 and, therefore, saw no action in the
course of the war.

Shortly before the start of the Sino-Japanese War, a contract was signed
at Elswick for a Japanese battleship with a five-year completion date.
Throughout the hostilities, Armstrong's was 'being pressed for provision of
all sorts of guns'.[16] Their swift response to this crisis in the East assisted in
securing a victory for Japan in April 1895. The North East firm had rallied
to Japan's assistance in a time of need and could now reap the rewards of
this timely success. For their role in aiding Japan in the Sino-Japanese War,
both Armstrong and Noble received the Order of the Sacred Treasure of the
Rising Sun. They also received a pledge of future orders from Japan.

The one major naval action of the Sino-Japanese War, the Battle of Yalu (17 September 1894), had underlined for the Japanese the importance of acquiring modern, well-armed and heavily protected battleships. At the end of the war, the surviving Chinese ships, some of them Armstrong-built, were incorporated into the Japanese fleet. In 1896, Japan decided to augment her existing naval resources with the passing of the Ten Year Naval Expansion Programme. This provided for the construction of four battleships, six armoured cruisers, six other cruisers, twenty-three torpedo boat destroyers, sixty-three torpedo boats and four other minor warships. In addition, base facilities, shipyards and training establishments were to be expanded.[17] Most of the orders went to British shipyards, with Armstrong's playing a major role in both building and arming new vessels.

For their part, the management at Elswick showed a clear determination to secure a fair share of the Japanese orders coming to Britain. At an Elswick directors' meeting in May 1895, Sir Andrew Noble reported a conversation that he had had with Sir Edward Grey of the Foreign Office. This concerned the likelihood of important naval and gun orders from both China and Japan following the end of the Sino-Japanese War. According to Noble, 'The Foreign Office had rather pressed the importance of English manufacturers being well-represented in the East at this juncture. We had taken steps to strengthen our representation in that quarter and should do what we could to secure orders'.[18]

Yashima, the Japanese battleship ordered before the war, was launched on 28 February 1896 at Elswick. The 12,330-ton vessel was the largest warship to be launched on the Tyne by that date. Among the distinguished guests who attended the luncheon at the start of the proceedings was Madame Kato, wife of the Japanese Minister. She performed the christening ceremony and invoked Japanese tradition by liberating a flock of pigeons to mark the occasion. Lord Armstrong's speech summed up both local and national feelings towards Japan at the time:

> Whatever may be the destiny of this splendid ship,
> we may be sure that she will be handled with the ability,
> the skill, and the courage recently displayed in the
> Japanese navy, and that she will prove worthy of the
> highly civilised and progressive nation to which she
> belongs.[19]

Shortly after the launch of the *Yashima*, Sir Andrew Noble set off for Japan and China, returning to Newcastle in July 1896. We can be certain of the success of his visit from the number of orders that quickly followed his return. Contracts were negotiated for a first-class battleship of 15,000 tons displacement, and a first-class cruiser of 9500 tons displacement.[20] A second-class protected cruiser, the *Takasago*, was launched for Japan on 18 May 1897 and completed in 1898. These were important commissions which further added to the firm's prestige in Japan.

Some corporate changes were taking place within Armstrong's company during these years. In 1896, Mitchell's name was dropped from the business which became known as Sir W.G. Armstrong & Company Ltd. One year later, a merger with Joseph Whitworth's Openshaw Works in Manchester resulted in the formation of Sir W.G. Armstrong, Whitworth & Company Ltd. This amalgamation had no real effect on the foundations of the company and Japanese orders went on as scheduled. In March 1898, the armoured cruiser *Asama* was launched for Japan, as was the *Tokiwa* in July 1898, the *Idzumo* in September 1899, and the *Iwate* in March 1900. In July 1900, Sir Andrew Noble responded to rumours of a new naval programme under consideration by the Japanese government by proposing that his son Saxton and Captain Honner visit Japan.[21]

On 27 December 1900, at the height of Armstrong-Whitworth's relationship with Japan, Lord Armstrong died. His life had spanned the Victorian age and had reflected its ambitions, tastes and values. If his death marked the end of an era, it did not break the bond that had been so carefully built up between Japan and Elswick during his lifetime. When the first-class battleship, *Hatsuse*, was launched at Elswick on 27 June 1899, Mr Watson-Armstrong spoke on Lord Armstrong's behalf in what stands as a fitting epitaph to the man and his vision for the future greatness of the Imperial Japanese Navy:

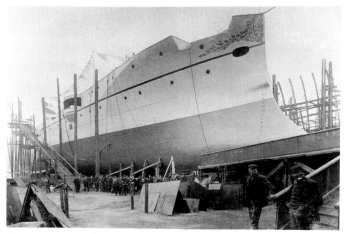

Construction work proceeds on the *Takasago* at Armstrong-Mitchell's Elswick shipyard. Photograph taken on 18 May 1897 (Newcastle City Libraries).

Lord Armstrong has always taken the keenest interest in
Japan and the Japanese people. His lordship has watched
with deep admiration how they had built up out of a
remarkable ancient and picturesque civilization, a
mighty and formidable power until, within a
comparatively short space of time, out of an ancient and
exclusive, yet, withal beautiful Nipon [sic], had evolved
a glorified Japan, the greatest Naval power of the East.[22]

On completion, in 1901, the *Hatsuse* sailed to Portsmouth to take part in a
naval pageant, symbolically representing the Emperor at Queen Victoria's
funeral before assuming her place within the increasingly formidable
Japanese fleet.

That the building of warships involved close collaboration between
designer and customer is reflected in some of the exchanges that have been
recorded. The *Hatsuse*, for example, was one of the four battleships
provided for under Japan's Ten Year Naval Expansion Programme of 1896.
As such, great ceremonial importance was attached to her launch, which
was attended by a number of Japanese Embassy staff and naval officials,
including a large contingent of Japanese naval constructors. Mme Arakawa,
wife of the Japanese Consul General, named the vessel and Sir Andrew
Noble spoke of the ship setting another Elswick record – at 15,000 tons, she
was 'one of the largest battleships afloat'. Sasow S., Chief Constructor to
the Japanese Navy, was invited to speak at the launch and registered his
appreciation for the excellent performance of Elswick-built ships, 'especially

This Japanese armoured cruiser, *Asama*, was launched at Elswick on
22 March 1898 and completed in 1899. Two further vessels of the
same type, *Idzumo* and *Iwate*, were launched by Armstrong-
Whitworth in 1899 and 1900 (Newcastle City Libraries).

Launch of the Japanese battleship, *Hatsuse*, at Elswick shipyard on 27 June 1899. At the launch ceremony, Mr. Watson-Armstrong spoke of Japan as 'the greatest Naval power of the East' (Newcastle City Libaries).

for their speed, which always exceeded that contracted for'. The designer of the *Hatsuse*, Philip Watts, was also present at this occasion. He had visited Japan three years earlier with Andrew Noble and had discussed with Mr Sasow the specific requirements of the Japanese Navy and Sasow's views on design. The *Hatsuse*, he acknowledged, had been the product of those discussions.

Captain Misu of the *Idzumo*, which was due to be launched at Elswick in September 1899, also attended the launch of the *Hatsuse* and clearly spent many months in Newcastle awaiting the completion of the ship. Japanese officers and crews were a not-uncommon sight in Newcastle in the 1880s and 1890s. While a ship was under construction, overseers were sometimes appointed and sent to liaise with the shipyard engineers at Armstrong's. During the construction of the *Naniwa-kan* (1884–6), the engineers Haji Sotojiro and Niahara Jiro were among those who assumed this role. The latter became famous in Japan for the introduction of water-tube boilers. The Japanese construction engineers allocated to the *Yoshino* (1892–3) and *Tatsuta* (1893–4) were Matsuo Tsurukaro and Yamamoto Ryotaro. Overseeing the building of the *Yashima* (1894–7) were Iwata Yoshiaki and Kosaka Ritaro.[23]

The *Hatsuse* passing through the Swing Bridge, Newcastle upon Tyne, in 1901. All of Newcastle would mourn the loss of this important battleship and two-thirds of her crew during the Russo-Japanese War (Vickers Defence Systems).

A Japanese dignitary photographed beside the battleship, *Hatsuse*, just before its launch on 27 June 1899 (Newcastle City Libraries).

Japanese construction engineer at Elswick
supervising work on the *Takasago*, completed
in 1898 (The Science Museum, Newcastle).

James Donnelly, a foreman at the Elswick Works, provided accommodation for a number of Japanese officers and construction engineers over these years. Lieutenant Akemoto was among those who temporarily resided at Donnelly's Pink Hall in Whickham. After his return to Japan, he maintained contact by periodically sending gifts and greeting cards to his former host. A Christmas card[24] sent by Akemoto to the Elswick foreman was, in itself, indicative of the cross-cultural exchange that went hand-in-hand with such residencies abroad. The imagery of the British and Japanese flags on the card spoke of the spirit of the Anglo-Japanese Alliance of 1902 (see p. 39) which strengthened the already existing bonds between Armstrong's and the Imperial Japanese Navy.

Following the launch of the *Tatsuta* in 1894, this Armstrong ship, like many others, proceeded to Hawthorn Leslie's St Peter's yard on the Tyne for machinery before returning to Elswick. While Armstrong's certainly played a key role in equipping the Japanese Navy, other North East shipyards shared in the training of Japanese engineers and contributed to the Meiji modernization process. Two Okayama clan samurai came to Newcastle for training as early as the 1870s. Mizutani Rokuro was at

Hawthorn Leslie between 1871 and 1874. On his return to Japan, he became an engineer and later vice-chairman of the Nagasaki shipyard. Matsuda Kinjiro similarly trained at Hawthorn Leslie between 1871 and 1878 and attended night school classes in Newcastle during this period. He went on to become a leading engineer at the Yokosuka naval yard and, eventually, president of the Hyogo shipyard.

While Newcastle University (Armstrong College) records do not list night school students for this period, the lists of non-matriculated students attending day classes do include some Japanese names. The 1885–6 session calendar for Durham College of Science lists Moritomo Hikoroku, Seki Shigetada and Asaoko Misutoshi. All three naval engineers were present at the launch of the *Naniwa-kan* and had supervised its construction. Seki had later written of this experience. Day courses on offer at the college included practical mineralogy, coal and metal mining, geology and geological surveying, mechanical drawing, mathematics, natural history and chemistry. Night classes for the same session dealt with steam and steam engines, applied mechanics, and, among other subjects, chemistry. Such courses would certainly have been

Lieutenant Akemoto inspecting a naval gun at Elswick in the late 1890s. Akemoto was one of a number of Japanese naval officers who stayed with James Donnelly, a foreman at Elswick, while his vessel was under construction (The Science Museum, Newcastle).

Christmas card sent by Lieutenant Akemoto to James Donnelly after his stay in Newcastle. The symbolism of the two flags suggests a post-1902 (Anglo-Japanese Alliance) date (The Science Museum, Newcastle).

of direct relevance to Japanese engineers and students in the early years of Meiji.

In September 1887, a request was received by the management at Elswick for permission for a 'Mr Bungihono' to study hydraulics at the works. This was complied with on the agreement that 'no tracing or drawings be taken out of the works'.[25] Armstrong's, too, played a part in the more general engineering training that was made available to Japanese in the North East in the second half of the nineteenth century.

The North East Coast Institution of Engineers and Shipbuilders was founded in 1884 to act as a professional body 'for the advancement of the science, and practice of engineering and shipbuilding, and the interchange of ideas and information amongst its members'.[26] Japan's links with North East industry can be further measured by the number of Japanese members elected to the Institution from the 1890s. The earliest of these was Wadagaki Yasuzo, elected in 1891, who was an engineer-draughtsman at Hawthorn Leslie's Marine Engine Works at St Peter's yard on the Tyne from November 1890 to September 1893.[27] Wadagaki's name appears among the Japanese naval constructors present at the launch of the *Hatsuse* in June 1899 and, again, in the visitors' book of Glasgow's Barr & Stroud Company on 6 February 1900.[28] The progress of shipbuilding and engineering research in Japan through this period is reflected in a paper written by Wadagaki and presented to members of the North East Coast Institution on 23 April 1909. The paper, on 'The Adaptation of Steam Turbines for the Propulsion of Vessels at Moderate Speeds', proved that the former Hawthorn Leslie apprentice had learned his lessons well. In setting out the benefits of using exhaust steam from a steam-reciprocating engine, he went on to describe the experiments performed at the Sasebo naval dockyard in this connection.[29] The application of such acquired knowledge to the modernization of Japan was evident. Other Japanese engineers and naval architects followed his lead in becoming members of the North East Coast Institution, including Kaneda Wasaburo of Grove Street, Newcastle, a ship inspector, and Haramishi M. of Eversley Place, Newcastle, a student of naval architecture. Both were elected in 1897. The following year, two engineers who resided at Warrington Road, Newcastle, Hayashi Kazuo and Matsuda Mantaro, became members. Ito Kumezo, an engineer from Mitsubishi's Nagasaki Dockyard, was elected in 1900 and Hayashida N., a marine engineer from Mitsubishi's Dockyard and Engine Works, joined in 1902. By this stage in the Institution's history, the total membership was in excess of one thousand and its importance was internationally acknowledged. Mitsubishi's Nagasaki shipyard certainly looked to the North East for technology and training from the 1890s. Their commitment to the importing of western technology was indicated by the twenty-one engineers and workers sent on study missions abroad between 1896 and 1901.[30] The Japanese membership of the North East Coast Institution reflected the priorities of such firms at a time of rapid and continuing progress.

In addition to the Japanese construction engineers and students who came to Newcastle from the 1870s onwards, there were, of course, the officers and crews who, on completion of their Elswick-built ships, came to the North East to collect them. Periods of months could be spent training on board the new vessels and mastering the use of unfamiliar gunnery and technical equipment. During these lengthy stays in Newcastle, there were some sad, perhaps inevitable, deaths of both Japanese seamen and students caused by accident or illness. In St John's Cemetery at Elswick, overlooking the river Tyne and the former site of the Armstrong shipyard, several Japanese graves stand today as a reminder of the casualties of modernization.

Kato Iwamoto died at Greenfield Place at the age of twenty on 21 June 1877. No other information is available regarding his stay in Newcastle though the date of his death would suggest that he was a student rather than a seaman. On 23 February 1886, Fukamachi Takezo was buried at St John's.

Photograph of the Paymaster of the *Naniwa-kan*, Fukamachi Takezo, taken in Newcastle shortly before his death in 1886 (Mr Shinohara Hiroshi).

Grave of Fukamachi Takezo at St. John's Cemetery in Newcastle. There are several other graves of Japanese seamen at this cemetery which overlooks the site of the former Elswick shipyard (M. Conte-Helm).

He was the paymaster of the *Naniwa-kan*, built at the Low Walker yard, and died from an accidental fall into the hold of the vessel. He was twenty-eight years old. The seaman Yamazaki Katsujiro died at Gresham House Hospital on Kenilworth Road at the age of thirty-three on 12 November 1899. The cause of his death was not recorded. He was most likely attached to one of the armoured cruisers, *Asama* or *Tokiwa*, completed earlier that year at Elswick. The final grave commemorates Ito Chiotaro, another naval seaman who died on 2 June 1906 on Hawthorne Street at the age of forty. He was probably a crew-member of the *Kashima*, the last battleship built for Japan on the Tyne.

Another of the four battleships provided for under Japan's Ten Year Naval Expansion Programme of 1896 was the *Mikasa*, Admiral Togo's celebrated flagship during the Russo-Japanese War (1904–5). Built by Vickers-Maxim & Sons of Barrow-in-Furness in the North West of England, the *Mikasa* was launched on 8 November 1900 and completed in 1902. While the *Mikasa* was a Vickers' ship, its armament, like that of the other three 1896 programme battleships, *Shikishima*, *Hatsuse* and *Asahi*, consisted completely of Armstrong guns and calibres, perhaps a harbinger of the growing association between the two competing firms which were eventually to amalgamate in 1927.

The years following the Sino-Japanese War saw Japan spending considerable sums of money on military expansion. While the war had ended in victory for the Japanese, it was a victory made bitter by the forced

Officers and crew of Japanese battleship, *Mikasa*, photographed with British officers and soldiers at Barrow-in-Furness in 1902. Togo's flagship in the Russo-Japanese War, the *Mikasa* was built at Barrow but its armament consisted completely of Armstrong guns
(The Furness Museum, Barrow).

relinquishing of her claims to Port Arthur and the Liao Tung Peninsula due to Russian, French and German intervention. Just one week after the signing of the Treaty of Shimonoseki (17 April 1895) by Ito Hirobumi and the Chinese envoy, Li Hung-Chang,[31] Japan's unexpected and dramatic defeat of China was turned to ignominy with the so-called 'Triple Intervention'. The Russian, French and German ministers in Tokyo strongly advised her abandonment of the spoils of war on the grounds of the threat posed by their possession to 'the peace of the Far East'.[32] Japan, without allies and with the Russian fleet standing at Vladivostock, had no alternative but to acquiesce. Her public humiliation was heightened as Russia, within five years of the Treaty of Shimonoseki, obtained control of Port Arthur and the Liao Tung Peninsula. The defeat of China and the ever-worsening relationship with Russia after 1895 fuelled the military fever in Japan which so benefited shipyards in Britain in the 1890s. A further deterioration in Russo-Japanese relations prompted the passing of the Supplementary Naval Construction Programme of 1903 which provided for three battleships, three armoured cruisers and two smaller vessels.[33]

The *Kashima* was ordered from Armstrong's yard under the 1903 programme and was one of the last major battleships to be built outside Japan. Construction of the *Kashima* began at Elswick in mid-April 1904, two months after the start of the Russo-Japanese War. It has often been said that this was a war fought not only at Port Arthur and in the Korean Straits but also in the boardrooms of the great Tyneside shipyards.[34] Charles Mitchell had, as early as the 1860s, built warships for Russia. Andrew Leslie's Hebburn shipyard, which merged with the engineering firm of Hawthorn in 1886, also had an established relationship with Japan's adversary. Eleven of Leslie's first seventeen ships represented orders from Russia and, between 1888 and 1896, Hawthorn Leslie built eight cruisers for the Russian Volunteer Fleet. In addition, the Tyneside firm had engined the Russian flagship, *Petropavlovsk*. Swan Hunter's, another Tyneside shipbuilder, had also built three cruisers for the Russians in 1883. It was Charles Mark Palmer, however, who was Armstrong's main competitor for overseas business. By 1893, his Jarrow yard had launched twenty-eight warships, including some for Russia. Early in 1905, the *Ashtabula* left Palmer's yard on the Tyne to join the Russian fleet. The great naval battles of the Russo-Japanese War were, thus, closely monitored at Elswick and other North East yards with a heated debate raging as to the performance of local ships and guns.

The signing of the Anglo-Japanese Alliance in 1902 provided both Japan and Britain with a much-needed counterweight to Russian infiltration in the East. The humiliation of the 'Triple Intervention' following the

Sino-Japanese War was replaced by tremendous pride in Japan's equal partnership with a major western power. The 'Britain of the East', as Japan came to be called, lived up to the challenge of this new status. Pushed to the point of no return by the Russians, Japan, in February 1904, master-minded a surprise attack on the Russian fleet at anchor outside Port Arthur. Her new ally's response was unequivocal. The *Times* declared: 'The Japanese Navy has opened the war by an act of daring which is destined to take a place of honour in naval annals.'[35] Just fifty years before, Japan had been brought to heel by western nations seeking access to her shores. In 1895, she was defenceless and without an ally when confronted with the combined weight of Russia, France and Germany. By 1904, however, Japan could turn a different fact to the West. Allied to Britain, with a major programme of military expenditure behind her,[36] Japan stood squarely on her feet before the Russians and earned the admiration of the western world for her courage and daring. That her modernization had been successfully accomplished was evidenced by the performance of her military men. Well-disciplined and trained in western tactics, Japan's army and navy combined the boldness of the samurai with the science of war as taught in the West.

The Japanese fleet owed its existence chiefly to British yards. Its six principal battleships – *Fuji, Yashima, Hatsuse, Shikishima, Asahi* and *Mikasa* – were all British-built; among these, the *Yashima* and *Hatsuse* originated at Elswick. Armstrong guns were so widely used that Sir Andrew Noble could later boast that 'all the ships engaged in the Battle of the Japan Sea (Tsushima) were armed with guns from Elswick'.[37] The Tyneside yard congratulated itself on such important naval victories as the Battle of the Yellow Sea (10 August 1904) and the most decisive Battle of Tsushima (27 May 1905) which saw the virtual destruction of the Russian Baltic fleet. The first vessel in the Japanese fleet to sight the Russians entering the Straits of Tsushima had, in fact, been the high-speed cruiser *Idzumi* (formerly *Esmeralda*), built at Elswick for Chile in 1883 and later acquired by the Japanese.

In Japan, such historic naval encounters were immortalized in the patriotic woodblock prints which always recorded the successes and never the defeats which were more quietly endured by the Japanese Navy.

All of Newcastle mourned the losses of the *Hatsuse* and *Yashima* on 15 May 1904. The two ships had been sunk by mines on the same afternoon; the *Hatsuse* with the loss of two-thirds of her crew. Throughout the war, British naval attachés were assigned to the Japanese fleet. One of them, Captain William C. Pakenham, was singled out by Admiral Togo to the Emperor as the bravest man in his fleet at Tsushima. Pakenham had

Naval engagement at Port Arthur on 13 April 1904 which resulted in the sinking of the Russian flagship, *Petropavlovsk*. Armstrong-built ships can be seen in many of these patriotic woodblock prints which celebrated Japanese naval victories during the Russo-Japanese War (Victoria & Albert Museum).

apparently continued dispassionately taking notes through the most violent action, leaving his wicker chair on the forward deck of the *Mikasa* only to change his blood-splattered uniform for a fresh white one when a nearby gun crew was blown apart by a shell.[38]

Armstrong's were in close contact with the Japanese Navy throughout the war. In January 1905, Mr Boyle was dispatched by the firm in response to a request from the Japanese that 'an expert should be sent to view damage received by ships in action'.[39] John Noble spent a lengthy period in Japan from early 1904 to 1905. The memoirs[40] of his wife, Amie Noble, who left for Japan with him in December 1903, leave no doubt as to the close ties between Elswick and Japan at this stage and the key role played by the Noble family in Japanese business dealings. She later recalled the spring of 1905 when 'war conditions needed Johnny's advice at the Japanese Admiralty where most of his days were spent'.

Amie Noble's own convictions were, ironically, pacifist; indeed, when John Noble proposed to her in 1902, she tried to persuade him to give up the armaments business and become a barrister with a London practice. The lady apparently disliked war and such 'large, dirty, noisy, industrial towns' as Newcastle upon Tyne. When Sir Andrew intervened and told her that John only dealt with the financial side of the business, she retorted, 'Yes! But his money comes from the sale of armaments!'

In Japan in 1905, Amie Noble reflected: 'I suppose it must strike Easterners as odd that we accept Christianity which to them is even more the religion of a peacemaker (compared with Buddhism) and Japs know us as war lords who have for ten years taken on their training for war.' She went on to describe her shock upon discovering:

> that we were building the Japanese navy and that on four of the battleships supplied by the Elswick works our Admiralty had sent four of our best Captains to insure success and engineers, also British, to see that our ships were kept as perfectly seaworthy as those of our own navy. Small wonder that the Russians lost what we call the Russo-Japanese War.

During this, her first of three visits to Japan, Amie Noble developed an innocent but flirtatious friendship with Captain Pakenham, the naval attaché, who mercilessly teased her about her pacifist beliefs. Very much the arms dealer's 'widow', she often went alone to parties and functions in Tokyo and was escorted home by Captain Pakenham. It is evident from her account that, due to work commitments, she saw little of her husband John in Tokyo. As a pacifist married to an arms merchant, she did not relish tales of war but could not avoid hearing reports of Russo-Japanese naval encounters. These did not always reach her via John Noble as she later recounted: 'Captain Pakenham used to tell me if and when he was going into action at Port Arthur where he stood on the bridge of an Elswick battleship directing the Japanese captain. I had to swear great secrecy until news came through as to the results of the fight. Often I didn't even breathe of it to my husband.'

Amie Noble returned to Japan with John in 1906 and 1908. During her final visit in 1939, war was declared in Europe. To have been in Japan at the start of the Russo-Japanese War and just before Japan's entry into the Second World War must have tried her pacifist conscience.

The Nobles clearly moved in high circles in Japan. There was lunch at the Palace with Prince Fushimi, brother of the Emperor of Japan, in 1905;[41] attendance at many grand social events; and the Nobles had, after all, sailed for Yokohama in 1903 on the same P.&O. liner as the Duke and Duchess of Connaught, who, themselves, had a longstanding connection with Japan.

Superior ships and guns, the brilliant leadership of Admiral Togo, and the courage of his men won for Japan a resounding naval victory in the Russo-Japanese War. The war was concluded with the signing of the Treaty of Portsmouth (New Hampshire) on 5 September 1905. Russia agreed to recognize Japanese interests in Korea and the lease of the Liao Tung Peninsula, and the Port Arthur-Mukden Railway was transferred to Japan, along with the southern half of Sakhalin which was ceded to Japan with

At the launch of the *Kashima* on 22 March 1905, Sir Andrew Noble stated that 'all the ships engaged in the Battle of the Japan Sea (Tsushima) were armed with Elswick guns' (Newcastle City Libraries).

The completed battleship, *Kashima*, with her crew at Elswick in 1906 (Newcastle City Libraries).

special fishing rights.[42] The lack of a Russian indemnity caused a great public outcry, including major riots, in Japan but national pride in the defeat of Russia remained strong. Japan had achieved Great-Power status through the Russo-Japanese War, and the contribution of British advisers and firms like Armstrong's to her naval victory would not soon be forgotten.

Throughout the war, the construction of the battleship *Kashima* went on, unabated, at Elswick. She was launched on 22 March 1905 and the friendship between Japan and Britain, sealed by the Anglo-Japanese Alliance, was reflected in the warmth of the gathering. Mme Arakawa christened the ship *Kashima*, after one of Japan's gods of war, and the Japanese Minister and his party stayed with the Nobles at Jesmond.[43]

In April 1906, the crew of the *Kashima* arrived in Newcastle to collect their ship and were hailed as 'Togo's Heroes'. The twenty-four officers of the *Kashima* and Captain Ijichi were invited to a luncheon by the Lord Mayor and Lady Mayoress of Newcastle, Alderman and Mrs J. Baxter Ellis, in the concert room of the town hall on 24 April 1906. The officers, immaculate in their British-style uniforms, were welcomed to the large gathering by the Mayor and reminded of the long connection between Japan and the Elswick shipyard which, from its earliest days, had built over sixteen war vessels for Japan and armed over twenty-two others.[44] The Alliance and Japan's recent victory over Russia set the tone for all the speeches at the luncheon and, indeed, for the events that followed. That evening, 150 members of the *Kashima*'s crew and a group of officers were taken to a football match between Newcastle and Stoke-on-Trent at St James's Park. They had spent the afternoon wandering about the town and were surprised to find a welcome written in Japanese when they reached the gates of the football ground. The welcome would be sustained within, as the *Newcastle Weekly Chronicle* (28 April 1906) later reported: 'After the men had had tea with the directors, they received a hearty cheer on ascending to seats on the stand, and the crowd again cheered when the officers stood at attention during the playing of the Japanese national anthem.'

This was perhaps the peak of Anglo-Japanese relations and certainly the peak of Japan's shipbuilding relationship with the North East. The Anglo-Japanese Alliance was revised and renewed in 1905 and renewed once again for a further ten years in 1911. The *Kashima* was the last of the great Japanese battleships to be built in Newcastle for, as Japan's victory over Russia had shown, she had as a military power truly come of age. Naval expenditure from the 1880s had been directed towards British yards like Armstrong's but was also channelled into the development of Japan's own shipyards. By 1914, these yards had the expertise and resources to build ships at home rather than abroad.

The officers and crew of the *Kashima* at Newcastle's football ground,
St. James's Park, in April 1906. They were hailed as 'Togo's Heroes'
(Newcastle City Libraries).

Armstrong's last major business involvement with Japan was the establishment of the Japan Steel Works (*Nihon Sei-Ko-Sho*) at Muroran on
Hokkaido in 1907. The formation of the company was initiated by the
Japanese government, concerned, after the tremendous drain on military
resources resulting from the Russo-Japanese War, that the nation should
have an indigenous ordnance facility. Vickers' and Armstrong's were
invited to co-ordinate with Japanese financiers to this end. From March
1905, John Noble was involved in negotiations in Japan over this important
development which, through a joint-venture agreement between *Hokkaido
Tanko Kisen* (the Hokkaido Coal and Steamship Company), Armstrong
Whitworth, and Vickers-Maxim, would provide for 'the manufacture of war
material and other steel and iron products' in Japan. Incorporated into the
deal was an agency agreement for the sale of the two British firms' products
which were not made in Japan.[45] As equal shareholders, Vickers' and
Armstrong's held a 50 per cent interest in the company which was founded
with a capital of £1,000,000 and increased in 1909 to £1,500,000.[46] The
new ordnance factory did receive its share of government orders and the
partnership with the two northern firms led to a continued flow of British
technological expertise into Japan.

John Noble played an important part in the setting up of the Japan Steel
Works which was fully operating by 1911. He was in Japan for extended
periods each year from 1904 to 1909. During the Russo-Japanese War, as
has been mentioned, he advised the Japanese Admiralty on the use and
maintenance of Armstrong guns and ships. The long-established relationship

Armstrong-Whitworth's last major business involvement with Japan was the establishment of the Japan Steel Works at Muroran on Hokkaido. The undeveloped site is shown here in 1907 (Company Prospectus).

between Armstrong's and the Japanese Navy entered its final phase in the establishment of this new business venture. A key figure on the Japanese side was Yamanouchi Masuji. Former head of the Kure naval yard, Yamanouchi went on to become the first president of the Japan Steel Works. The armaments factory that was constructed at Muroran with the help of Armstrong's and Vickers' must have had an historic significance for the man who was introduced to the principles behind the Armstrong gun on a deer-shooting expedition with Andrew Noble in the 1880s and who, in 1893, headed a naval mission to Elswick. The reputation of Britain's foremost arms manufacturer instilled the agreement with an air of auspiciousness that would mark the company's progress in the years to come.

While the completion of the *Kashima* saw the end of Elswick's battleship construction for Japan, the North East still held a special fascination for the Japanese. In Japan, people regularly visit Shinto shrines to pay homage to the dead and to their heroes. So, too, did the North East become a special

The Japan Steel Works in 1911. Armstrong-Whitworth managers and engineers played an important part in the development of the Works (Company Prospectus).

place of pilgrimage in the years that followed. In July 1911, Admiral Count Togo, the 'Nelson of Japan', came to Newcastle after attending the coronation of George V in London. He had come to fulfill his 'long-cherished desire' to visit the city of Newcastle and the Elswick shipyard which had so contributed to Japan's emergence as a world power.

Togo Heihachiro was widely known in Britain by the time of his visit. In 1863, as a fifteen-year-old member of the Satsuma clan, he had taken part in the Battle of Kagoshima, manning one of the city's hillside guns against the British squadron that was seeking redress for the murder of Richardson. Togo, who had joined the Satsuma navy as a junior sub-lieutenant in 1866, served on board the warship *Kasuga* during the Battle of Hakodate (1868) which brought the Shogunate's navy under the control of the Satsuma and, ultimately, the Imperial Japanese Navy.

Britain, for Togo, became the epitome of the western teacher who so helped in the transformation of Meiji Japan. In 1871, he signed on as a cadet on the marine officers' training ship, *Worcester*, anchored at Portsmouth. After a training cruise to Australia on board the *Hampshire*, Togo returned to Britain to study mathematics at Cambridge and, eventually, naval engineering at Greenwich.[47] During the period he spent at Cambridge, Britain received orders for three warships for Japan. Togo's last months in England provided the opportunity for a direct application of his

Admiral Count Togo, naval hero of the Russo-Japanese War on a 'pilgrimage' to Newcastle's Elswick shipyard in July 1911 (*Newcastle Daily Chronicle*).

training in supervising the construction of the *Fuso*, the first armoured war-ship to be built in England (at Samuda Brothers' Poplar yard) for the Imperial Japanese Navy.[48] In 1878, he returned home on one of the other ships built under the 1875 naval programme, the *Hiei*. Both ships were designed by Sir Edward Reed who would later establish links with Armstrong's. Togo acquired a more direct knowledge of Armstrong ships when, in 1890, he was appointed Commander of the *Naniwa-kan*, the protected cruiser built at the Walker yard on the Tyne between 1884 and 1886.[49] Finally, during the Russo-Japanese War, Togo would command an outstanding fleet of ships which had been either built or armed at Elswick.

When Togo and General Nogi (the hero of Port Arthur) were invited to attend the coronation of George V in 1911 as members of Prince Fushimi's party from Japan, Togo planned his pilgrimage to the North East. Accompanied by his aide-de-camp, Commander Taniguchi, and Commander Saito, Togo, on 18 July 1911, realized his great ambition. He arrived in Newcastle as the guest of Sir Andrew and Lady Noble at Jesmond Dene House and spent the next two days of his visit meeting the men and perusing the shipyard associated with the rise of the Japanese Navy.

The 19th of July was completely taken up with Togo's inspection of the Elswick Works. He was accompanied by Admiral Charles Dundas (former naval attaché at the British Embassy in Tokyo), Ide Kenji (naval attaché at the Japanese Embassy, London), Taniguchi, Saito and a party of officers from the Japanese cruiser, *Tone*, which had been completed the year before at Sasebo. The visitors were received by Saxton Noble and various other directors of the Elswick firm and the early part of the day was spent inspecting the steel works and ordnance department where 'Admiral Togo displayed great interest in the different stages through which the Elswick guns pass, and listened with keen interest to the officials' explanations of the different processes.'[50] Models of Elswick warships built for Japan were shown to the visitors before they were given the opportunity to examine Elswick's latest ships. Togo inspected the crew of the HMS *Calliope*, lined up along the quay beside their ship, and placed his signature in the ship's visitors' book for posterity. The *Calliope* had, in fact, sailed to Japan in 1887, arriving in Nagasaki harbour on 20 July, whereupon she saluted the Japanese flag with twenty-one guns.[51]

During their visit to the high-level shops where the finer mechanism of the Armstrong guns could be observed more closely, notices welcoming the Japanese visitors were prominently displayed. To underline these messages, tools and castings had been arranged on the floor of the forge to read: 'Welcome to Admiral Togo, O.M.'[52]

The Elswick shipyard was the point of departure on the following

Left – Elswick Ordnance Works at about the time of Togo's visit to Newcastle in 1911 (Newcastle City Libaries).

Above – Admiral Togo inspecting the crew of HMS *Calliope* at Elswick, 19 July 1911 (*Newcastle Daily Chronicle*).

Below – Togo signing the Visitors' Book of HMS *Calliope* on 19 July 1911 (*Newcastle Daily Chronicle*).

Signature of Admiral Count Togo in the HMS *Calliope* Visitors' Book (HMS *Calliope*).

morning for a cruise down the river Tyne. The Armstrong Whitworth vessel chosen to carry the famous seaman to the landing at North Shields was aptly and proudly named *Armstrong*.

At the Mansion House luncheon hosted by the Lord Mayor of Newcastle and the Tyne Commissioners, Togo paid the following tribute to Elswick and the legacy left by one of Newcastle's most illustrious citizens:

> It is a well-known fact that the name Newcastle is inseparable from the pages of the history of the Japanese navy, so many men-of-war have been either built or armed by the famous works of Elswick, which the city of Newcastle is very proud to possess. A great number of our officers and men have studied in this city how to build ships and how to make guns. I believe I am not flattering you too much if I say, that but for the kind help of your people, the history of the growth of the Japanese navy might have been written in a different way.[53]

Lord Armstrong had died in 1900. Sir Andrew Noble would follow him in 1915. Perhaps the great days of the Elswick shipyard were drawing to a close but Togo's visit to Newcastle in 1911 represented a memorial and a gesture of thanks to these men and to the shipyard that had guided Japan into the twentieth century.

During his stay, news of the renewal of the Anglo-Japanese Alliance was announced. Cheering him wherever he went, the city and its people gave voice to the spirit of the Alliance. Togo alluded, in his speech, to the larger sphere of Anglo-Japanese relations to which his visit to Newcastle made more than a nostalgic contribution: 'The voice of your welcome to me, I believe, is the voice of your welcome in the new Treaty, which is the assurance of the peace of the world, and the continued friendship of our two nations.'

Armstrong's ships and guns had helped to foster the friendship between Britain and Japan in the last decades of the Victorian period. Now, in the final year of Meiji, that friendship was cemented as Japan's greatest hero paid homage to the past.

Principal warships built on the Tyne for the Imperial Japanese Navy

Naniwa-kan   Protected cruiser, 3700 tons, Armstrong-Mitchell, Walker Yard.
Launched 18 March 1885, wrecked 26/7/12.

Takachiho-kan Protected cruiser, 3700 tons, Armstrong-Mitchell, Walker Yard.
Launched 16 May 1885, lost 17/10/14.

Yoshino   Protected cruiser, 4180 tons, Armstrong-Mitchell, Elswick Yard.
Launched 20 December 1892, lost 15/5/04.

Tatsuta   Torpedo boat destroyer, 920 tons, Armstrong-Mitchell, Elswick Yard.
Launched 6 April 1894, scrapped 1926.

Yashima   Battleship, 12,330 tons, Armstrong-Mitchell, Elswick Yard.
Launched 28 February 1896, capsized 15/5/04.

Takasago   Protected cruiser, 4160 tons, Armstrong-Mitchell, Elswick Yard.
Launched 18 May 1897, lost 13/12/04.

Asama   Armoured cruiser, 9700 tons, Armstrong-Whitworth, Elswick Yard.
Launched 22 March 1898, scrapped 1947.

Tokiwa   Armoured cruiser, 9700 tons, Armstrong-Whitworth, Elswick Yard.
Launched 6 July 1898, lost 9/8/45.

Hatsuse   Battleship, 14,967 tons, Armstrong-Whitworth, Elswick Yard.
Launched 27 June 1899, lost 15/5/04.

Idzumo   Armoured cruiser, 9733 tons, Armstrong-Whitworth, Elswick Yard.
Launched 19 September 1899, scrapped 1947.

Iwate   Armoured cruiser, 9733 tons, Armstrong-Whitworth, Elswick Yard.
Launched 29 March 1900, scrapped 1947.

Kashima   Battleship, 16,400 tons, Armstrong-Whitworth, Elswick Yard.
Launched 22 March 1905, scrapped 1924.

3 Japan in the North East: Images, Artefacts and Culture

During the fifty years which witnessed Japan's emergence from feudal isolation to world power, the North East of England had a significant role to play. The direct involvement of the West in Japan's transformation accelerated the modernization process but it was the nation's firm grasp of *fukoku kyohei* ('enrich the country, strengthen the army') as a guiding principle which made what the North East had to offer indispensable to a changing Japan. Within half a century, a modern military establishment had evolved out of Japan's samurai class. The North East provided ships, guns and training to aid in this metamorphosis and, by 1904, the dragon was reborn wearing a new and strengthened suit of armour.

Heightened by Japan's success in the Sino-Japanese War (1894–5), the relationship between Japan and the North East was consolidated into a close economic partnership as preparations were made for the war with Russia. Japan's unexpected victory over a major western power in 1905 was accomplished with the vital assistance of Tyneside warships and Armstrong guns.

The development of Armstrong's business connections with Japan in the second half of the nineteenth century illustrates clearly that commercial transactions do not take place in a cultural vacuum. The cultural implications of technical transfer are by no means so easy to trace or define, however, as the material consequences of economic co-operation. Japan's image in Britain and the North East in this period of flourishing trade was the product of increased contact and the acquisition of knowledge about her history, culture and institutions. Along with knowledge, however, came personal interpretation and the building of stereotypes which, once established, were treated as fact. Certain images of Japan and the Japanese dominated Anglo-Japanese relations and the cultural interchange that took place between Japan and the North East in the days of modernization and military expansion. They represent an important aspect of the cross-cultural communication that surrounded the visits of Japanese to the region in the nineteenth century and the business associations that subsequently developed.

After more than two centuries of isolation, Japan, to western eyes, seemed a mysterious and paradoxical place. There was, on the one hand, the natural unspoilt beauty of the country, likened to a 'fairyland' by so many authors. The image of Japanese womanhood – small, fragile, gentle and ever-serving – complemented the physical attraction of the surroundings. Add to this a universal aestheticism and love of nature affecting all levels of society and Japan seemed paradise itself.

Japan, on the other hand, was also the home of the samurai and the warrior arts. Britain's diplomats and merchants dived head-first into a political turmoil which was partly initiated by their very presence in the country. Numerous incidents of violence in the 1860s taught westerners that all was not perfect in paradise and that codes of behaviour in Japan were decidedly different from those of the West. Bold, brave and fearless, the samurai posed a constant threat to the foreign community who had dared to interfere with the future of Japan. The rigorous discipline and seemingly wanton violence of the samurai lifestyle counterbalanced the image of smallness, quaintness and '*Madame Butterfly*-ness' that also represented Japan.

What then were the perceptions of Japan in the North East of England from the first experience of contact in 1862 to the commemoration of the region's special relationship with her through Togo's visit in 1911? The rhetoric generated by the stay of the Bakufu ambassadors in Newcastle upon Tyne in May 1862 left no doubt that Japan was little known, little understood and was somewhat suspiciously regarded, if regarded at all, by the population at large. These 'dark-haired sons of the mysterious East', as one newspaper described them, were deemed to be 'men of great energy and industry, notwithstanding that they are Orientals'.[1] The treaty revision which had brought them to Britain was largely forgotten as the image of the eager pupil coming to the heartland of coal in pursuit of practical knowledge was pressed home to the Newcastle readership. A certain magnanimity characterized the accounts of the visit in the local press. If Japan was willing to learn, then the North East, of course, was willing to teach.

Dress contributed powerfully to the aspect of total foreignness exuded by the Bakufu representatives. The *Newcastle Daily Journal* (27 May 1862) was forthright in its response to their appearance: 'All were dressed in the most outlandish garments, resembling somewhat those of Chinese women, and the costumes of one or two of them, that of the chief ambassador more especially, bore a very strong resemblance to that of a woman.'

When they were taken to the Theatre Royal during their stay, it was further commented upon that pathetic episodes of the popular melodrama *Peep O'Day*, alas, gave rise to misplaced chuckles among the Japanese party. Whether theatre-going, inspecting a coal-mine, or travelling on the Newcastle to Carlisle Railway, the presence of the Japanese visitors in the region excited great interest. Indeed, if anything was shared between the Bakufu party and the people of the North East, it was the overwhelming curiosity with which they regarded one another. From the first-class waiting room of the Central Station at the start of their visit, an enlightened 'Newcastleonian' sounded a note of caution:

> I sincerely hope, for the credit as well of our town as for
> our name as a civilised nation, that during the stay of
> these royal personages amongst us, the populace who
> may be thrown across their path in their peregrinations,
> will not allow their curiosity to approach ridicule. As a
> very ancient people, the Japanese are very far advanced
> in the arts and sciences, and for the purposes of their
> own trades and manufactures, are as erudite as many
> much nearer home; and though their costume may differ
> from our notions of propriety and the beau monde, we
> must remember that, in their country, our peg-tops,
> baloon [sic] sleeves, hoops, and chimney-pot hats, will
> be equally conspicuous and interesting, should the
> contact between the two nations become as we wish it. I
> believe the rush of the populace in the South has already
> offended their rather sensitive notions of hospitality, and
> the liberty of the British subject. Let it not be so here.[2]

That the local populace did comport themselves reasonably well was confirmed by another writer who observed, following their departure:

> If we laughed at their dress a little, they laughed at ours;
> and as I sat perched upon the porter's table in front of
> the saloon carriage, when they were about to leave for
> Carlisle on Tuesday, I was glad to see that at least one of
> the mission held up our chimney pot hats to derision.[3]

The Bakufu ambassadors who came to Britain to negotiate a postponement in the opening of Japan's 'treaty ports' represented the old order. The isolationist policy of Tokugawa Japan had only been broken in the 1850s. Information about Japan was slow to reach the West until the conclusion of agreements establishing trade and diplomatic representation allowed for the presence of westerners in Japan. In the case of the British, Yokohama was the 'treaty port' from which observations of the country as a whole were made; in itself, a misleading microcosm of the real Japan. Reports by British diplomats and traders of life in Japan subsequently percolated through to British readers. Newspapers and illustrated magazines devoted an increasing proportion of space to the anti-foreign movement and the trials and tribulations of British citizens in Japan. In 1860, the *Illustrated London News* appointed the artist, Charles Wirgman, as its special correspondent in Japan. To the murder of Richardson in 1862 and the bombardments of Kagoshima in 1863 and Shimonoseki in 1864, Wirgman applied both his pen and brush. All of these incidents and many others were described and reproduced in the pages of the *Illustrated London News*. This journal and a variety of similarly popular magazines acted as vehicles for instructing the nation about Britain's involvements in Japan.

There were opportunities to learn about Japan from other sources in these early years of trade, both nationally and within the North East. The Newcastle Literary and Philosophical Society on Westgate Road, for example, had a significant library which, through the second half of the nineteenth century, developed considerable holdings on Japan. Like so many other societies of this period, the 'Lit and Phil' devoted itself to the pursuit of knowledge and the satisfaction of the intense curiosity with which the Victorians regarded the outside world. Its lecture programme focused on the topical and the newsworthy from new inventions, the march of science, to the opening-up of Japan. Sir William Armstrong who was president of the Society from 1860 to 1890, periodically gave lectures and demonstrations of his machinery there. On one occasion, the hall was so crowded with interested members of the public that he had to climb through a window to gain access to the platform.[4]

It was a very large gathering that assembled for the two lectures delivered by Dr C.T. Downing on 20 and 22 December 1852 at the Newcastle Literary and Philosophical Society on the 'Empire of Japan'. News of the contemplated American expedition to Japan had prompted this very early analysis of China's little-known neighbour. Alternately describing the Japanese as the 'Children of the Rising Sun' and the 'English of the East', he spoke on a wide range of subjects from the physical characteristics of the place and the people to the position of the Emperor, the role of the samurai and the artistic qualities of the nation as a whole. Downing lauded the 'triumph of the principle of free trade' and accordingly went on to assess Britain's potential trading partner in the East: 'Formerly it was supposed that they [the Japanese] were a barbarous and unenlightened people, but it had been ascertained that they were considerably advanced in science and that their proficiency in art was almost unrivalled, while their manners, customs and institutions were by no means undeserving of respect.'[5]

It was with a sense of being similarly pleasantly surprised following Perry's successful expeditions of 1853 and 1854 and the opening of Japan to trade that commentators registered their approval of the Bakufu representatives in Britain in 1862. That their visit combined attendance at London's International Exhibition, at which the arts of Japan were first displayed, with more pressing matters of political and economic concern helped to reaffirm some of the conflicting stereotypes that had already emerged at the time of Downing's lecture. Japan was represented by the party of men who inspected Armstrong guns at Woolwich and coal-mining in the North East but she was also represented in the Japanese Court at South Kensington by

---

LITERARY AND PHILOSOPHICAL SOCIETY.

SYLLABUS OF TWO LECTURES

ON THE

EMPIRE OF JAPAN,

BY C. T. DOWNING, ESQ., M.D.,

OF LONDON,

AUTHOR OF "THE FAN-QUI IN CHINA," &c.,

TO BE DELIVERED

IN THE SOCIETY'S LECTURE ROOM, ON THE DAYS MENTIONED BELOW.

EACH LECTURE TO COMMENCE AT 8 O'CLOCK, P.M.

LECTURE I.—MONDAY, 20th DECEMBER, 1852.

THE Exclusive Countries—The English of the East—The Japanese Islands—General Description—Their Approach, Soil, Climate, and Population—Origin of the Nation—The Jewelled Staff—History of Sik-wo—Japanese and Chinese compared—Test of Language—Personal Appearance—Manners and Customs—Dress—Females—Novel Aids to Beauty—Sumptuary Laws—National and Individual Character—Heroism—The Happy Despatch—Anecdotes illustrative of Wit, Fancy, Justice, and Sagacity—Literature—Arts and Sciences—The Running Post—Money—Internal Traffic—Land Carriage—Water Carriage—Extraordinary Voyages—Agriculture—Horticulture—Portable Groves—Laws of Etiquette—Position of Women, the test of Civilization—Japanese Lucretia—Industry and Resources of the Children of the Rising Sun.

LECTURE II.—WEDNESDAY, 22nd DECEMBER, 1852.

INSTITUTIONS of the Country—The Feudal System in Japan—Hereditary Classes—Samlai or Soldiers—Respectable and disreputable Men—Merchants—Serfs and Slaves—Outcasts—The Jetta—Government of the Empire—Liberty in Chains—The Mikado—Spirit of Sun-Goddess—His Invisibility—His Hair, Beard, and Nails—The Zio-goon, or Temporal Emperor—Council of State—Practice of Inkioe—Domestic Arrangements of Princes and Nobles—Feasting the Zio-goon—The Police—Universal Espionage—Duties of Householders—Native Religions—Adventures of Darma—History of Japan—European Intercourse—Progress of Christianity—Its Final Abrogation—Present Policy—Foreign Trade—Position of Dutch—Nagasaki—Life at Dezima—Contemplated American Expedition—Future Prospects.

ADMISSION—Free to Members, and to Persons proposed as or elected Members, at the Monthly Meeting in January, 1853.—STRANGERS' TICKET—for the Two Lectures, Gentlemen, each Four Shillings; Gentlemen under 16 years of age and Ladies, each Three Shillings ; Single admission, Two Shillings and Sixpence.

JOHN ADAMSON, } SECRETARIES.
JOSEPH WATSON,

Westgate Street, 7th December, 1852.

The earliest lectures on Japan delivered at the Newcastle Literary and Philosophical Society were given by Dr. C.T. Downing in 1852 (Newcastle Literary and Philosophical Society).

a 'curious and interesting collection' of *objets d'art*, from inlaid lacquer boxes and quaint porcelain utensils to 'such high marks of civilization as masking-armour for fencing' and elaborate samurai swords.[6]

The Bakufu ambassadors took Britain and the North East by surprise in 1862 but their successors in the Iwakura mission of 1872, while of a different political persuasion, elicited no less of a response. The dark silk tunics of the Bakufu guests were replaced by 'ordinary English costume'; for the fact that there was 'little distinctive of the Oriental about them',[7] the members of the Iwakura party made no apologies. They stood for the advances and the liberal policies of the new Meiji government, and western dress was taken on as the uniform of modernization. That the mirror-image was somewhat disturbing to the western observer was evident from the reactions of the press. The *Newcastle Courant* (25 October 1872) remarked on Japan's change of image after 1868:

> Japan is certainly the strangest of many strange countries
> in the east. After isolating itself almost entirely from
> foreign intercourse for so many centuries, it has suddenly
> thrown open its doors to all nations, and casting away its
> own ancient culture has begun to recivilise itself after
> the European fashion with a rapidity which promises to
> place it in a few years in this respect, if behind England,
> France and Germany, nearly on a level with Russia, Italy
> and Spain.

The concept of 'recivilization' was given some currency in reports of Japan's progress and, as for her projected status among nations, these were prophetic words indeed, uttered just thirty years before the Anglo-Japanese Alliance and Japan's preparations for war with Russia.

The visit of the Iwakura mission to the North East encompassed a much more thoroughgoing tour than that of the 1862 ambassadors. Coal-mining was, once again, a focus but many other local industries came under the scrutiny of the Japanese. Their overwhelming interest in Armstrong's Elswick Works on the Tyne pointed to a purposeful reordering of national priorities through the acquisition and updating of military resources. Their industriousness and demonstration of faith in Britain and the North East appealed to the deeper sensibilities of their work-oriented and self-confident Victorian hosts. As Japan took up the challenge of westernization, so local commentators ceased to pull their punches in predicting the course of the nation's future:

> Unlike the Chinese Emperor, wrapped up in his descent
> from the sun and the moon, the Japanese monarch has
> recognised at once the superiority of Western over

eastern civilisation, and the despotic power he wields,
together with the lively, industrious, and versatile
character of his subjects, will in all probability enable
him to achieve, in an inconceivably short space of time,
his purpose of exchanging one for the other.[8]

Japan was frequently compared to China in accounts from this period: a
logical frame of reference given Britain's relatively informed acquaintance
with the one country and almost total ignorance of the other. The features
of the Iwakura ambassadors were, therefore, described as 'slightly Chinese'[9]
just as ten years earlier the garments of the Bakufu party were seen to
resemble 'those of Chinese women'.[10] The attentiveness with which the
Iwakura visitors inspected the various manufactories of the region was such,
however, that, eventually, direct comparisons were abandoned. It was
remarked upon with admiration that 'intelligent men among the Japanese
must surely have a capacity for noting and comprehending a multitude of
new facts which is possessed by the inhabitants of few other countires.'[11]

As Japan became better known in the 1870s, similar opinions of the
Japanese were expressed by those who came into direct contact with them.
In the early years of Meiji, many students travelled abroad to study and the
North East had its share of resident Japanese, several of whom trained at
Hawthorn Leslie & Company in Newcastle from 1871. Among the *yatoi*
('government foreign employees') hired by the Japanese government during
these years, the North East was again represented. R.W. Atkinson was
Professor of Chemistry at the Imperial University of Tokyo between 1874
and 1881. Born in Newcastle and educated at the Royal Grammar School
before going to University College (London) and the Royal College of
Chemistry, Professor Atkinson briefly returned to the North East in 1878
and delivered a lecture on 8 November 1878 at the Newcastle Literary and
Philosophical Society. The subject, 'Progress of Science in Japan', was
appropriate to the tenth anniversary of the Meiji Restoration. In his
lecture, Atkinson pointed to the advances of the last decade. Referring to
the strides made by the Japanese, he enthused:

> They had already made great progress in the arts and
> sciences of Europe. They built their own men-of-war,
> and their own engines; and will soon lay down their own
> railways. They possess abundant stores of iron and coal;
> and there are large blast furnaces erected and in course of
> construction.[12]

Atkinson eventually returned to Newcastle to teach at the Durham
College of Science at Barras Bridge but, during his years in Japan, he clearly
saw the government's commitment to education as tied to material progress

and as an investment in the nation's future. In his 'Lit and Phil' lecture, Atkinson spoke highly of:

> the ability, earnestness, and application of the students,
> and also of their buoyant nature and good humour. In a
> generation or two, we might find them rivalling the
> older nations of Europe in the number and importance of
> their scientific achievements; and he saw nothing to
> prevent Japan becoming the England of the East!

Atkinson's views were not foreign to Japan-watchers in the 1870s. His experience of living and working in Japan through these years would, on his return to the North East, provide yet another form of contact with the reality rather than the fleeting images of Japan that were so prevalent at the time.

There were other personalities, better known than Atkinson, with connections in the North East, who contributed to spreading an awareness of Japan. Algernon Bertram Mitford, later Lord Redesdale, was one of Britain's first diplomats in Japan in the precarious days following her

The *Cragside* Visitors' Book contains the names of many Japanese ministers and naval officials who were conducting business at Elswick from the 1880s (Vickers Defence Systems).

opening to trade. The Mitford family originated in Northumberland and Mitford adopted the name of the Northumbrian valley of Redesdale for his title. He was in Japan from 1866 to 1870 and, in 1906, took part in Prince Arthur of Connaught's Garter Mission to Japan. On this latter occasion, a visit to Yokosuka naval yard underlined for the party the reasons for Japan's success in the recent war with Russia. The sight of the conquered Russian ships under repair and the 19,000-ton *Satsuma*, the first ironclad battleship

The Japanese signatures in the *Cragside* Visitors' Book include those of two future Prime Ministers, Saito Makoto (September 1886) and Kato Takaaki (August 1895) (Vickers Defence Systems).

H.I.J.M.S. "ASAMA."

BUILT FOR THE IMPERIAL JAPANESE NAVY BY
SIR W. G. ARMSTRONG, WHITWORTH & CO., LTD.,
NEWCASTLE-UPON-TYNE

LAUNCHED FROM ELSWICK SHIPYARD BY MADAME ARAKAWA,
MARCH 22ND, 1898.

Launch card for the armoured cruiser, *Asama*. The traditional
Japanese imagery of fan and bamboo was juxtaposed with details of
armament and displacement statistics (Newcastle City Libraries).

to be built in Japan, lying on the stocks, spoke of the progress that this small
island nation had made in his lifetime.

Mitford's *Memories* (1915) and *Further Memories* (1917) shed much light
on political developments and social change over this period just as his
earlier translation of *Chushingura*, the famous *Tale of the Forty-Seven Ronin*
and his eyewitness account of the ritual disembowelment (*hara-kiri*) of a
Bizen clansman in *Tales of Old Japan* (1871) had helped to foster an interest
in the cult of the samurai in late-nineteenth century Britain. The *hara-kiri*
victim, though deserving of his fate, was described by Mitford as 'brave and
chivalrous' and the ceremony as 'characterized throughout by that extreme
dignity and punctiliousness which are the distinctive marks of the proceedings of Japanese gentlemen of rank'.[13] Mitford was among those who would
read these same characteristics into the performance of Japan's latter-day
'warriors' during the Russo-Japanese War.

Lafcadio Hearn, one of the leading literary interpreters of late-Meiji
Japan, represents yet another North East-Japanese connection. Hearn spent
part of his youth at Ushaw, a Roman Catholic college in County Durham,
before making his way to Japan via America in 1890. *Glimpses of Unfamiliar
Japan* (1894) and *Japan: An Attempt at Interpretation* (1904) were two of his
most famous attempts to chronicle his relationship with his adopted
homeland. His books, like Mitford's, certainly contributed on a national
level to the sphere of contemporary British knowledge about Japan.

From 1883, Japan and the North East were drawn closer together as
Sir W.G. Armstrong Mitchell & Company began receiving orders to build
ships for the Imperial Japanese Navy. When Newcastle mounted an
international exhibition in 1887 to celebrate Queen Victoria's Jubilee, the
illustrious local firm was well represented. Among the central attractions,
was a full-sized model from Elswick of the 110-pound naval gun which had
so impressed the Japanese at Shimonoseki. The shipbuilding exhibits

included models of the fast protected cruisers that had been recently built for Japan. The Victoria Jubilee exhibition was attended by more than 100,000 people on its first day (11 May),[14] and focused attention on the city's achievements which were also becoming increasingly apparent to visiting Japanese.

In this same period, important naval delegations began making their way to Elswick and to Cragside, the country home of Sir William Armstrong. The Cragside visitors' book contains the names of the many Japanese ministers and naval officials with business at the Tyneside yard – Chief Engineer Yoshida T. in April 1886, General Count Saigo, Minister of Marine, in September 1886, Kawara Y. in May 1891 and Commander Iwasaki T. in February 1898. Over these same years, two future prime ministers, Saito Makoto (September 1886) and Kato Takaaki (August 1895), also stayed at Cragside.

The launching of a ship for Japan was a festive occasion in which Japanese Embassy representatives from London mingled with visiting naval officials and Elswick managers to provide the appropriate send-off. Launch cards were produced to commemorate the building of the ship by the yard and usually included a colour engraving of the vessel at sea as well as details of the launch. The displacement statistics, armament and dimensions of the vessel would be entered on one side along with the date of the launch and the name of the dignitary performing the honours.

Launch cards for Japanese ships built in the latter years of the nineteenth and early years of the twentieth centuries seemed to compete with one another in their efforts to incorporate what was seen to be traditional Japanese imagery. The stark and asymmetrically placed branch of a pine tree adorns the launch card of the armoured cruiser *Tokiwa* (1898), while the *Idzumo* (1899) bears a Japanese naval ensign, a sprig of blossoms and a flock of birds. The *Iwate* (1900) launch card is a testament to the impact of the decorative arts on ephemera during this period. An art deco design dominates the card which bears the sixteen-petalled chrysanthemum, motif of the Imperial house, a stylized bank of water-marked patterning and snake-like linear motifs.

As Japan and Britain became allies in 1902 and Japan progressed towards war with Russia, the pictorial symbolism of launch cards became richer and more effusive. The peak was perhaps reached with the launch card for the *Kashima* (1905). This first-class battleship was launched during the Russo-Japanese War and the card designer combined a wealth of traditional symbols in a very crowded and un-Japanese blend to convey something of the enthusiasm of the times. The trellised frame with Imperial chrysanthemum encloses a trail of heart-shaped blossoms and a bold rising sun, the

Launch card for the armoured cruiser, *Tokiwa*, featuring the stark and asymetrically-placed branch of a pine tree (Tyne and Wear Archives Service).

The *Idzumo* launch card was adorned with a Japanese naval ensign, a sprig of blossoms, and a flock of birds (Tyne and Wear Archives Service).

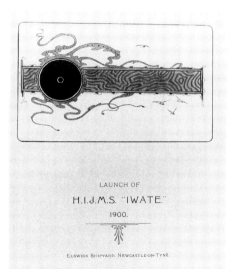

Launch card for the *Iwate* – a testament to the impact of the decorative arts on ephemera during this period (Tyne and Wear Archives Service).

The *Kashima* was launched during the Russo-Japanese War. Its imagery reflected the diverse strains of contemporary interest in Japan (Tyne and Wear Archives Service).

THE ELECTRIC BELL
will ring in the
ROYAL BARS,
In Grey Street and Market Street,
adjoining the Entrance to the Theatre,
3 MINUTES
Before the rising of the Curtain for
EACH ACT.

GIBSON & CO., PROPRIETORS.

STYLISH MILLINERY.
LADIES SHOULD VISIT
S. PITTS,
28, NUN ST., NEWCASTLE,
For LATEST FASHIONS AS PRODUCED.
PRICES STRICTLY MODERATE.

G. CARRICK, FIRST-CLASS BOOT MAKER, 49, NORTHUMBERLAND STREET, NEWCASTLE, AND HIGH STREET, GOSFORTH.

MONDAY, SEPT. 6th, 1886,
And Every Evening during the Week, at 7.30,

THE

MIKADO!

OR, THE TOWN OF TITIPU.

Written by W. S. GILBERT. Composed by ARTHUR SULLIVAN.

The Mikado of Japan .... Mr. ALLEN MORRIS
Nanki-Poo (his Son, disguised as a Wandering Minstrel, and in love
with Yum-Yum) .... Mr. CHARLES HILDESLEY
Ko-Ko (Lord High Executioner of Titipu) ...... Mr. GEORGE THORNE
Pooh-Bah (Lord High Everything Else) .... Mr. JAMES DANVERS
Pish-Tush (a Noble Lord) .... Mr. GEORGE GORDON
Yum-Yum ...... } Three Sisters, { .... Miss ETHEL PIERSON
Pitti-Sing ...... } Wards of Ko-Ko { .... Miss HAIDEE CROFTON
Peep-Bo .... } { .... Miss SIDDIE SYMONS
Katisha (an elderly lady, in love with Nanki-Poo) Miss FANNY EDWARDS

Chorus of School Girls, Nobles, Guards, and Coolies.

ACT I.

COURTYARD OF KO-KO'S OFFICIAL RESIDENCE.

ACT II.

KO-KO'S GARDEN.

The Incidental Dances by Mr. J. D. AUBAN.

The Ladies' Dresses by Messrs. LIBERTY & Co., and Madame LEON.

The Gentlemen's Dresses designed by Mr. WILHELM, from Japanese
authorities, and executed by Madame LEON.

The Wigs by Mr. CLARKSON.

Acting Manager ...... { For { ...... Mr. R. REDFORD
Musical Director ...... { Mr. D'Oyly Carte { ...... Mr. GEORGE ARNOLD
Stage Manager ...... { { ...... Mr. R. WEATHERSBY

MONDAY, SEPTEMBER 13th, 1886,
The Eminent Comedian,

MR. EDWARD TERRY

Supported by his SPECIALLY SELECTED COMPANY.

Gilbert and Sullivan's comic operetta, *The Mikado*, had its northern debut at Newcastle's Theatre Royal in October 1885 and was repeatedly performed to packed houses (Newcastle City Libraries).

most recognizable symbol of Japan. Two pictures set within the frame conjure up Mount Fuji, a Buddhist temple precinct, a Shinto gateway and an ancient warrior bearing cuirass and arrows in Robin Hood-like pose. The incongruity of the juxtapositions resulted, of course, in some very un-Japanese images but the temptation to combine quaint picturesque symbols with Japan's weapons of war nevertheless prevailed.

From what had been described as 'the contest of two civilisations',[15] Japan emerged the victor. When the officers and crew of the *Kashima* came to Newcastle following the Russo-Japanese War in 1906, 'Togo's heroes' were received with great enthusiasm. Yet *Madame Butterfly* had survived unscathed in the popular mind. A description of the town hall in which the Japanese officers of the *Kashima* joined the Lord Mayor and Lady Mayoress of Newcastle for lunch underlines the persistence of such perceptions:

The balconies were draped in red and white; extending
from the roof were strings of flags, in the centre of the
ceiling was a gigantic paper umbrella, and everywhere

were palms, and the glowing symbol of the rising sun
upon bunting. The long tables were gracefully adorned
with white lilies, and purple irises and ferns, and every
napkin held a tiny Japanese fan.[16]

The hall was clearly decorated as for a victory celebration but the umbrella, fans, flags and flowers signified certain assumptions about Japan and the Japanese which lingered from the past.

F.T. Jane in *The Imperial Japanese Navy* (1904) went some way towards righting the balance by pointing to Japan's naval achievements, on the one hand, while contradicting popular opinion about the artistic sensitivity of all Japanese, on the other hand. He summed up his observations as follows:

Art books tell us of Japanese art instinct, of their feeling
for decorative art, and so forth. Japanese artists may
possess, or have possessed, this feeling, but it is
conspicuous for its absence in Japanese naval officers,
who are as 'philistine' as British officers – if possible,
more so. The decorative art that their nation is supposed
to live for they cordially despise . . . We may note,
therefore, that 'art-instinct' was the first thing flung
behind him by the Japanese when he 'advanced'.[17]

It should be remembered that, while Japan was building a modern navy in the 1880s and 1890s, western writers and artists were, as far as Japan was concerned, frozen in time, looking to the images of old or sometimes the traditional that coexisted with the modern. Hence, in the year in which the *Naniwa-kan* was launched for Japan at Wallsend, Gilbert and Sullivan's comic operetta, *The Mikado*, was first performed (1885). As Japan was implementing her first Navy Expansion Bill and directing orders to the North East, Pierre Loti's novel of a French naval officer's liaison in Japan, *Madame Chrysanthème*, (the inspiration for Puccini's *Madame Butterfly*) was published (1887). Images of gentle damsels in kimono floated through the paintings of James McNeill Whistler, Mortimer Menpes, George Henry, E.A. Hornel, John Varley Jr. and many other artists in Britain in the latter years of the nineteenth century. The North East of England may have been well acquainted with Japan's naval progress and technological achievements, but one of its leading poets, Wilfred Wilson Gibson, chose to evoke a more picturesque image in his poem, 'A Lyric of Japan' (1896):

My love is an almond-eyed girl;
    Her face is as round as the moon;
  In her hair there is never a curl;
    And her smile is the sunshine of noon.

Her name is Li-Kinta-Sim-Poo,
  She dwelleth in Tokio's town,
And peacocks in silver and blue
  Emblazon the fold of her gown.

We sat by the river one day,
  She twanging a sounding guitar,
And watching the smoke curl away
  From the end of my fragrant cigar.

When shyly I asked her to wed
  While the summer still reigned in the land,
She replied with a nod of the head
  Which no one could misunderstand.[18]

Audiences in the North East were soon treated to performances of *The Mikado* following its London debut. It was first performed at the Theatre Royal in Newcastle in October 1885 and February 1886 and, shortly after, at the Avenue Theatre in Sunderland. The operetta, while hardly providing insights into Japan itself, nevertheless afforded the opportunity to indulge in Japanese costumes and settings, all of which contributed to the region's collective impressions of Japan.

'Tannakers Japanese' grave at
Bishopwearmouth Cemetery, Sunderland.
Dated 21 February 1873 (M. Conte-Helm).

As early as 1873, a Japanese acrobatic troupe, 'Tannaker's Japanese', performed in Sunderland at the Victoria Hall. A rather poignant memorial of their stay in the North East can be found in Bishopwearmouth Cemetery in Sunderland where Godie, the young son of the touring performers, was buried following an illness. His gravestone reads:

Here lies Little Godie, who died February 21, 1873.

Aged 15 months, the only son of Omoterson and Godie, natives of Japan, members of Tannakers Japanese.

This is the first Japanese monument erected in this country.

Tannaker Buhicrosan was a Dutchman married to a Japanese who brought his touring troupe around Britain in the 1870s ('Tannaker's Japanese' also performed in Hartlepool in 1873) and, following their success, returned in 1885 to establish a 'Japanese Village' in Knightsbridge. At a time when the Japanese government was seeking revision of the 'unequal treaties', such traditional entertainments did not prove very popular with the Japanese authorities.[19] By September 1887, the village had closed and the performers either returned to Japan or were dispersed throughout Europe.

A 'Japanese Village Fair' was held in Newcastle at the Central Exchange Art Gallery in January and February 1886. This may have been an off-shoot of 'Tannaker's Japanese' as the programme of events was similar to the Japanese entertainments being offered to London audiences. In addition to 'real Japanese artists at work' and 'fan painting by real Japs', the programme included jugglers, illusionists and Mlle deLonn, 'charming Japanese balancer', followed by Motto Kitchee, 'a marvellous rope walker – a real Jap'.[20] The search for a reality to fuel the lingering image of a quaint and curious Japan was assisted by such travelling performers. In creating a suitably styled

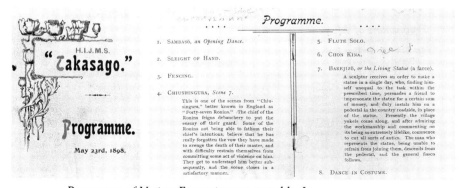

Programme of Variety Entertainment staged by Japanese crewmembers of the *Takasago* in Newcastle on 23 May 1898 (Newcastle City Libraries).

Albert Howard Higginbottom (d. 1930),
Newcastle wine and spirits merchant and
collector of Japanese art (Sanderson family).

ambience to house such entertainments, local firms were called upon to
enter into the spirit of *japonisme*. The 'Yokohama Tea Lounge' and other
display areas of the Central Exchange Art Gallery were fitted and decorated
by the North of England School of Furnishings and the local department
store, Bainbridges, which supplied the silks.

Along with such commercially organized ventures, the presence of
Japanese seamen in the North East sometimes led to cultural exchanges
of a rather unusual nature. On 23 May 1898, the crew of the protected
cruiser, *Takasago*, who were in Newcastle to collect and train on their
Elswick-built ship, brought another manifestation of traditional Japan to
the region. The Programme of Variety Entertainment[21] which they presented to a Tyneside audience consisted of eight traditional items of
entertainment including costumed dances, a fencing display and a performance of scene seven of *Chushingura* (*The Tale of the Forty-Seven Ronin*),
first translated by A. B. Mitford in 1871. Japan's most famous legend of
samurai loyalty was aptly juxtaposed against the ship and the guns
with which these latter-day warriors would soon do battle. In an atmosphere of fluctuating images, the First Newcastle Artillery Band contributed
musical offerings from Wagner and Sullivan. Selections from the *Mikado*
conjured up the western image of Japan just as the *Takasago* crew gave its
audience a glimpse into the traditions from which this image had sprung.
The programme ended with '*Kimi-gayo*', the Japanese national anthem, and

The *Mechanics Arms* was one of a chain of pubs along Scotswood
Road owned by A.H. Higginbottom and patronised by the shipyard
workers at Elswick (Newcastle City Libraries).

'God Save the Queen', respectfully acknowledging the contrasting roots of
the performers.

Though aspects of her native culture were often submerged in Japan's
quest for a modern image, the opposite process generated an active interest
in traditional Japan in the West. In Britain and many other countries, an
enthusiasm for the traditional arts of Japan resulted in the formation of
numerous collections of Japanese artefacts in the late-nineteenth century.
At a time when artists in Japan were abandoning their own artistic
traditions and looking to those of the West for inspiration, British

The garden of A.H. Higginbottom's house
overlooking Jesmond Dene, complete with
Japanese stone lantern (Sanderson family).

collectors were seeking to acquire the discarded remnants of Japan's past which were favourably compared to western examples. Collectors in the North East shared in this interest.

One of the largest collections of Japanese art[22] formed in the North East in the nineteenth century belonged to Albert Howard Higginbottom, a wine and spirits merchant, who moved to Newcastle from Derbyshire in 1876. Higginbottom came to the North East as the representative of the brewers Ind, Coope, & Company Ltd, but subsequently started his own business which consisted of a large chain of pubs, many of which were situated along the Scotswood Road. The public houses in this part of Newcastle tended to take their names from the heavy industry that dominated the west end of the city. Scotswood overlooked Elswick and pubs like the *Hydraulic Crane*, the *Crooked Billet* and the *Mechanics Arms* (owned by Higginbottom) provided relaxation for the shipyard and factory workers employed by Armstrong's at Elswick. A 'keen connoisseur' of Japanese art, Higginbottom collected more and more items as his business prospered. His collection was displayed at the house which he built in 1900 overlooking Jesmond Dene. The house no longer stands but an old estate agent's brochure shows the garden complete with Japanese stone lantern.

Many of Newcastle's leading industrialists escaped from the noisy labours of the day to the peace and tranquillity of their houses on the Dene. Lord Armstrong built his house to the west of Jesmond Dene and the existing park was his own private woodland until he generously gave it, in 1883, to the Corporation of Newcastle upon Tyne for the use of its citizens. Andrew Noble and his family lived nearby at Jesmond Dene House (now a school) and some of the city's most prominent shipbuilders, including Charles Mitchell, Charles Mark Palmer, Henry F. Swan and G.B. Hunter, similarly gravitated to this haven on the outskirts of a heavily industrialized Newcastle. Higginbottom would have been known to these men of industry. As a successful merchant, he was proposed for associate membership to the North East Coast Institution of Engineers and Shipbuilders in 1913 by Sir Charles Parsons, inventor of the steam turbine.

Higginbottom shared with his neighbours a taste for good living and was much affected by the contemporary fascination for things Japanese. A number of Japanese visitors had made their way to Jesmond Dene over the years to be entertained by the Armstrongs and the Nobles but Higginbottom's associations with Japan were of a different sort. He does not appear to have ever visited Japan but, in his lifetime in England, he accumulated a vast store of Japanese material, all of which, in later years, was donated to Newcastle's Laing Art Gallery.

The Higginbottom collection offers a representative sampling of the kinds of Japanese artefacts available to the reasonably well-to-do buyer in the late-nineteenth century. It contains some eighty-three woodblock prints of traditional subjects, among them works by Eizen Kitugawa, Kunisada Utagawa and Hiroshige Ando. There are some forty wood and lacquer *inro* (pouches), some with *netsuke* (fasteners). Japanese metalwork of the Tokugawa period is represented by a finely crafted articulated iron carp. There is, in addition, an eighteenth-century picnic set, inlaid iron boxes, wooden mask ornaments, ivory and lacquer combs and hairpins, pipes and pipecases, a tea caddy, *sake* cups, letter containers, chopsticks, a few bronze buddhas, an iron vase, a bronze fan and a variety of other unrelated objects. The *Madame Butterfly* enthusiast looking over the array of Higginbottom possessions would have had all prejudices confirmed.

Higginbottom's interests were wide-ranging, however, and his purchases of Japanese swords, sword fittings and armour completed both his collection and the paradox of Japan's image in the West. Swords and daggers of different types with lacquered and inlaid scabbards summoned up the world of the samurai which, by the waning years of the nineteenth century, had already been transformed into a modern military machine. Higginbottom acquired some 700 *tsuba* or swordguards, but also examples of *kogai* (a small knife carried in a slot in the scabbard), and assorted other fittings. Such quantity items as the *tsuba* would have been purchased in large lots, probably from salerooms in London. Two full sets of armour, a helmet and a saddle and stirrups offered further reminders of Japan's warring past which was generating so much attention among collectors of the day throughout Britain.

The Higginbottom collection provided the North East with a portrait of traditional Japan which both supported and contradicted the contemporary

Some examples from among the seven hundred *tsuba* or Japanese swordguards in the A.H. Higginbottom collection (Tyne and Wear Museums Service).

Eighteenth century Japanese saddle and stirrups from the A.H. Higginbottom collection bequeathed to Newcastle's Laing Art Gallery (Tyne and Wear Museums Service).

image of an increasingly formidable naval power looking to the region for both ships and guns, the equipment of modern warfare. If *Madame Butterfly* personified one side of traditional Japan, then the samurai warrior encapsulated the other.

By 1905, the translation of the samurai spirit into the feats of Admiral Togo's fighting men was being recognized in many quarters. A Russian commentator, reporting on the naval encounters of the Russo-Japanese War, described the spirit of *bushido* which lived on in the performance of the Japanese navy:

> War is very terrible and unpleasant, especially against
> savages armed with all the best of modern weapons and
> of dauntless courage, such as none except our sailors
> were in any way able to face; for be it known it was our
> sailors who held the forts to the last man when the
> Japanese rushed on like a dust storm, finding death a joy.
> It is impossible to do many things against such men.[23]

W. Petrie Watson in *The Future of Japan* (1907) placed a rather different interpretation on the relentless fighting spirit of the Japanese: 'To link fanaticism with this loyalty to a lofty tradition is to traduce the character of a thousand heroes of old Japan, as well as to malign and misconstrue the battle-motive of the Japan of today!'[24] For such authors, *bushido* was seen as a religion to which the Japanese sailor, like the samurai before him, adhered.

It is not unlikely that a fascination with and admiration for the samurai fighting spirit which so readily adapted to modern methods of warfare would have informed the purchases of traditional Japanese weaponry by collectors at the turn of the century. In addition to the Higginbottom collection, the Hancock Museum in Newcastle also owns Japanese swords and suits of armour donated from this period. The Gray Art Gallery in Hartlepool received similar donations of arms, armour and other traditional items from local collectors. Further Japanese weaponry can be found in the Sunderland Museum and Art Gallery. Bamburgh Castle in Northumberland, perhaps most appropriately, houses Japanese armour owned by the Armstrong family. That the family which supplied Japan with modern armament should look to her weapons of old is of particular significance.

One can point to various paradoxes and ironies in assessing the contemporary interest in such material but, in the case of the Higginbottom collection, there is an additional curiosity in the particular circumstances of its formation. Higginbottom funded his Japanese purchases from the proceeds of his public houses located along the Scotswood Road. Consequently, wages earned in part by the construction of guns and warships for

Japan at Elswick were converted into profits which were, in turn, used to finance samurai swords and armour, the traditional weaponry of Japan's warrior class. This may represent a somewhat intangible link with the shipyard that dominated Japan's naval modernization but it points up the economic sub-text of Japan's image in the region.

Public and private collections of Japanese art have found their way to the North East via a number of different routes. The Bowes Museum in County Durham, for example, houses the nineteenth-century collection of John Bowes, son of the tenth Earl of Strathmore, and his wife, the actress Josephine Benoite. It includes some fine examples of *imari*-ware porcelain which was highly popular in the late Victorian period. George W. Squires, the general manager of the North Eastern Paper Mills at Marsden (Sunderland) between 1915 and 1930, represented another type of local collector. Between 1898 and 1907, he was general manager of Shenju Kaisha (a paper-manufacturing company) in Japan. The diverse assortment of material which he amassed during this period has recently been donated to Durham University's Oriental Museum. Opened in 1960, the Oriental Museum contains a range of Japanese artefacts collected in the North East and beyond over the last hundred years.

Missionary societies were well represented in Japan in the later years of the nineteenth and early-twentieth centuries and some gifts to local collections, as with the Hancock Museum, can be traced to such sources. In

Japan display in Medical Missionaries Exhibition in Newcastle organised by the Church Missionary Society in March 1907 (Newcastle City Libraries).

1891, Henry Baker Tristram, Canon of Durham, travelled to Japan to investigate the position of missionary work there and particularly that of the Church Missionary Society. The Canon's daughter had been a missionary in Japan for some time and assisted him with his research, the results of which were finally published in his *Rambles in Japan: the Land of the Rising Sun* (1895).[25] Tristram was optimistic about the progress of Christianity in Japan but, throughout his travels, like so many other visitors, viewed his surroundings in relation to the more familiar world he'd left behind. Thus, the 'old Tokaido' highway was compared to 'our own Great North Road'; Nagoya Castle was seen as 'the Alnwick Castle of Japan'; and the hills above Kyoto likened to 'our own Pennine Range'. Of Japan's more modern facade, he did acknowledge that the first-class warships of the Japanese fleet at Yokohama appeared 'as smart and trim as any English man-of-war'. Indeed, some of these would have shared the same origins. Japan was destined, Tristram concluded, 'when it had embraced Christianity . . . to be the Britain of the Pacific'. Despite the Christian context, this echoed a popular theme in the contemporary British response to Japan.

In October 1897, the Reverend Walter Weston presented a lecture on 'Travel and Exploration in Unfamiliar Japan' to the Newcastle Literary and Philosophical Society. At the height of the region's trade with Japan, such a topic, like that of Canon Tristram's book, could not help but attract a large and eager audience. Some ten years later, in March 1907, the Church Missionary Society opened a Medical Missionaries Exhibition in Newcastle's Exhibitions Building. The Japan display was dominated by the conical shape of Mount Fuji which provided a backdrop to a scene in which blossoming trees, pagoda, a Chinese junk and many other misplaced images served to symbolize the nation that had won the Russo-Japanese War with the aid of sophisticated battleships and armaments purchased from the North East.

Another illustration of the contradictory perceptions of Japan that persisted into the twentieth century can be found in the *Memoirs*[26] of Amie Noble who was in Japan during the Russo-Japanese War and had some knowledge of Japan's naval strength and Armstrong's contribution to it. Her thoughts on arrival, however, were centred on Mount Fuji and her observations matched the tone of less well-connected visitors: 'How wonderful to have been wafted here to Japan. My only picture of it so far had been that play 'Madame Butterfly', showing a western idea of a geisha girl's emotions and kimonos.' Amie Noble broadened her observations after a year of living in Tokyo where she stayed at the western-style Imperial Hotel ('such an ugly copy of our worst type'). As her husband, John, went about the firm's business, she filled her days and informed her opinions, shopping in Yokohama, cherry-blossom-viewing among the temples of Kyoto, and attending the 'At Homes' of the diplomatic set in Tokyo. She was not much touched by the war, though a reference to rolling bandages with the 'royal princesses' suggests that it was more than just a distant backdrop to her expatriate existence in Tokyo. Whether Japan was perceived at first hand, as was the case with Amie Noble, or at a distance, the image retained would always depend on the breadth of the beholder's vision.

The 1910 Japan-British Exhibition at White City (London) accorded Japan more space than she had ever previously enjoyed in such ventures. The exhibition, which had the full support of the Japanese government, united the two island nations by portraying their traditions but also their industries. A sizeable section was devoted to shipbuilding, with models of Armstrong Whitworth ships built for Japan on display. It was inevitable, as Japan took full control of her own destiny, that a new image would begin to replace the old.

The arrival of Admiral Togo at Elswick in July 1911 drew attention to Japan's changing status. The crew members of the *Tone* who accompanied him had travelled to Britain on a ship built totally in Japan. Togo and his party stayed with the Nobles at Jesmond; the hero of the Russo-Japanese War appeared very much at home among the wealthy industrialists of the North East. Lady Noble later recollected his visit:

> We were delighted with him, and with his simplicity and dignity. We had a large reception for him, and later in the evening I asked if he would not like to slip off and go to bed, after such a tiring day and evening, and shaking hands with more than a hundred people. – 'No, I thank you, I should like to billiard a little with Mr. Saxton'.[27]

There are few personal insights into the nature of this reserved man who was one of Japan's greatest naval tacticians. The head gardener at Jesmond Dene House, Walter Rutter, often recalled Togo's visit, however, and the pleasure which the great seaman seemed to take in the Nobles' 'natural and almost wild garden' on the Dene. Just prior to his departure from Newcastle, Togo asked Mr Rutter to provide one final tour of the lovely garden, a hint of the nature-loving soul within the samurai.[28]

In looking to the perceptions of Japan in the North East of England in the late-nineteenth and early years of the twentieth century, one is inevitably forced to paint with a broader brush. The years surrounding the Anglo-Japanese Alliance and the Russo-Japanese War saw a wealth of observations made about Japan on a national level which had their necessary impact on views of Japan in the region. The special relationship

The close ties between Japan and Britain at the time of the Russo-Japanese War were reflected in this cover of the *Illustrated London News* (19 March 1904) showing Admiral Togo, the 'Nelson of Japan', and the British-built battleships at his command (*ILN*, 19 March 1904).

between Japan and the North East through the decades of business collaboration led to particular and often lasting friendships being formed and a steady stream of Japanese visitors coming to Tyneside and Northumberland. Yet the image of Japan was multi-faceted and the cultural awareness engendered by the process of technical transfer represented the other side of this mutual exchange. With the emergence of the modern warrior in the making of the Imperial Japanese Navy, the trade in Tyneside warships and guns and traditional Japanese weaponry acquired a symbolic focus.

Togo and the men who served him in the Russo-Japanese War embodied the fearlessness and loyalty of *bushido*, the code of the samurai, which excited much admiration in Britain in the first ten years of the twentieth century. *Bushido* as a code of honour was compared to the tradition of 'conduct or morale' in the British Navy and to the unwritten laws governing the behaviour of the English 'gentleman'.[29] A measure of the popular interest in the roots of contemporary Japanese heroism could be seen in the enormous readership for Nitobe Inazo's *Bushido, The Soul of Japan*, which was written in 1902 and had gone into its tenth edition by 1904. Leading socialist intellectuals like Sydney and Beatrice Webb saw in traditional samurai values a remedy for the ills of Britain. The Fabian socialist H.G. Wells wrote *A Modern Utopia* in 1905 and actually used the word 'samurai' to describe his ideal of a ruling élite. In it, he advocated the remodelling of the Fabian Society into an 'Order of the Samurai', which would 'embody for mankind a sense of the State'.[30] Other proponents of National Efficiency[31] equally looked to Britain's ally, who had survived trial by fire, and was thus deemed worthy of further analysis.

The spirit of the Anglo-Japanese Alliance was the spirit of co-operation and exchange. The responses to Japan in the North East in the years leading up to and beyond the 1902 Alliance were partly coloured by economic ties and the regular presence of Japanese in the region; they were also coloured by the palatability of certain prevalent images. How the Japanese perceived the North East during this period is also worthy of reflection. From the 1862 Bakufu mission through the years of naval expansion, a steady stream of Japanese visitors came to the region and enjoyed the hospitality of Britain's new ruling class, industrialists like Armstrong and Noble, whose origins were humble but who, in attaining economic success, adopted the paraphernalia and style that went with 'old money'. The factories and shipyards of Newcastle generated great wealth but the new aristocrats spent their profits on building projects, art collecting and country pursuits. The lifestyle of the English country house and castle which Japanese visiting the North East therefore had the opportunity to experience must have generated some equally curious images of the British. The Japanese guests at Jesmond, Cragside and Chillingham Castle went hunting and shooting, played billiards and acquired a taste for western art. The cultural codes that underlay the assumptions and practice of such pastimes and rituals were as difficult to decipher as those that determined the seemingly peculiar manners and customs of the Japanese in the eyes of their hosts.

As the Meiji period drew to a close, the cultural ramifications of Japan's relationship with the North East were apparent. The North East, which had contributed so much to Japan's future, discovered that there were some

Admiral Count Togo pictured here at the entrance to Jesmond
Dene House where he stayed with Sir Andrew Noble (to his right)
and Lady Noble in July 1911. Commander Saito (centre) and
Commander Taniguchi, A.D.C., (far right) were in his party
(Newcastle City Libraries).

important lessons to be extracted from her past. The Japanese returned from
the North East with the training and technology to determine their own
fate. Each society had gleaned from this partnership something of the
culture and traditions of the other. In this important respect, the relationship was not one sided, nor would its consequences be short lived.

4 Merchant Ships and Traders: Japan's Merchant Navy and its Links with the North East

The transformation of the Imperial Japanese Navy was accompanied by the simultaneous development and expansion of the country's merchant marine. The North East of England, with its thriving shipyards on the rivers Tyne, Wear and Tees, became a supplier to the leading Japanese shipping companies and forged particular links with the Japan Mail Steamship Company (NYK). The merchant shipping connections between Japan and the North East are often overshadowed by the romance of warship history, but they were substantial, none the less, and provide important insights into the region's wider associations with Japan and the continuing trading relationship between Japan and Britain.

While the Tokugawa Shogunate's policy of enforced seclusion precluded the building of full-scale ocean-going vessels from the seventeenth to mid-nineteenth centuries, coastal shipping in Japan, reliant on small wooden sailing vessels, was nevertheless central to her commercial economy. Japan, as an island nation of mountainous terrain, looked to the fleets of the various coastal domains for the conduct of domestic trade. With the start of the Meiji period, came the realization of the importance of adapting mercantile traffic to the requirements of industrial and economic expansion. This coincided with the revolution in world shipbuilding which rapidly saw iron-built and steam-powered vessels replacing the wooden sailing ships of old.

It was against this setting that the Japanese government agreed to lend its support to the former Tosa samurai Iwasaki Yataro's shipping business, Mitsubishi Company (Yubin Kisen Mitsubishi Kaisha), which, from 1870, had been operating between Tokyo, Osaka and Shikoku. In 1875, Mitsubishi was given control of government-owned steamships and was directed to open a new route to Shanghai. This line, carrying coal as its main cargo, was inaugurated in the same year and marked the start of Mitsubishi's lucrative overseas service. From this period, direct government sponsorship played an important part in the development of the firm. Another partially subsidized concern, the Union Transport Company (Kyodo Unyu Kaisha), was established in 1882 and became Mitsubishi's chief competitor. When, under government pressure, the two firms amalgamated in 1885 to form the Japan Mail Steamship Company (Nippon Yusen Kaisha), shipping history was made. NYK would enjoy an unrivalled position as Japan's largest shipping company from that day forward. The merged company was guaranteed an 8 per cent annual dividend by the government, in return for which its management and operation of routes came under the supervision of the Ministry of Communications.[1] A Kobe to Bombay service was instituted in 1893, at which time NYK employed 370 Japanese and 121 foreign officers,[2] reflecting the general pattern of technical co-operation which affected so many spheres of industry in the Meiji period.

The government-industry relationship in shipping was put to the test during the Sino-Japanese War. Almost all of NYK's ships were requisitioned and emergency purchases of foreign vessels made. NYK's direct participation in the war led to the doubling of its fleet from 64,000 to 128,000 tons in 1894–5. Just as the Sino-Japanese War had prompted the passing of the Ten Year Naval Expansion Programme (1896) with such important consequences for Newcastle's Elswick shipyard, new post-war legislation similarly addressed itself to the development of Japan's merchant fleet. The Navigation Encouragement Law (1896) provided aid to shipping companies utilizing vessels of over 1000 tons, with a speed of more than ten knots, and less than fifteen years of age. The same conditions applied to those ships built abroad which were less than five years old.[3] As Japanese yards were not sufficiently advanced to produce the types of overseas liners in demand from 1896, the new legislation provided a form of indirect subsidy to foreign yards, including those in the North East of England.

Profits from the Sino-Japanese War and the subsidies provided under the Navigation Encouragement Law enabled NYK, in 1896, to begin operating its European Line, initially planned as an extension of the Bombay Line. At a time when Japan's railway network was rapidly expanding, thereby diminishing the future potential of coastal shipping, NYK's focus shifted to foreign shipping and the development of overseas trade. This trade revolved around the exporting of raw silk to America and cotton yarn to Korea and China along with the importing of raw cotton from India and America and machines and metal goods from Europe and America.[4] It was much affected by the 'shipping conference' system whereby a cartel-like organization of

European shipping companies, dominated by the British, adopted protectionist measures to maintain control over foreign routes.

In planning its new service to Europe, NYK was obliged to negotiate with the European-Far Eastern Conference (formed in 1879). Shoda Heigoro, an NYK company director, travelled to Europe in this connection late in 1895. From his arrival in London in February 1896, he attended to the preparations for the opening of the European Line – touring ports, setting up branch offices, appointing agents and ordering new ships. The arranging of NYK's ports of call in Europe brought Shoda into direct conflict with the European-Far Eastern Conference over port access. The Conference agreed to allow NYK to discharge cargo at London on its westbound route before going on to the Line's terminus at Antwerp. On the return journey, however, European Line vessels were not allowed to load eastbound goods at London. It was out of this restriction that NYK's important association with Middlesbrough evolved.

Middlesbrough was selected as the European Line's loading port for the eastbound journey and it was from there that metal goods, heavy machinery (spinning machines, etc.), iron rails and 'Lancashire and Yorkshire goods' (cotton and woollen cloths and yarns) were exported to Japan. A certain share of locomotive machinery, wheels and axles, normally carried from Liverpool by the Ocean Steamship Company, was, by special arrangement, also loaded for NYK at Middlesbrough. Even after 1899, when NYK won

Postcard illustrating the *Hakusan Maru* (1922), one of the many ships which called into Middlesbrough as part of NYK's European Line service (Betsho family).

the important concession of London loading rights for the eastbound journey, Middlesbrough, with its iron and steel and chemical industries, remained an important port of call well into the twentieth century. The NYK trade from Middlesbrough also encompassed the sole handling of Japanese government cargo, including munitions, from Britain. Indeed, military cargo, between 1899 and 1900, accounted for 4 per cent of the total eastbound freight receipts. By the end of the century, NYK ships were calling into Middlesbrough twice per month. As it was the coaling port for the European Line's eastbound route, this volume of traffic led to significant purchases of Durham coal and increased prosperity for the port of Middlesbrough. The European Line provided a passenger as well as a cargo service, transporting 29,777 passengers between Japan and Europe from 1896 to 1902 while 1984 million tons of cargo were handled over this same period.[5]

Although NYK was and remains Japan's leading shipping company, developments in domestic and foreign trade led to the formation of several other large shipping concerns in the late-nineteenth century. Osaka Mercantile Steamship Company (Osaka Shosen Kaisha) emerged in 1884 out of a freight agreement between small steamship owners in the Kansai region. After obtaining the annual mail subsidy in 1888, OSK began operating a regular service to almost all the ports in the western part of Japan. In the 1890s, it extended its services to Korea, Formosa and China, and, following the Russo-Japanese War, launched a full ocean-going service with its Hong Kong to Tacoma (Washington) route and, from 1913, Bombay Line.

Japan's third largest shipping company, the Oriental Shipping Company (Toyo Kisen Kaisha), owed its origins to the Shipbuilding Encouragement Law of 1896. From a small coastal shipping firm, TKK became a trans-Pacific passenger liner company and, by 1898, was operating a monthly service to San Francisco. Like NYK and OSK, TKK expanded its operations following the Russo-Japanese War, extending its west coast route to South America. All three companies, operating under government subsidy, grew and prospered (along with the Japanese economy) through Japan's successes in two wars. By the close of the Meiji period (1912), NYK owned vessels amounting to more than 280,000 tons; OSK, vessels of more than 130,000 tons; and TKK, vessels of more than 70,000 tons.[6]

Mitsui and Company (Mitsui Bussan Kaisha) also played a key part in the shipping history of this period. Established as a trading house in 1876, Mitsui became the sole agency for sales of coal from the government-owned Miike mine in Kyushu and for its transport to Hong Kong and Shanghai where it was supplied to western steamships. To cope with the demands of this trade, Mitsui purchased steamships in London, sailing ships from domestic yards, and chartered foreign sailing vessels and steamships. As trade increased and diversified towards the end of the century, Mitsui enlarged and modernized its own fleet and chartered large-scale foreign ships to carry growing consignments of coal to Singapore. Although its own shipping section was established in 1897, Mitsui, by the late 1890s, was importing substantial quantities of iron products (amounting to some 30,000 tons per year) via NYK's European Line and had become Japan's principal importer of locomotive machinery, iron rails and spinning machinery. By handling such a volume of heavy industrial cargo for Mitsui, NYK was compensated for the greater costs of shipping from the east coast port of Middlesbrough, an illustration of the kind of business alliance so prevalent in Japan.

The tremendous growth in mercantile shipping over these years led to a demand for ships and ship machinery which Japanese yards could not always meet. In 1887, Mitsubishi, with its origins in shipping, had purchased the Nagasaki shipyard from the government. Developed with western assistance, it represented the largest shipbuilding facility in the country.[7] Hitachi Shipbuilding had been similarly set up in the 1880s with the help of the Tyneside firm of C.S. Swan & Hunter Ltd.[8] In 1889, the Ishikawa shipyard was founded. There were, in addition, important naval yards at Yokosuka and Kobe (Hyogo). The development of overseas liner routes after the Sino-Japanese War, however, put a strain on the technology of Japanese yards. Foreign-built ships continued to be purchased by Japanese shipping companies under the favourable terms of the Navigation Encouragement Act of 1896. When, in 1899, the government reduced the level of subsidy for foreign-built vessels to one-half that allowed for ships constructed in Japan, the role of British yards in supplying Japanese merchant ships was considerably diminished. After 1900, NYK purchased most of its large ocean-going vessels from Mitsubishi rather than from overseas. In 1911, just before the government raised the rate of import duty on ships, there was a sudden rush of buying activity abroad but the new rate further strengthened the position of Japanese over foreign yards and sounded the death-knell for this particular form of trade.[9]

In the later decades of the nineteenth century, the shipyards of the North East of England, with their established reputation for the building of passenger and cargo ships, made a considerable contribution to Japan's merchant fleet. While the regional history of warship production for Japan revolves around Newcastle upon Tyne and the Elswick shipyard, Japanese merchant ships were built over these same years by a variety of yards on the rivers Tyne, Wear and Tees.

The carriage of coal had resulted in the creation of an elaborate transport network in the North East by the middle of the nineteenth century. Railways and shipping provided solutions to the problems of moving coal efficiently over both long and short distances. As in Japan, coastal shipping was crucial to the region's economy in catering to the coal markets of London. The growth of shipbuilding firms in the early-nineteenth century can be seen as a response to the demands of the coal trade as well as other types of commerce.

It was the building of the screw-propelled iron collier, *John Bowes*, in 1852 at Palmer's Jarrow shipyard on the Tyne which determined the future of the modern cargo vessel.[10] The iron-built steam colliers which succeeded the wooden sailing ships in mercantile use contributed greater capacity and speed to the efficiency of transport from this period onwards. The shipyards on the region's three rivers, all important centres of the coal trade by the 1850s, gradually adapted their production to iron shipbuilding. By 1863, the annual output of iron ships on the Tyne was 51,236 tons; on the Wear, 25,000 tons; and on the Tees, 15,060 tons.[11]

The river Wear was the earliest centre of commercial shipbuilding in the North East, with shipbuilding in Sunderland dating back to at least the mid-seventeenth century. Of the firms that had risen to prominence in the second half of the nineteenth century, James Laing & Company was formed in 1793, S.P. Austin & Company on the North Sands in 1826, Bartram's at Hylton in 1838, Pickersgill at Southwick in 1851, Doxford at Ox Green in 1840 and at Pallion from 1870, J.L. Thompson on the North Sands from 1846 and Short Brothers at Claxheugh in 1850.

The earliest shipbuilding sites on the Tyne can be traced back to the mid-eighteenth century though the growth of the industry was a mid-nineteenth-century phenomenon. Smith's Dock Company was established at St Peter's yard in east Newcastle from 1810, Charles Palmer opened his yard at Hebburn in 1851 as did Andrew Leslie two years later. In 1852, Charles Mitchell started his Walker yard at Wallsend which, from 1867, was building warships in collaboration with Armstrong's Elswick Company. With the amalgamation of the two firms in 1883 and the opening of the Elswick shipyard, Walker went on to specialize in merchant shipping. In 1871, R & W Hawthorn converted the St Peter's yard into an engineering works, while Smith's established a new yard and repair facilities in North and South Shields. C.S. Swan & Hunter Ltd opened their shipyard at Wallsend in 1872. These and a number of other companies built the Tyne's reputation for both merchant and naval ship construction.

While there were early shipyards on the Tees at Stockton, the development of the river and its facilities was generally later than on the Tyne and Wear. Of the port towns associated with shipbuilding in the North East,

The River Wear was the earliest centre of commercial shipbuilding in the North East. Merchant ships were built for Japan from the 1870s by various Sunderland yards (Newcastle City Libraries).

Middlesbrough's history is unique. With the extension of the Stockton to Darlington Railway to Middlesbrough in 1830, what had been a small agricultural community developed into a boom town. Middlesbrough, with its deeper harbour, provided a crucial link in the coastal shipping of Durham coal. Such was the importance of the coal trade to this quintessential Victorian town that its population of 150 in 1831 had grown to a remarkable 5463 just ten years later. The carriage of coal also led to the revitalization of the old port of Hartlepool, the population of which had quadrupled over the same period.[12]

Along with coal, the mining of iron-ore deposits in the Cleveland hills by Bolckow and Vaughan transformed the fortunes of Middlesbrough. Henry Bolckow and John Vaughan became partners in 1839, setting up blast furnaces at Witton Park and a small forge iron works at Middlesbrough. Vaughan's discovery of a main seam of iron-ore at Eston in 1850, however, resulted in an escalation of mining activity and the tremendous expansion of the business. When the Iwakura mission visited the Bolckow and Vaughan Iron Works in 1872, they paid tribute to the growing international importance of iron and steel to industry and to the firm that had done so much to heighten the reputation of Teesside. By 1881, Middlesbrough's population had grown to 56,000 an understandable leap when viewed in the context of the changing face of local industry. While

Teesside lacked even a single blast furnace in 1850, by 1881 it could point to twenty-seven smelting plants, operating a total of ninety-nine blast furnaces, with an annual output of over two million tons of pig iron.[13] Coal, iron-ore, and, in the latter years of the nineteenth century, a burgeoning chemical industry transformed Middlesbrough and led to the rise of shipbuilding concerns along the river Tees. A number of yards sprang up in the late-nineteenth and early-twentieth centuries including William Gray at Hartlepool in 1862, R. Cragg & Sons, Sir Raylton Dixon & Company, and, in 1909, Smith's Dock at South Bank, Middlesbrough.

In addition to shipbuilding, there were those North East firms which concentrated on marine engineering, including Parsons' and R & W Hawthorn of Newcastle, George Clark of Sunderland and Blair & Company of Stockton. Such companies supplied ship engines to local yards and dealt with foreign orders as the transfer of shipping technology increased.

Yards in the North East varied in the types of ships produced but some considerable success was achieved by narrowing the range and handling repeat orders for similar vessels. Teesside yards adopted this policy as did certain shipbuilders on the Tyne and Wear. Doxford's of Sunderland, for example, built 178 fairly standardized turret-deck cargo ships between 1893 and 1911 while Palmer's continued production of their highly successful iron colliers.[14] On the Tyne, meanwhile, some standard models of passenger and cargo ships were repeatedly produced, with Armstrong's specializing in oil tankers from the 1880s.

In considering the associations between Japanese shipping companies and North East yards, it is important to realize that more than one-half of

Middlesborough became the eastbound loading and coaling port for NYK's European Line in 1896. Among the vessels in the NYK fleet, were some ships built on the Tees (Newcastle City Libraries).

the world's new tonnage at the start of the twentieth century emanated from British yards and that over one-half this amount was built in the North East.[15] As Japan adapted her merchant fleet to the rigours of industrial commerce and international trade, imported British ships contributed to mercantile expansion and the establishment of overseas routes in the last decades of the nineteenth century. North East shipyards supplied NYK, OSK, TKK and Mitsui with numerous vessels, either purchased directly or at second hand.

In the case of NYK's fleet, over fifty North East-built ships were acquired between the 1870s and 1914. The fleet consisted initially of Mitsubishi steamers and then government vessels transferred to Mitsubishi. Among the latter were the *Seimyo Maru* (1858) built in Hartlepool and the *Taganoura Maru* (1869) built by James Laing of Sunderland. Both had changed hands a number of times before passing into Mitsubishi ownership. The NYK fleet also incorporated those Kyodo Unyu Kaisha ships purchased from abroad in pre-merger days.

In Mitsubishi's early years of development, the former P. & O. seaman and navigator, A.R. Brown,[16] played a key role in training merchant seamen and ordering new ships from the UK for the Japanese government. By the mid-1870s, with the reorganization of Mitsubishi under government subsidy, Brown's position was formalized as their marine superintendent. In that capacity, he purchased many ships to support the Meiji leadership's trade and military initiatives. The Taiwan expedition of 1874 had prompted emergency ship purchases, resulting in the acquisition of thirteen transport ships for government use which were then transferred to Mitsubishi in 1875. Of the thirteen, six – all iron screw-steamers – were Sunderland-built ships. The *Hyogo Maru* (1874) and *Sumida Maru* (1875) had been ordered directly by A.R. Brown from Robert Thompson's Southwick yard, while the remaining four vessels[17] were purchased from existing owners.

The *Hyogo Maru* was actually built as the *Min* but, on completion, was sold by Brown to the Japanese government and renamed. The *Sumida Maru*, designed as a troop-ship, was the first vessel built to order by Robert Thompson's for Japan. Morimichi Motono, the Japanese Minister, was present in Sunderland for the *Sumida*'s trial journey. During his stay, he toured many of the town's sights including the docks area, the River Wear Commissioners Chain and Anchor Test Works, Robert Thompson's shipyard, George Clark's engine works at Southwick (which had supplied the *Sumida*'s engines), as well as a number of public buildings. The Minister went down the pit at Wearmouth Colliery and looked to other important Sunderland industries as he inspected Hartley's glass works, Scott's pottery and Austin's bottle works. With the trial of the *Sumida*, the *Sunderland Echo* (5 February 1875) claimed for the town the first instance that the Japanese flag 'had ever floated in an English harbour'. The contemporary European dress of the Japanese Minister and sailors was somewhat predictably remarked upon. While the crew consisted of seventy Japanese and Lascar sailors, the *Sumida's* officers were all English. Descriptions of the vessel certainly indicated that there was an artistic dimension to technical transfer. In addition to elaborate wood carving in the saloon and berths, paintings of Japanese subjects by a local artist, 'Mr Smith of Villiers St', decorated the ship's windows.

Mitsubishi extended its coastal routes and inaugurated its first overseas shipping line from Yokohama to Shanghai over this same period. The Satsuma Rebellion of 1876 had directly involved Mitsubishi ships in military transport activities with thirty-two of the firm's forty coastal vessels requisitioned. The resulting disruption to coastal trade was compensated for by a government loan. This enabled the firm to purchase seven large steamships and several smaller vessels. Of these, three were recently built iron screw-steamers from North East yards which A.R. Brown acquired at second hand in 1877. It is thought that the *Takachiho Maru* (1873) was chartered to the Japanese government as a transport vessel during the Satsuma Rebellion before its sale to Mitsubishi.[18] This ship and the *Kumamoto Maru* (1875) were constructed at Charles Mitchell's Walker yard. The third North East ship financed by government loan at this time was the *Kokonoe Maru* (1875), built by J.R. Redhead & Company of South Shields. A smaller steamer, the *Kaihei Maru* (1865), a Pile, Hay & Company of Sunderland ship, was purchased by Mitsubishi the following year.

The competition between Mitsubishi and Kyodo Unyu Kaisha in the 1880s is well documented. KUK, established in 1882 under partial government subsidy, was tightly controlled with regard to its acquisition of ships. The new company was required to obtain government permission to purchase ships for its fleet, all of which had to be less than two years of age. A trip to the UK made by the KUK president, Ito Shunkichi, in 1883 resulted in the sale of sixteen such vessels to the firm.[19] Ito was, somewhat surprisingly, assisted by Mitsubishi's A.R. Brown in this shopping expedition. Of the sixteen ships, four were ordered directly from North East yards. The *Totomi Maru* (1883) was built by Robert Thompson & Sons of Sunderland while the other three, all dated 1884, were built at Armstrong-Mitchell's Walker yard. Each followed an interesting course.[20] The *Yamashiro Maru* carried the first consignment of Japanese emigrants to Hawaii in 1885 and, by her fourteenth voyage, had transported a total of 13,943 emigrants. In

Launch of the *Yamashiro Maru* at the Walker shipyard, Wallsend, on 12 January 1884. Lady M.D. Noble can be seen in the foreground (Newcastle City Libraries).

The *Yamashiro Maru*, built by Armstrong-Mitchell in 1884, carried the first consignment of Japanese emigrants to Hawaii in 1885 (Newcastle City Libraries).

The *Omi Maru* was built for Kyodo Unyu Kaisha by Armstrong-Mitchell in 1884 and, like the *Yamashiro Maru*, was successfully converted into a torpedo boat during the Sino-Japanese War (NYK).

1896, she became the first NYK vessel to be put into service on the Australian Line to Melbourne. The *Omi Maru* was the second vessel to serve on this Line. These two ships and the *Sagami Maru*, also ordered by Ito in 1883, won Armstrong-Mitchell early accolades in Japan for their adaptability to military use. Both the *Yamashiro Maru* and the *Omi Maru* were successfully converted into torpedo boats during the Sino-Japanese War while the *Sagami Maru* was remodelled as a supply ship. Later in 1883, the *Ecchu Maru* (1881), built by Short Brothers of Sunderland, was bought by Mitsui & Company and then transferred to KUK.

When Mitsubishi and KUK finally merged in 1885, each firm contributed twenty-nine steamships and, together, eleven sailing ships to the fleet of the new company, Nippon Yusen Kaisha. As thirty of the steamships were more than ten years old, a modernization programme was put into effect and twenty-five of the out-moded vessels disposed of. Of the replacement ships purchased between 1886 and 1892, many were built in the North East. These included the *Fushiki Maru* (1885) from the Tyne Shipbuilding Company at Willington Quay and the *Sakata Maru* (1887) from Andrew Leslie & Company, both purchased in 1887. New and high quality vessels like the steel screw-steamer *Miike Maru* (1888), built to order by Robert Thompson of Sunderland were assigned to NYK's growing overseas routes. The *Miike Maru* was the first ship put into service on Japan's US (Seattle) Line which began in 1896. The *Hokkai Maru*, another direct order, was purchased from Craig Taylor & Company of Stockton in 1890. Robert Thompson & Sons of Sunderland built the *Hiroshima Maru* for NYK in 1891 and, two years later, this ship sailed from Kobe to Bombay, marking the beginning of the company's wider ocean-going service. In 1892, the *Mikawa Maru* (1884), another Robert Thompson vessel, was acquired. By that year, NYK could claim ownership of twenty-eight ships less than ten years old and nineteen others that were over that age.

The *Fushiki Maru* (1885), built by the Tyne
Shipbuilding Company at Willington Quay,
was purchased by NYK in 1887 (NYK).

The Sino-Japanese War and the Russo-Japanese War resulted in a major escalation of shipping activity, ship purchases, and shipyard development in Japan. Even before the outbreak of war in 1894, the demand for ships to serve Japan's trade routes was mounting. The *Wakanoura Maru* (1885), built by Sir Raylton Dixon of Middlesbrough, and the *Asagao Maru* (1888), built by James Laing of Sunderland, were bought by NYK in 1893. The *Izumi Maru* (1894), built by William Dobson & Company of Newcastle, was purchased just before the start of the war.

As Japan declared war on China, virtually all NYK ships were requisitioned and many foreign ships were chartered in order to maintain the company's regular services. Ultimately, the war greatly benefited Japanese shipping, however, with NYK's fleet increasing from forty-five to sixty-eight ships by 1895. A number of North East ships were purchased second-hand by NYK and the Japanese government as troop transport vessels in 1894–5: the *Moji Maru* (1877), *Genzan Maru* (1868) and *Eijyo Maru* (1880) were built by Andrew Leslie & Company at Hebburn, and the *Tiensin Maru* (1887) by William Gray & Company of West Hartlepool. A further eight vessels from yards on the Tyne, the Wear and the Tees were bought by the Japanese government during 1894–5 and transferred to NYK in 1896.[21]

It was due to its increased tonnage following the Sino-Japanese War that NYK was prompted to launch services on new lines; in this way, the European Line, the Seattle Line and the Australian Line were born. In addition, eighteen new ships were built to serve these routes, including twelve for the European Line service. Each of the new vessels, with a gross tonnage of 6000 and a speed of fourteen knots, contributed to the success of NYK's expansion programme. In 1889, A.R. Brown had returned to Glasgow and established his own shipping business. As Honorary Japanese Consul, he maintained his links with Japan, selling, in the first thirteen years of his business, twenty Clyde-built ships to NYK. That North East

The steel screw steamer, *Miike Maru*, was built by Robert Thompson of Sunderland for NYK in 1888 and was the first ship put into service on the U.S. (Seattle) Line in 1896 (NYK).

The *Wakanoura Maru* (1885), built by Sir Raylton Dixon of Middlesborough, was bought by NYK to serve Japan's expanding trade routes in 1893 (NYK).

yards were not represented among the suppliers for these post-war purchases is, therefore, hardly surprising.

The merchant navy followed the pattern of the Imperial Japanese Navy in building up its resources at the turn of the century as Japan's relationship with Russia deteriorated. The *Bombay Maru*, built by Sunderland Shipbuilding & Company in 1900, joined the NYK fleet in 1902. In 1904, NYK acquired a number of vessels which were put to government use as troop, water supply, communication, guard and transport ships. At the start of the Russo-Japanese War, seventy-five NYK ships, totalling 24,000 tons, were requisitioned by the Army and the Navy, causing a temporary suspension of the overseas lines. Japan's other shipping companies were not spared their contribution to the war effort; the government requisitioned 48,000 tons from Osaka Shosen Kaisha and approximately 25,000 tons each from Toyo Kisen Kaisha and Mitsui.[22]

Among the purchases made by NYK in 1904 in response to the resulting shortage of vessels were seven North East-built ships.[23] These represented emergency purchases and were not ordered directly from the region's yards but bought from existing owners. NYK's losses during the war amounted to eleven ships, totalling 252,000 tons. In the post-war period, reorganization of the fleet led to the acquisition in 1906 of the *Hirosaki Maru* (1902) and *Kamikawa Maru* (1903) built by Sir Raylton Dixon & Company of Middlesbrough. Captured Russian ships were transferred from the Japanese Navy to NYK in 1912. Three of these had originally been built in North East yards.[24]

NYK's emergency purchases of vessels at the start of the Russo-Japanese War included the *Totomi Maru* (1901), built by S. P. Austin & Sons of Sunderland (NYK).

From the first purchases made by A.R. Brown in 1874 to the transfer of these last three ships in 1912, NYK had utilized a total of fifty-one North East-built vessels in its Japanese coastal trade, overseas liner service, and, in 1894–5 and 1904–5, for military transport. Many of these had been purchased from existing owners but a certain percentage were ordered directly from the yards. Armstrong-Mitchell had contributed some highly adaptable vessels before the Sino-Japanese War and Robert Thompson's of Sunderland supplied troop ships and other passenger and cargo steamers for NYK in the 1880s and 1890s.

NYK was not the only Japanese shipping company which made use of ships built in the North East. Osaka Shosen Kaisha, formed in 1884, extended its services to Korea, Formosa and China in the 1890s, which resulted in orders placed with yards on the Tyne and Wear. The *Tai Tou Maru* was built for OSK in 1896 by Blyth Shipbuilders while the *Anping* (1896) and *Takao* (1897) were ordered from Wigham Richardson's (Swan

The *Tainan Maru* was one of three passenger and cargo steamers built for Osaka Shosen Kabushiki Kaisha (OSK) by Joseph L. Thompson & Sons of Sunderland in 1897 (Tyne and Wear Museums Service).

Hunter) Neptune yard. James Laing of Sunderland built the *Taichu Maru* for OSK in 1897 and, during that same year, Joseph L. Thompson & Sons of Sunderland supplied three vessels – the *Keelung*, *Tamsui* and *Tainan* – to cater to the shipping company's new services. All three passenger and cargo steamers were launched within a six-month period from Thompson's North Sands building yard. The engines and boilers were supplied by John Dickinson & Company Ltd, another Sunderland firm, at their Palmer's Hill Engine Works. Sugiyama Komei, OSK's managing director, was present at the launch of the *Keelung* (4 November 1896).[25] Attending the launch of the *Tainan* (3 June 1897) were various other representatives from OSK including Mr Konishi S., the Chief Superintendent, Mr Atsumi, Superintendent Engineer, Captain Tarao G., Captain Negata S. and Captain Hubback.[26] Among the naval officers present was Commander Fukuda N. who was, most likely, attached to one of the IJN warships in preparation at Elswick. Finally, Armstrong Whitworth built a cargo vessel, the *Chosen Maru*, for OSK in 1911 at their Walker yard on the Tyne. This was launched at Wallsend on 11 September 1911.

Toyo Kisen Kaisha went into business in 1896 and, in December 1898, as Japan's third largest shipping company, started its liner service to San Francisco. the *Nippon Maru*, *Hong Kong Maru* and *America Maru* were built by yards in the North East in 1898 specifically to serve this new route. The first two ships were produced by James Laing of Sunderland with a Japanese overseer, Captain Tomioko of TKK, resident in Sunderland during 1898 to

Launch of the OSK cargo vessel, *Chosen Maru*,
at the Walker shipyard, Wallsend, on 11 September 1911
(Newcastle City Libraries).

supervise construction of the vessels at Laing's Deptford yard.[27] At the launch of the *Hong Kong Maru* (7 July 1898), Sir James Laing admitted to a changing awareness of Japan and the Japanese which matched the sentiments being expressed at similar functions on the Tyne:

> Fifty years ago the islands of Japan were mere geographical names to the people of this country, and the way the natives had developed the resources of their country and taken advantage of European education and methods was one of the most astounding advances of the century.

Sir Marcus Samuel, London agent for TKK, replied to this toast, acknowledging in turn a growing awareness of the skill of North East shipbuilders in the international market-place:

> At one time it was generally supposed that passenger and mail steamers could only be built on the Clyde, but no one who had seen the two fine vessels that had been built for them by Sir James Laing could doubt that the North East could build as fine a vessel as could be built anywhere.[28]

The third vessel ordered by TKK at this time, the *America Maru*, was built at Wigham Richardson's Nepture yard on the Tyne. In 1908, Toyo Kisen looked to Armstrong-Whitworth for their purchase of the oil tanker, *Buyo Maru*. By then, the firm had built up a particular specialization in this field.

Mitsui & Company, with its significant shipping interests, purchased

Toyo Kisen Kaisha purchased the oil tanker, *Buyo Maru*, from Armstrong-Whitworth's Walker shipyard in 1908. The Newcastle firm specialised in oil tanker production during this period (The Science Museum, Newcastle).

several vessels from Sunderland shipyards in 1911. Glover Brothers of London acted on behalf of the Japanese trading house in ordering a steel screw-steamer, the *Takaosan Maru*, from John Priestman & Company of Southwick. The *Sunderland Daily Echo* (17 April 1911) noted that 'Mrs Mitsui' was on hand to perform the christening ceremony in April 1911. The ship was considered of special interest given its construction on the self-trimming cantilever principle that had been patented by Priestman, Harroway and Dixon. Two Mitsui employees, Mr Nagataki and Mr Kurata, were resident in Sunderland during the construction of the ship and acted in a supervisory capacity on the firm's behalf. Joseph L. Thompson of Sunderland built another vessel for Mitsui in 1911, the *Tenpaisan Maru*. The engines and boilers for both ships were supplied by Blair & Company of Stockton, another illustration of the wider business links established with the region through such orders.

While NYK maintained its premier position in Japanese shipping, Osaka Shosen, Toyo Kisen and Mitsui, in expanding their services, made use of North East shipyards and engineering works. The yard lists for some local shipbuilders also point to orders placed directly by the Japanese government. Palmer's of Jarrow, for example, built and engined an 800-ton iron screw-steamer for the Japanese government as early as 1863, referred to in the company listings and press reports only as 'Number One'. Floating dock gates were ordered by the Meiji government from Wigham Richardson's Neptune yard and were listed as the fifty-three-foot 'Japanese Caisson' (1899), and the 280-foot 'Japanese Dock Number One' (1902) and 'Dock Number Two' (1903).

Further orders were placed with North East yards by private companies in Japan as when Holme, Ringer, & Company of Nagasaki purchased the *Asagao* from James Laing of Sunderland in 1888 for the Takashima Colliery Company. The steel screw-steamer was engined by George Clark of Sunderland and was destined to carry coal from Nagasaki to Hong Kong. In addition to the ordinary galley for Europeans, the ship was fitted with a 'native' galley for the use of the Japanese sailors who made up the majority of the crew.[29] The Takashima Colliery had been jointly operated by the British and Japanese since 1868 when the Nagasaki-based merchant Thomas Glover entered into an agreement with the Saga clan to develop the mine.[30] By 1888, Glover no longer had any personal involvement in the Takashima coal mine but some of his original business partners acted on the colliery company's behalf in purchasing the *Asagao* from Sunderland.

Specific references have been made to North East marine engineering establishments, such as Clark's of Sunderland and Blair's of Stockton, who provided engines and boilers for Japanese vessels built in the region. A more

direct Japanese link was established with Parsons Marine Steam Turbine
Company at Wallsend in the early years of the twentieth century.
Following their successful development of the first turbine-driven vessel,
Turbinia, in 1897, Parsons received orders from all over the world. Not
surprisingly, the Japanese placed a number of orders with the Tyneside
marine engineering firm for turbine engines to be fitted in both merchant
vessels and warships. In 1906, Mitsubishi ordered Parsons turbines for the
Toyo Kisen passenger ships, *Tenyo Maru* and *Chiyo Maru*. These, Japan's
first turbine-driven ships, were built in 1908 at Mitsubishi's Nagasaki
shipyard. The turbine orders were handled through Brown MacFarlane,
A.R. Brown's Glasgow-based company which placed orders with firms like
Parsons on behalf of Mitsubishi. Through this same channel, two Japanese
torpedo-boat destroyers, *Umikaze* and *Yamakaze*, built by Mitsubishi between 1909 and 1911, were supplied with Parsons turbines ordered in 1908.
In 1910, Vickers-Maxim ordered engines for the battleship *Kongo* being
built for the Japanese Navy at Barrow-in-Furness. Brown Macfarlane placed
another order with Parsons in 1911 for engines for the Toyo Kisen South
American liner, *Anyo Maru*, built by Mitsubishi in 1913. Parsons supplied
engines for the NYK vessels, *Toyooda Maru* and *Toyama Maru*, completed
by Mitsubishi in 1915. In that same year, an order was placed by
Commander Yoshida, representing the Nagasaki shipyard, for turbines for
the battleship *Hyuga*, completed in 1918. These represent verifiable
orders[31] placed with Parsons though many further purchases appear to have
been made by Mitsubishi from this North East firm over the years.

In some cases, licensing agreements were drawn up which involved the
manufacture of a particular turbine model for Mitsubishi by Parsons with
training for Japanese engineers built into the agreement.[32] The *Tenyo Maru*
turbine order thus provided design and manufacturing experience for one
senior engineer and one senior worker from Mitsubishi at Wallsend. Under
the terms of the licence, the next model would be built in Japan to Parsons'
designs and future ones designed at Nagasaki but checked by Parsons. This
mode of importing technology began in 1904 and resulted in a close
relationship between the two firms. Parsons sent several engineers to
Nagasaki in 1908 to supervise the fitting of the *Tenyo Maru* turbines. When
problems developed with the first geared turbine adapted for the *Anyo Maru*
in 1913, a Japanese engineer and two workers were sent to Parsons to study
gear hobbing. In this way, Parsons generated a steady stream of traffic
between the North East and Japan.

The strong regional link with the Mitsubishi shipyard at Nagasaki is
further illustrated by the membership lists of the North East Coast
Institution of Engineers and Shipbuilders. The names of Mitsubishi engineers,

naval architects and even managing directors appear from 1900 onwards.

The shipbuilding associations between Japan and the North East of England from the 1880s were important on a number of levels. It was not only the Imperial Japanese Navy but also Japan's merchant shipping companies which absorbed the latest in shipbuilding technology through the ships being purchased from the North East and the direct contact with the yards, engineering works and local shipbuilding institutions which visits to the region afforded. There is clear evidence that Japanese engineers and technicians supervised the construction of both naval and merchant vessels built in the North East and that some spent very lengthy periods in the area, apprenticed to firms, attending night classes and learning – at first hand – how to build the best possible ships. The goal, in the case of both navies, was to cut the umbilical cord which bound them to British expertise and to attain the knowledge and independence crucial to the development of their own shipbuilding skills. It was a goal that could be easily understood in the wider context of Meiji coming of age. It was, by 1914, a goal that was largely achieved as Japan's shipyards acquired the resources and self-confidence successfully to construct their own men-of-war, cargo and passenger ships. While some shipbuilding technology links between Japan and the North East continued beyond 1914, yards like Mitsubishi at Nagasaki were fully operative by the start of the First World War and no longer looked to foreign yards for instruction. The shipyards of the North East, meanwhile, experienced a steady decrease in foreign orders, particularly in the area of naval shipbuilding, which did not bode well for the future of the industry.

If Japanese ships were no longer being built on the region's rivers, there was nevertheless an important shipping connection with the North East which survived well past the years of the Great War. NYK's European Line had gone into operation in 1896 with Middlesbrough as the loading and coaling port for its eastbound journey. As trade links between Japan and Britain flourished, Teesside exports continued to make their contribution to the growth of Japanese industry.

Middlesbrough was one of the few British cities in the early years of the twentieth century to have an Honorary Japanese Consul. Waynman Dixon of the local shipbuilders, Sir Raylton Dixon & Company, took on this role in 1901 as NYK made its bimonthly calls into Middlesbrough. The intensive development of heavy industry in Japan necessitated the ongoing import of machinery, metal goods and pig iron from the Cleveland area. In addition to its other sources for such materials, Mitsui & Company placed orders for locomotives with Hawthorn Leslie's engineering works in the first decade of the twentieth century. According to the firm's records, at least one such order provided for the supply of locomotives to the Japan Steel Works at Muroran in 1911, the year in which the Armstrong Whitworth and Vickers joint-venture operation went into production. As NYK was Mitsui's sole transport agent, such goods would have been loaded at Middlesbrough for shipment to Japan. The NYK ships which served the European Line and called into Middlesbrough were, until 1900, mainly built in Britain. By 1914, virtually all new ships were being built in Japan. The trade with this east coast port and the history of NYK's links with the region can be seen to highlight certain larger issues central to Japan's modernization and her changing relationship with the West.

The First World War brought Japan's shipbuilding industry and merchant shipping into a new phase. Between 1914 and 1918, the Japanese mercantile marine doubled in size from a tonnage of one-and-a-half million in steamships and motor vessels at the start of the war to three million in 1918.[33] The war in Europe provided a tremendous boost to the Japanese economy with the pace of industrialization quickening to fill the trading gaps created by the more pressing involvements of the nations in conflict. Japan found herself with new and expanded export markets, many of which, particularly in textiles, were retained after 1918. Her munitions factories and shipyards dramatically increased production to fill the orders for guns and ships now being placed by her western allies. Despite the amazing shift in the fortunes of this once-hailed 'fairyland', western imports of engineering equipment and other industrial raw materials were still needed to keep Japan's factories running and the lifeblood of heavy industry flowing. Although steel production, for example, had risen from a quarter-of-a-million tons in 1913 to approximately half-a-million tons in 1919, this latter figure represented less than one-half of contemporary consumption. In order to export, Japan was dependent on imported raw materials, a 'Catch-22' situation which has persevered to the present day and from which she has acquired her 'fragile superpower' status. The implications of this trading relationship for the growth of merchant shipping in the 1914–18 period were considerable. Japan's position as a trading nation soared as her annual income from freights multiplied ten times over the war years. NYK, previously hidebound by the European 'conference' system, enjoyed a wartime shipping boom as it kept its trading routes open (though the European Line service was suspended for this period) and established new services on thirteen ocean-going lines and three lines around Japan. By the end of the war, Japan was the third largest shipping nation of the world, after Britain and America.

The cessation of hostilities, however, brought with it a world-wide slump in shipbuilding which affected British yards as well as Japanese. In the North East, this change in the fortunes of the industry had dramatic and, ultimately, lasting effects. Associations with Japan were reinforced through trade but, in the years following the First World War, the building of ships for Japan would become part of the region's memory of a truly great industrial past. In the world of images, this one would be retained by the Japanese as the one, more than any other, which summed up the character and legacy of the North East of England. It was a lingering image which did not confine itself to the time-scale of the immediate post-war period but was to be sustained far into the future.

The Troubled Years: A Friendship Under Strain

The First World War accelerated the pace of industry in Japan and, for the North East, meant a revitalization of shipbuilding and heavy industry, with the region's shipyards working to capacity from 1914 to 1918. An average of five ships per week were produced in North East yards throughout the years of the war, in addition to a vast undertaking in ship-repairing work resulting from the German submarine offensive. By 1917, a shortage of labour and of steel was pushing the industry to its limits, with Lloyd George, the then-Prime Minister, seeing victory as very much 'a question of tonnage'.[1] The standardization of vessels helped to boost production levels and firms like Armstrong-Whitworth emerged from the war in considerable profit, if somewhat stretched. The prospects for the post-war future were not so bright however, given the diminishing demand for warships and armaments in a world at least temporarily at peace.

British merchant shipping had suffered a severe set-back due to the wartime disruption of trade. The loss of export markets, as with the European coal trade, had serious implications for shipbuilding, particularly in the North East where the multi-purpose cargo vessel was the backbone of the industry.[2] This, and the emphasis on naval construction from 1914, saw merchant shipping in a state of decline. The first two years after the war were prosperous ones as North East shipyards replaced wartime losses and filled a backlog of mercantile orders. With 1920, however, came a world-wide slump in shipbuilding which led to the closure of many North East yards and a change in the employment structure of the region. Just three years later, Sunderland could sadly claim 14,000 unemployed shipyard workers and Jarrow, 6000.[3]

While Japan had benefited economically from the war, the post-war recession in trade most strongly affected those industries like coal-mining and shipbuilding which had undergone rapid expansion in recent years. Industrial unrest followed at the Kawasaki and Mitsubishi shipyards as prices rose and workers fought to maintain levels of employment.[4]

In the North East, the traditional industries of coal-mining, iron and steel, shipbuilding and engineering, all so interconnected, suffered from the same international pressures as were affecting Japan. The Washington Conference of 1921–2, which focused on naval disarmament, imposed restrictions on naval building and armament production and set levels for the relative strengths of the British, American, and Japanese navies. This heightened the dilemma of shipyards like Armstrong-Whitworth, Palmers and Hawthorn Leslie whose prospects for naval work had already suffered with the end of the war. In instituting the Four Power Pact in December 1921, involving Britain, Japan, France and the United States, the Washington Conference brought about the demise of the Anglo-Japanese Alliance, which finally lapsed in 1923. With its conclusion, two decades of close friendship between Japan and Britain came to a close. That an alliance which hinged to such an extent on naval links should be superseded at a Conference focused on naval disarmament has been seen as fitting.[5] The North East of England had enjoyed a close and fruitful relationship with Japan up to the start of the First World War. What then did the demise of the Alliance mean for the region's future associations with its former economic partner?

While naval shipbuilding for Japan had declined in the first decade of the twentieth century, Armstrong Whitworth maintained its direct involvement with the country through the Japan Steel Works Ltd. Established at Muroran on Hokkaido in 1907, the Japan Steel Works was a joint-venture company formed by Armstrong-Whitworth, Vickers and the Hokkaido Coal and Steamship Company. Like latter-day *yatoi*, engineers and advisers

Hydraulic press produced by Armstrong-Whitworth's Manchester Works for the Japan Steel Works at Muroran (Company Prospectus).

from Elswick and Sheffield steel workers travelled to Japan to direct operations and training at Muroran. In 1911, the year in which the Japan Steel Works went into production, the company issued a prospectus in which British technical assistance was gratefully acknowledged and the teacher-pupil relationship between Japan and Britain highlighted. Although some Japanese came to the UK for training, Armstrong-Whitworth reported sending a designer and gunnery expert from Elswick and an accountant, a foreman and four steel smelters from Sheffield to Japan in 1911.[6] In 1912, a 'passport to travel to Japan' was issued to George Adamson Atkinson, an engineer from the Elswick Works who went to Muroran to provide instruction in the manufacture of large naval guns.[7] That same year, a Mr Trevelyan was sent by the company to assist in the management of the Japan Steel Works. By 1913, it was suggested that he be appointed a resident director.[8] Admiral Yamanouchi, the first President of the Japan Steel Works, who had earlier naval ties with Armstrong Mitchell's, was invited to Newcastle in 1912 to discuss the financial postion of the steel works.[9] Though it is not clear whether he actually made the journey, continued associations were obviously quite considerable even before the First World War increased the respective demands for steel and armaments in Japan and Britain.

By 1917, a new agreement had superseded the original 1907 contract, appointing the Japan Steel Works as sole agents in Japan for both the armament and commercial products of Vickers and Armstrong-Whitworth.

Passport for travel to Japan issued to George Adamson Atkinson, a gun engineer from Elswick, in 1912 (Tyne and Wear Archives Service).

Tokugawa Yorisada and his wife, Tame (centre) uncle and aunt of the Empress of Japan, visit *Cragside* in 1929 (The National Trust).

The successful growth of the company saw its capital reaching £4,000,000 in 1919 with Vickers' and Armstrong's share of the company's assets reduced to 25 per cent.[10]

The decisions reached at the Washington Naval Conference and the ultimate demise of the Anglo-Japanese Alliance resulted in a much altered relationship between Vickers', Armstrong's and the Japan Steel Works. Contracts were cancelled and the British firms sought means of withdrawing from their Japanese commitments. This they failed to do; it was not until the 1930s that what had begun as the consolidation of an earlier relationship came grindingly to a halt.

When the first Lord Armstrong died without a direct heir in 1900, his estate passed to his great-nephew William Watson-Armstrong (1863–1941) who, in 1903, became the first Lord Armstrong of the second creation. Lord Armstrong of Cragside and Bamburgh, as he was known, pursued the friendships of his illustrious forebear and entertained many Japanese visitors over the years at his Rothbury home. In 1916, Tokugawa Yorisada and his wife, Tame, uncle and aunt of the Empress of Japan, paid the first of several visits to Cragside, during which gifts of Japanese prints and other items were presented to the family. Sir William Armstrong's original 'Business Room' came to house such gifts and was later named the 'Japanese Room' in their honour. In the year of that first visit, the Cragside visitors' book was inscribed with a poem by another guest from Japan, Yamada Nakaba, who in an eight-month period (from December 1915 to August 1916) stayed several times with Lord and Lady Armstrong. The poem, written in both

English and Japanese, is a tribute to the first Lord Armstrong and to the spirit of Victorianism with which the house is so imbued. The poignancy of this testament to Japan's identification with Britain's past is reflected in the changed perspective of her own achievements by 1916. Yamada dedicated his poem – 'To the Honour of Cragside'. It reads as follows:

> One day I came to Rothbury
> Where a norman cross solemnly stands,
> Bearing some epitaph of a man,
> A greatest geneous [sic] since Eve span,
> Of both his grand virtue and work.
> I trod my pace toward a river,
> Where he ever used to throw his flies
> Where, by the bank, now his graveyard lies.
>
> Paused where's the meadow green and soft,
> My eyes were musefully laid,
> Upon a fairly old cross tombstone;
> To the carved words, my attention was paid,
> 'Whatever thy hand findeth to do, do it with thy might',
> Which shone my heart as a flash of light.
> Here lies the soul of the Cragside Herbe
> Who with his gift and arduous work
> Had won the day to make his mark.
>
> His greatest mind and marvellous task,
> Has blessed all as the sunbeam ray,
> Has made them come homage to pay.
> Alas he is no more on the earth,
> Yet his fame will everlastingly glow,
> As if the waters forever flow.
> His soul rests by the Coquetdale,
> Still pleased with the stream from the vale,
> Which had ever been his greatest mate,
> The sole master of his epoch-making plan,
> To unite the powers of water and man,
> 'The flowing of water, the wheeling of crane'.

For Yamada and other Japanese visitors to Cragside in the 1920s and 1930s, the Armstrong name conjured up memories of an age in which Japan's links with the region had first been forged.

During the inter-war period, the North East of England continued to be identified in Japan as a centre of industrial know-how. Even after Japanese

shipyards had proven their capabilities through increased levels of pro-
duction in the years of the Great War, membership of the North East Coast
Institution of Engineers and Shipbuilders remained much sought after. If
Japan had caught up with British shipbuilding skills, she did not intend to
be left behind in the development of new technology. In October 1918,
Ota Dai, a shipbuilding engineer from the Uraga Dock Company near
Yokohama, was elected an associate member of the Institution. Exactly one
year later, Baron Tokudaiji Tsunemaro, a naval architect at Mitsubishi's
Kobe shipyard, was proposed for full membership by Ito Kumezo, Haramishi,
M. and Sir Charles Parsons. New Japanese members in the 1920s included:
Hamada Hyo (October 1922), managing director of Mitsubishi Zosen
Kaisha (shipbuilding company) in Tokyo, who was proposed by Shiota T.,
Haramishi M. and Baron Tokudaiji; Takagishi Otojiro (October 1924),
chief engineer of the Military Transportation Office (Hiroshima); and
Captain Shiozawa Koichi, Naval Attaché to the Japanese Embassy in
London, who became an associate member in 1927. The last Japanese to be
proposed for membership to the Institution before the outbreak of the
Second World War was another managing director of Mitsubishi, Shiba
Koshiro, elected a full member in February 1933.[11]

Pilgrimages to Elwick[12] by Japanese naval and industrial missions in the
1920s underlined the lingering prestige of this North East shipyard which
had formed so many important ties with Japan. Armstrong Whitworth had
opened a new naval yard at Walker in 1913 but the mystique of Elswick
remained considerable. On 11 May 1921, twenty officers of the Imperial
Japanese Third Squadron visited the celebrated shipyard. This visit was
followed by that of the Japanese Naval Attaché which included a tour by
five senior officers of the Elswick works on 11 July 1921.

On 16 January 1922, an important Japanese industrial mission came to
Elswick. The party of fifty-two business leaders, who had arrived in Britain
in December 1921, was on a tour of key industrial locations in the UK and
the United States. Led by Dr Dan Takuma of Mitsui & Company, they
were granted an audience with George V in London and met with the
Foreign Secretary, Lord Curzon, during their stay. The visit to Newcastle
was made by nineteen members of the mission and included detailed tours
of the Elswick works and the Walker naval yard.[13] Among the group were
leading industrialists from Tokyo, Yokohama, Osaka, Kyoto and Kobe. All
were to go on to careers in the fast lane of the Japanese industrial and
political establishment: Fujiwara Ginjiro, then president of the Oji Paper
Manufacturing Company and benefactor of Keio University's engineering
faculty, became Minister of Commerce and Minister of War Production
during the Second World War; Ohashi Shintaro headed various leading
companies and established the Hakubunkan Publishing Company, later

Signatures of leading Japanese industrialists
in Elswick shipyard Visitors' Book, 1922
(Tyne and Wear Archives Service).

becoming a member of the Upper and Lower House; Nakajima Kumakichi rose to top positions in Furukawa Gomei, Yokohama Rubber, Furukawa Denko and the Nihon Kogyo Club. He went on to become Minister of Commerce and Industry and was the founder of Nihon Boekikai (the Japan Foreign Trade Council). Hara Kunizo was president of Daihyaku Bank and Aikokuseimei (life insurance) and headed other important industrial concerns before becoming chairman of Japan Air Lines. The calibre of the visitors suggests that North East industry was still felt to have something to offer Japan in this period.

Of the names which stand out in the Elswick shipyard visitors' book from these years, those recorded on 22 October 1923 were clearly of the greatest historical significance. The naval delegation was headed by Vice-Admiral Ide Kenji who knew Elswick well, having accompanied Admiral Togo on his own pilgrimage to Newcastle in 1911. At that time, Ide was Naval Attaché to the Japanese Embassy in London. By 1923, he had risen in rank and it was as a military councillor that he returned to the North East, attended by colleagues of some stature. Rear Admiral Tosu Tamaki was in the party, as was Commander Yamamoto Isoroku, the man who would be remembered for masterminding the Japanese attack on Pearl Harbor in 1941. Yamamoto left Japan with Ide in July 1923 on a nine-month tour of England, France, Monaco, Germany, Austria, Italy and the United States.[14] It is of some interest that Elswick, despite the shipping shortages of the 1920s, was on the itinerary. In treading in the footsteps of Togo, Japan's most famous naval tactician, the future Commander-in-Chief of the Combined Fleet was perhaps already absorbing some of the lessons of history.

Signatures of Japanese officers in Elswick shipyard Visitors' Book. Yamamoto Isoroku went on to become Commander in Chief of the Combined Fleet (Tyne and Wear Archives Service).

Armstrong-Whitworth had tried to survive the difficult times by diversifying. A shortage of artillery orders after the Boer War led to the firm's first move into motor car and commercial vehicle production. After some experimentation, the Armstrong-Whitworth car went into manufacture from 1906 and carried on until the outbreak of the First World War. Then, in 1919, Armstrong's purchased the Siddeley-Deasy Company and formed a new holding company, Armstrong-Whitworth Development Company Ltd, with Armstrong-Siddeley Motors Ltd as a subsidiary.[15] Motor car production was taken up again at Coventry but eventually, in 1926, the two firms parted ways to pursue their independent careers. The North East's only foray into the motor industry had come to an end.

Financial problems precipitated a forced merger between Armstrong-Whitworth and its former rival, Vickers' in 1927. The new company, Vickers-Armstrong Ltd, lived on to preserve the armaments and shipbuilding interests of both firms, but symbolized in the demise of Armstrong-Whitworth as an autonomous enterprise was the end of the economic ascendancy of the North East.

Heavy industry on the Tyne, Wear and Tees had suffered irrevocably through the post-war depression years. On Teesside, however, the rise of the chemical industry helped to counteract some of the losses of employment otherwise incurred. With the establishment of ICI at Billingham in 1926, the region was revitalized as the industry expanded to meet growing markets both at home and abroad. NYK had maintained its shipping link with Middlesbrough throughout these years and had added chemicals to the list of goods loaded at the Teesside port. Between 1912 and 1926, the principal cargo shipped from Middlesbrough to Yokohama and Kobe consisted of

Armstrong-Whitworth motor car, c 1914. Armstrong-Whitworth moved into car production in 1906, eventually forming Armstrong-Siddeley Motors Ltd. which located its production base in Coventry after the First World War (The Science Museum, Newcastle).

steel, pig iron and ammonium sulphate. After 1926, chemical exports to Japan broadened to include nitric acid, 'cyan natrium' and raw zinc.[16]

NYK's bimonthly stops at Middlesbrough brought a visible presence from Japan to the region. Japanese businessmen, families and students could be seen mingling with other travellers as the ships were loaded for their return journey to Japan. On the North Continental Cruise of the *Terukuni Maru*

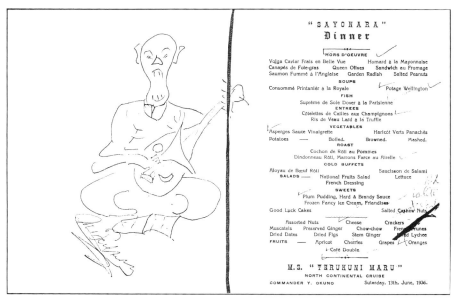

'Sayonara' dinner menu from NYK European Liner's North Continental Cruise, 13 June 1936 (NYK).

in June 1936, the passenger list of 107 names included only thirteen from Japan. This smaller proportion of Japanese passengers was fairly standard but the European Line, nevertheless, made much of its eastern origins. The *Terukuni Maru*'s was not the only voyage to feature a 'Sayonara Dinner' with suitably styled menus. Indeed, many of the ships themselves were decorated with traditional paintings and woodwork designs redolent of the old Japan.

One of NYK's early European liners, the *Awa Maru*, developed a more personal association with the area when, on the night of 27 December 1906, she was stranded on the sands at Redcar. The crew of 112 officers and men were all rescued and were much fêted on shore. Local legend has fed on the incident. The captain, known as 'Togo', was said to have left an illegitimate child behind. In later years, the Redcar fish-shop owner Margaret Crawford recalled her brother receiving a Yorkshire terrier on his birthday which was named 'Togo' – with all due respect to the skipper of the *Awa Maru*.[17]

Apart from this rather unusual Redcar connection, the NYK ships of the European Line were crewed by Japanese sailors who found in the port of Middlesbrough a home away from home.[18] Over the years, a succession of Japanese boarding houses sprang up along Marton Road in the docks area of the city. The first of these, run by Tommy Amori, was opposite the Borough Hotel at 96 Marton Road. Amori's café and boarding house appears to have had direct NYK links and to have provided facilities for Japanese seamen in transit. Eventually, its lodgers would include those Japanese seamen who found their way to Middlesbrough independently of NYK. The existence of a seagoing Japanese population in Middlesbrough in the 1920s and 1930s gave rise to the establishment of Otani's boarding house at 42 Marton Road and the very popular Suzuki's at 48 Marton Road. In considering the presence of Japanese in Teesside during these years, NYK may offer an initial framework, but wider developments in mercantile traffic were the context out of which Middlesbrough's Japanese community evolved.

The boom in trade and shipping which led to the opening of NYK's European Line in 1896 had also resulted in an increased mobility for merchant seamen from all over the world. Many Japanese seamen followed different paths to Middlesbrough during the First World War. In a number of cases, work aboard British vessels had led them to northern ports. Middlesbrough, with its Japanese boarding houses and NYK link, proved a popular land-base for securing future employment. The association with NYK also made Middlesbrough one of the few cities in Britain to have an Honorary Japanese Consul. That the Consul was also a shipping agent

An aerial view (1954) of Middlesborough Dock on the south bank of the River Tees. Marton Road can be seen running from right to left (lower centre) (Hunting Aerofilms).

enhanced the opportunities for work and settlement in the region. In 1899, NYK appointed T.A. Bulmer & Company as their Middlesbrough agents. Waynman Dixon of the local shipbuilding firm, Sir Raylton Dixon & Company, was Honorary Japanese Consul between 1901 and 1930. By the 1930s, this role had passed to Alfred W. Bulmer who was also the agent for NYK. For those seamen leaving Japan in the first decades of the twentieth century, a base in the North East of England had not been their set goal. The history of Japanese emigration in the nineteenth century provides some insights into the motivations of the Japanese who found themselves in Middlesbrough at the time of the First World War.

Between 1885 and 1908, many Japanese had emigrated to Hawaii where fixed contracts for work on the sugar-cane plantations meant a secure living and the possibility of future residence on the US mainland. By 1908, however, the US government had reduced the flexible options for emigration. Although the numbers of Japanese emigrants drastically declined after this date, America still held the promise of a brighter future, particularly for the poverty-stricken tenant farmers of south-western Japan. The greater proportion of Japanese emigrants had come from the prefectures of Hiroshima, Yamaguchi, Kumamoto and Fukuoka – districts known for

Doi Tomoji, born in Miyagi prefecture in 1893, arrived in Middlesborough in 1916 (Doi family).

the poverty, hardship and deprivation associated with the farming life.[19] Even after the contract system was abolished, some independent emigrants from this background made their way to America and other parts of the world. The Japanese who settled in Middlesbrough in a slightly later period did not form part of such formal emigration movements but, as *de facto* emigrants, were clearly affected by the hopes and ambitions of those who had preceded them in leaving Japan. Merchant shipping was the context for their migration and merchant shipping provided a lifestyle for those who chose to stay. By 1920, it has been estimated, some 250 Japanese were living in Middlesbrough. Many of these found employment on British merchant vessels and had contact with Japan only through the *maru* boats (a traditional term applied to Japanese merchant vessels) which they regularly visited for Japanese food, medicine and news from home.

A general picture of the circumstances of Middlesbrough's Japanese community can be pieced together by considering the individual stories of some of those seamen who found themselves based in the North East in the inter-war period. Doi Tomoji, born in Miyagi prefecture in 1893, arrived in Middlesbrough in 1916. Through Duncan's Shipping Company, Doi found work on a number of locally registered merchant ships. During his leave in Middlesbrough, he lodged at Suzuki's boarding house and it was there that he met his future wife, Gladys Wilberforce, whom he married in 1923. She was employed as a domestic servant at Suzuki's. After their marriage, they moved to 56 Marton Road so contact with the boarding house and its residents remained close. Doi continued to work as a merchant seaman until the 1920s when he opened a laundry with a Mr Kaiichi at North Ormesby. He returned to the sea when his business failed in 1932 and, until 1943, was a fireman and donkeyman aboard British ships operating out of North East ports.

Aliens Certificate of Registration issued to Kageyama Okuro in
1927. Kageyama's seaman's discharge papers show that he first
arrived in the U.K. in 1917 (Betsho family).

Kageyama Okuro, born in Hiroshima prefecture in 1893, was twenty-four
years old when he arrived in Liverpool on the British vessel, *Prairial*, in
1917. Having served in the Japanese Navy between 1911 and 1915,
Kageyama joined this ship at Karachi in 1916. For the next few years, he
worked out of Liverpool, Cardiff, Newcastle and Middlesbrough. From
1924, he served on the SS *Teesburn* and other Middlesbrough-registered
ships until 1940 when he retired from the sea. Kageyama never married but

Certificate of Nationality for a Seaman. Issued to Betsho Ryoichi,
one of Middlesborough's Japanese residents, in 1920 (Betsho family).

lived with Betsho Ryoichi, another of the Japanese seamen resident in Middlesbrough during these years.

Betsho, also born in Hiroshima prefecture in 1897, arrived in South Wales in 1917, apparently believing himself to be in America. His mistake realized, he worked on only one other British vessel before joining the *Morna* at Middlesbrough in 1920 as a fireman and trimmer. From 1920 onwards, Betsho served on different ships out of Middlesbrough, Blyth, South Shields, Sunderland and Newcastle. While resident at Suzuki's boarding house, he met Emma Morrow who became his wife in 1922. Margaret Suzuki was one of the witnesses at their wedding. Betsho continued to work as a merchant seaman into the 1940s when he took a land job with Cleveland Products on Cargo Fleet Road. He was later employed by the flour mills at Thornaby as an engineer fitter. After the death of his first wife, Betsho, at the age of forty-eight, married Theresa Gwendoline Roper, aged twenty-five, in 1946.

Family reminiscences, documents and various secondary sources permit some insights into the lifestyles of such men, but Akiyama Taichi's first-hand account of his arrival in Middlesbrough after the First World War conveys much of the spirit of the times and the circumstances which led to the emergence of a Japanese community in Middlesbrough. Born in 1898 in Yamaguchi prefecture, Akiyama left his farming family in 1917 and sailed

Akiyama Taichi arrived in Middlesbrough in 1920. His great ambition, at that time, was to emigrate to Hawaii (Akiyama family).

on a fishing boat to Port Said. It was there, in June 1918, that he joined HMS *Sallust* which brought him to Glasgow some six months later. He was to receive war medals for this period of service to the Admiralty. From Glasgow, Akiyama made his way in 1920 to Middlesbrough where he met Caroline Gresham who would later become his wife. His great ambition at the time was to settle, as so many Japanese had previously done, in Hawaii. After 1920, Akiyama's adventurous spirit led him to many foreign ports in America, Brazil, the Cape, India, the Mediterranean and Canada. In New Orleans, he pursued the possibility of emigration to Hawaii but, eventually, very much in love, returned to Middlesbrough to marry Caroline Gresham on 16 February 1924, his birthday. Akiyama worked as a merchant seaman until 1939 when he took up employment with Cleveland Products in Middlesbrough.

While the details vary, there are many common elements in the stories of the Japanese who came to Middlesbrough. All were of similiar ages and from farming backgrounds. Many, though not all, came from south-western Japan. The majority of these seamen arrived in Middlesbrough during the second decade of the twentieth century. Those who married seem to have met their wives at Suzuki's boarding house and to have continued to live there or in the Marton Road area.

That so little has been known about Middlesbrough's Japanese can perhaps be explained by the fact of intermarriage with local girls which provided another kind of distance between their lives in Middlesbrough and their roots in Japan. Many embraced their new lifestyle, losing contact with their families back home, though always gravitating towards the company of their fellow countrymen in Middlesbrough. The role played by the wives of the Japanese in raising their children was a key element in the losing of

Members of Middlesbrough's seafaring Japanese community. It has been estimated that, by 1920, some 250 Japanese were living in this northern port town (Doi family).

Anglo-Japanese group photograph taken in
Middlesbrough, 1920s (Betsho family).

one culture and gaining of another. Until the 1940s, little was seen of
the Japanese fathers who were so frequently away at sea. The elements
of culture, such as language and food, which a Japanese mother might
have transmitted to her children were not to be passed on to these
Anglo-Japanese offspring. For many of them, the only sight of a
Japanese woman was on the decks of the *maru* boats which called
into Middlesbrough. In the main, they were brought up by English mothers
in an English way and blended into the local community. When they
were ashore, the Japanese seamen did expose their families to aspects of
the Japanese way of life. Middlesbrough's Anglo-Japanese households
would have differed from those of their neighbors in the eating of rice
and the preparation of *sushi* and many other native dishes. All the families
dined frequently on *taki-taki*, a kind of minced beef stew served with
rice. Japanese soy sauce (*shoyu*) was used in cooking and chopsticks were
the standard eating utensils. Japanese *sake* (rice wine) and green tea
would be on offer when the men gathered in each other's homes to share
meals and conversation. The NYK ships were an early source for Japanese
goods and food supplies. Some Middlesbrough Japanese even had food
parcels sent to them directly from Japan. In later years, Japanese foodstuffs could be ordered from London. It was perhaps inevitable that some
basic greetings and expressions would be transmitted to the English-
speaking wives and children of these seamen. Language ties would reinforce

Left – Middlesborough's Japanese seamen often worked on board the same ships and, when ashore, met at the Japanese boarding houses along Marton Road (Betsho family).

Right – This photograph of the crew of S.S. *Morna*, c 1920, illustrates the ethnic diversity of the ship's company. Mr. Betsho and Japanese mates can be seen to the right (Betsho family).

the closeness of the male community who shared in the experience of being Japanese in the North East.

Middlesbrough's Japanese often worked on the same ships and, when ashore, socialized with one another either in their homes or at Suzuki's boarding house. Gambling was a favourite pastime; the playing of *hanafuda* (flower cards) would often be the focus of such gatherings at which Japanese food and conversation helped to restore any loss of identity. Although the seamen spoke Japanese in each other's company, communication was

Tommy Doi (left) and his brother Hideo. The children of Middlesbrough's Japanese seamen recall excursions to the NYK 'maru boats' which regularly called into port (Doi family).

Alfred W. Bulmer, Middlesbrough's
Honorary Japanese Consul (left of centre)
and Captain Y. Watanabe (centre) of NYK's
Kashima Maru planting Japanese cherry trees
in Pallister Park, North Ormesby, 19 May
1932 (The *Northern Echo*).

otherwise in broken English. Whenever NYK ships were in port, contact
was made with the Japanese crew members who visited the homes of their
Middlesbrough compatriots and joined in their meals and card games. This
was one way in which a link with Japan was maintained over the years.
Purchases of Japanese food and other goods were made on board the *maru*
boats and the men periodically visited the ship's doctor for Japanese

Japanese seaman and his son photographed in
Middlesbrough, 1930s (Doi family).

treatment and medicines. The children of the Japanese seamen were taken on excursions to the *maru* boats and were given dried fruits and other treats by the sailors as their fathers exchanged news and joined the crew for Japanese meals.

The arrival of the NYK vessels in Middlesbrough was greeted with enthusiasm by the wider community. Local schools and organizations were provided with escorted tours of the ships by the company which contributed to the popularity of the service within the community. NYK's close association with the town was highlighted as late as 1932 with the planting of cherry trees by representatives of the firm in the Stewart, Pallister and Albert parks.[20]

The homes of the Japanese seamen living in Middlesbrough contained traces of their origins and glimpses of native culture. The Doi family had a life-size samurai figure on display for many years. This was later donated to Middlesbrough's Dorman Museum. Their sitting-room was dominated by a large rising sun, fashioned from painted and varnished matchboxes, which adorned the mantelpiece. In the Betsho family home, a photograph of the Japanese Emperor and Empress was given pride of place. A child's silk kimono, sent from Japan, was worn by their daughter, Yuki, for fancy-dress parties and loaned out to friends. 'Uncle Nagasaki', as one of the local Japanese was known, made traditional Japanese kites for the children which were flown with great pride in Middlesbrough's Albert Park. In the 1920s and 1930s, the Japanese were a close community, mainly centred in the Marton Road area. The Japanese men were all referred to as 'uncles' and their wives as 'aunties'. Some of them shared accommodation so that the children grew up, if not speaking Japanese themselves, at least with strong

Mr. Betsho and Mr. Nagasaki (right) at Seaton Carew in the 1970s. The former seamen lived together for many years (Betsho family).

Japanese seamen take to the air in Middlesbrough fairground
photograph from the 1920s (Doi family).

community ties. Betsho, Kageyama and Nagasaki lived together for many years
and Betsho and Kageyama were eventually buried in the same grave. Shimura
lived with the Nishimis; Araki with the Saitos; and Fujiwara with the
Ikeshitas. Like so many of the other Japanese seamen who settled in
Middlesbrough during these years, Ikeshita Umetaro came from a Hiroshima
farming family and travelled to Britain on board a British merchant vessel.

The Saito family who eventually moved
to Blyth, another shipping port in the
North East (Doi family).

If the North East was down on its fortunes in the 1920s and 1930s, for the Japanese living in Middlesbrough it nevertheless had a great deal to offer. Many of them hailed from the same prefectures in south-western Japan that had given rise to mass emigration in the 1880s and 1890s. They left for similar reasons of poverty and deprivation though, in Akiyama's case, his departure from Japan was, according to him, motivated by the desire 'for a change' as much as anything else. Most of the seamen had hopes of reaching America when they first left Japan. The success stories of local villagers who had earlier emigrated to Hawaii and California no doubt inspired their own exodus. American emigration laws made such hopes fruitless by the time of the First World War, however, and the Japanese, having gravitated to Britain, decided to remain.

As long as the seamen retained their citizenship, they reported on a regular basis to the immigration authorities in Middlesbrough's town hall. Over the years, some became naturalized British citizens while others, inevitably, returned to Japan. In marrying Japanese nationals, the Middlesbrough wives adopted their husbands' nationality and were forced to register as 'aliens' in the same way. This created some unforeseen problems during the years of the Second World War.

While a large number of Japanese seamen had settled in Middlesbrough by 1920, they were gradually dispersed over the years. Some families moved to Blyth, like the Saitos; or, like the Matsokas and Otanis, to North Shields. Others went to London in search of employment. Furihata, Matsoka and Shimura were, at different times, employed making lamp-shades at T.K. Nakamura Ltd on 43 Howland St, London W1. Of those who stayed in Middlesbrough, some pursued factory work from the 1940s.

Furihata Mutsushi married Daisy Victoria Tickle in 1930 (Diane Furihata).

Schellenberg's glue hide factory on Cargo Fleet Road, known as Cleveland Products, provided employment for many Japanese ex-merchant seamen. Akiyama worked there for a total of twenty-eight years and, on his retirement, was commended for never once being late or absent in the whole of that time.[21] Betsho also spent a period of his career on land working for Cleveland Products as did Ikeshita, Kageyama, Furihata and Doi. Kageyama had been employed during some of his years in Middlesbrough at Anderson's Iron Foundry at Port Clarence. Some of the other Japanese went into business for themselves as with Doi and Kaiichi who opened a laundry in the 1920s and Mr Sano who ran a garage on Harris Street. There were those, too, who pursued that, to the uninitiated, somewhat unlikely sounding occupation of chicken-sexing. The Japanese skill in this area was highly valued by the poultry industry and provided a rather unusual form of employment.

That there were pressures associated with a life away from home, particularly in the 1940s, is clear. Mr Araki, who worked at Smith's Dock making sails, committed suicide by hanging himself, while another of the Middlesbrough Japanese ended his days at St Luke's mental hospital. Nagashima was found drowned on the beach at Redcar and Nishimi was drowned in an accident at Hull. Some Japanese finally chose to leave, as was the case with Mr Nakahara. Such departures mainly took place, however, before Japan entered the Second World War. The Japanese who were naturalized continued to work in and out of Middlesbrough after 1941.

There were, too, those Middlesbrough Japanese who served on British ships for all or part of the war. Furihata and Doi were at Dunkirk in 1940 and Betsho also completed a period of wartime service. Ikeshita was discharged from the navy as late as October 1945. Others, like Fujiwara and Kingo, joined the small number of their nationality in Britain who were dispatched to internment camps on the Isle of Man. In December 1941, thirty-four Japanese, primarily from the London business community, were interned at the Palace Camp in Douglas. By February 1942, this group had increased to ninety.[22] A small number of Middlesbrough's Japanese would have been among the later arrivals brought there from various parts of the UK.

Japan's entry into the Second World War placed the Middlesbrough Japanese and their families in a difficult position. The wives of unnaturalized Japanese, like Caroline Akiyama, though born and bred on Teesside, were forced to report to the local police station and to carry an alien's 'Certificate of Registration'. Akiyama Taichi seems to have been unusual in retaining his nationality yet continuing to live and work in Middlesbrough during the war. The Anglo-Japanese children of such alliances did not suffer unduly from being half-Japanese in wartime Britain. The prejudice

Aliens Certificates of Registration issued to Akiyama Taichi and his wife Caroline. In marrying Japanese nationals, the Middlesbrough wives assumed their husbands' nationalities (Akiyama family).

directed at the local Italian community was often more severe than anything experienced by the families of the Japanese seamen. Perhaps the war in the Pacific was too far away; perhaps, with English wives and many years of residence in Middlesbrough, the Japanese and their families had attained true local status. Certainly, those who stayed had few remaining ties with Japan. Betsho Ryoichi was the only member of his group ever to return to Japan to visit his family. In 1972, he spent six weeks in his village in Hiroshima, his one and only trip back to Japan in fifty-six years. The blending of cultures that occurred is best symbolized in the names given to the children of Middlesbrough's Japanese. As memories of Japan faded, Doi

Tomoji's son was named Tommy and Betsho Ryoichi's son became known as Roy.

The development of a Japanese community in Middlesbrough around the time of the First World War represents a unique phenomenon in the history of Japan's relationship with the North East. The culture of the Middlesbrough Japanese was primarily that of the merchant seaman and the way of life dictated not so much by being Japanese as by being part of a seagoing community. Their experience of coming to the region, intermarrying, and finding work both at sea and on land offers up a fascinating example of the multidimensional aspects of intercultural exchange. That these events took place as Japan's relationship with Britain was steadily deteriorating adds a touch of poignancy to the tale of Middlesbrough's 'forgotten' Japanese. The Second World War brought this sad deterioration to a climax. NYK had ceased to operate its service into Middlesbrough in 1939. As for more distant memories, to have armed the Japanese Navy in days of yore no longer seemed a matter for regional pride. The warm feelings once expressed for 'Togo's heroes' were overturned and a new and troubled phase in Japan's relationship with the North East was begun.

Japan's surprise attack on the US naval base at Pearl Harbor on 7 December 1941 catapulted America and Britain into a long and costly war in the Pacific. The universal denunciation of Japan's action was echoed in the North East press which hearkened back to earlier stereotypes in condemning Britain's former ally. The *Newcastle Journal and Northern Mail* (8 December 1941) reported on the Pearl Harbor debacle: 'In its flagrant disregard of all the usages of civilised peoples this attack is paralleled by that which the Japanese themselves made upon Russian ships in harbour at Port Arthur in 1904.' What had been applauded by the *Times* and celebrated as tactical cunning in the boardrooms of the Tyne in 1904 was seen from a

Betsho Ryoichi's family in Hiroshima prefecture. He left Japan in 1916 and returned for only one visit in 1972 (Betsho family).

Akiyama Taichi and his wife, Caroline, on
their sixtieth wedding anniversary in 1984.
The last of Middlesbrough's early Japanese
community, he died in 1986 and she, one
year later (*Middlesbrough Evening Gazette*).

different standpoint as Yamamoto Isoroku used history to guide Japan to
victory once again in 1941. Like Togo, Yamamoto had once been
welcomed to the Elswick shipyard in commemoration of the past. It was
with a sense of betrayal that the *Newcastle Journal* pronounced its verdict on
Japan's infamy: 'This is not merely to deny those standards of dignity and
behaviour which have been set up so laboriously between civilised peoples,
but to send them crashing down with a noise to startle the whole world.'

If Japan's samurai code had once been held up as a model for the West,
ballads like the 'Oriental Spider' which appeared in the region's press[23],
saw, in the 'duplicity' of her diplomats in Washington, the ultimate
contradiction to its lofty spirit:

> While their words were honorific –
>   Thoughts of war they both deny –
> Guns spat death in the Pacific.
>   Bombs hurled thunder from the sky.
>
> Japs resort to 'hara-kiri'
>   As a means of 'saving face'
> Suicide – by 'sword of honour'
>   Will atone for all disgrace!

> Surely lying – planning – plotting
>   Gangster tricks for gaining time,
> Demand wholesale hara-kiri
>   To wipe out a nation's crime?

Having hailed Japan the 'Britain of the East' just forty years before, the North East stood by and watched as the layers of 'civilization' were peeled from the image of Britain's former ally and the region's former friend.

The deterioration in Britain's relationship with Japan can be traced back to the Washington Conference of 1921–2 and the demise of the Anglo-Japanese Alliance. The economic pressures of feeding a population of sixty-four million in 1930 as compared with thirty-two million in 1868 resulted in the intensification of Japan's export drive. Japan became known for cheap labour, undercutting prices and producing unreliable copies of western goods. Colonialist expansion into China in the 1930s was done, once again, in the name of economic necessity and fuelled anti-Japanese feeling in the West. The signing of the London Naval Treaty of 1930 confirmed and further implemented the agreements made at Washington in 1922 regarding the respective naval strengths of Britain, America and Japan. By 1934, however, Japan had renounced the London Naval Treaty and was pursuing unrestricted rearmament. As a fanatical military rapidly assumed the reins of power, the nation was directed with dizzying inevitability towards war. The occupation of Indo-China in 1941 led to all-out American sanctions against the Japanese. The embargo on oil was the key element which prompted Japan's decision to bring matters to a head. With the bombing of Pearl Harbor and the immobilization of a large part of America's Pacific Fleet, Japan hoped to remove the threat posed by America to her invasion of South East Asia. That a war against Britain and America could never be won was, ironically, argued to no avail by the Commander of the Combined Fleet, Admiral Yamamoto Isoroku, who masterminded the attack on Pearl Harbor.

British perceptions of the Japanese, understandably, underwent a drastic turnabout as reports of Japan's victories in the Pacific reached home. The sinking of the *Repulse* and the *Prince of Wales* just a few days after the attack on Pearl Harbor prompted such headlines as 'Bushido Sank Our Ships' in the North East press. The 'way of the warrior' may have appealed to British Japanophiles in the days of Alliance but in the context of mutual war Japan's samurai past was viewed in a decidedly different light. Confirmed reports of the poor treatment of British POWs in Hong Kong in 1942 led Anthony Eden to protest to the House of Commons: 'the Japanese claim that their forces are assisted by a lofty code of chivalry (*bushido*) is nauseating hypocrisy.'[24]

There are, not surprisingly, no references in the wartime local press to the region's former links with Japan. Some older North East-built ships had survived to serve the Japanese Navy during the Second World War but such associations were quietly forgotten. Attention was directed instead to the North East ships which played a part in Japan's defeat. Most dramatically, when US and British vessels made their triumphal entry into Tokyo Bay in August 1945, the procession was led by HMS *King George V*, built at the Walker naval yard on the Tyne. The Royal Navy squadron which entered Singapore harbour one week later was headed by another North East ship, HMS *Cleopatra*, built by Hawthorn Leslie on the Tyne in 1938. Such landmarks provided a different focus for the region's pride in her shipbuilding prowess which had been exercised to the full throughout the course of the war.

The celebratory mood in the North East that followed the victory over Japan was much dampened by the tales of local POWs returning from Japanese camps in the Far East and South East Asia. The press carried daily lists of North East prisoners of war who had died in Japanese camps. Local reporters and MPs, such as Jack Lawson for Chester-le-Street, visited the Far East to see for themselves what toll the war had taken. As with all other parts of Britain, the North East had its own stories to tell. The Reverend John L. Wilson, Bishop of Singapore and former vicar of St Andrew's of Roker in Sunderland, had been incarcerated for three years and gave a graphic account of his life inside a Japanese POW camp. The return of the remnants of the Royal Northumberland Fusiliers from Changi prison near Singapore in October 1945 prompted extensive reporting of the indomitable spirit of the North East men who defied their captors by singing 'Blaydon Races' whenever life seemed at its hardest. According to one POW who worked on the Burma railway, '"Blaydon Races" was a rallying call in Thailand ... the Japanese could not understand it. They were willing to flog and to torture for obvious revolt but song and spirit were beyond their understanding.[25] Some thirty North East internees regularly gathered to sing 'Blaydon Races', 'Keep Your Feet Still Geordie' and other songs from home, led by Len Farrell, an accordionist from Blaydon, who was conductor of an orchestra at Kuala Lumpur when Singapore fell.[26] A Northumbrian Association was formed at Changi to keep local internees together. Here, as in other POW camps, the list of Japanese transgressions mounted and was recounted to a stunned audience at the end of the war. More than the war itself, reports of atrocities in POW camps fuelled anti-Japanese feeling in the North East as in other parts of Britain. Never had the symbolism of the samurai sword been more potent or more forbidding. The war and its legacy would pervade both the national and regional consciousness for some time to come.

Shipbuilding in the North East had survived the depression of the 1930s to reach new heights during the period of the Second World War. Yards that had been closed on the Tyne, Wear and Tees were rapidly reopened as the war effort intensified. More than four million tons of British shipping was lost by 1945 but over half that amount was to be replaced by North East yards. In the aftermath of the war, the North East figured strongly in such rebuilding and repairing programmes. For fifteen years after Japan's surrender, over half a million tons of shipping was produced annually in the region, amounting to some 40 per cent of the British total.[27] Britain's percentage of world output, however, was gradually declining, which led to an inevitable recession within the industry. The military defeat of Japan and Germany, Britain's two main shipbuilding rivals, left British yards, in the immediate post-war period, with the way clear to fill the enormous demand for world shipping. Once again, with the outbreak of the Korean War and the Suez Crisis, shipyards flourished as the pace of building was stepped up to meet new demands. Foreign competition eventually undermined Britain's lead in the industry, however. By 1956, Japan's escalation of tanker production in response to the Suez Crisis saw her overtake Britain as the world's major shipbuilding nation. The *North East Industrialist* (January 1956) addressed the growing threat of Japanese shipbuilding to North East yards: 'The significance of this advance in Japanese shipbuilding lies, perhaps, not so much in the present as in future potential output and its ultimate competitive strength in world markets.'[28] Japan's recovery following her defeat in the Second World War was no less dramatic than the all-embracing transformation effected by her during the years of the Meiji period. In just over seventy years, the nation that had once looked to the North East for ships and guns had lost the battle but, in some senses at least, had won the war.

The coronation of Queen Elizabeth II in 1953 saw the arrival in Britain of many foreign dignitaries and heads of state. This important event also occasioned the first post-war visit of a member of the Japanese royal family to Britain. Crown Prince Akihito, son of the Emperor Hirohito and heir to the throne, was only nineteen years old at the time of the Coronation but carried with him the burden of an entire nation seeking to heal the wounds of war. From his disembarkation at Southampton on 27 April to his departure five weeks later on 9 June, Akihito attended many official functions, and, through the Japanese Embassy, hosted some of his own.

The Japanese ex-seamen of Middlesbrough were among the guests invited to a garden party at the Japanese Ambassador's residence at Kensington Palace Gardens on 3 May 1953. The invitation sent by Mitani Takanobu,

By Command of
His Imperial Highness the Crown Prince of Japan
Mr. Takanobu Mitani has the honour to invite
Mr. Furihata
to a Garden Party at 23, Kensington Palace
Gardens W.8. on Sunday the 3rd of May 1953
at 3.30–5 o'clock.

Mr. Furihata's invitation to a garden party at the Japanese Ambassador's residence during Crown Prince Akihito's visit in 1953. Many members of Middlesbrough's Japanese community were invited to attend (Diane Furihata).

the Japanese Grand Chamberlain, on behalf of the Crown Prince must have aroused mixed feelings in the Middlesbrough Japanese who had long before severed their ties with their homeland. The two hundred guests who attended the garden party included members of the London Japanese community, embassy officials, Japanese business visitors and reporters. Such gatherings suggested that, some eight years after the war had ended, official relations between Japan and Britain were, once again, on an even keel.

During his stay in Britain Crown Prince Akihito (since January 1989, Emperor of Japan) visited many places of historic interest or of special significance in the century-old Anglo-Japanese relationship. On 9 May 1953, this same spirit of commemoration took him to Cragside in Northumberland, home of the first Lord Armstrong, where he was to stay for eight days as the guest of Lord and Lady Armstrong. Throughout his visit, the accent was placed on past associations and the reviving of old ties. Akihito spent his days at Cragside, riding, fishing, playing billiards and tennis and enjoying the pleasures of 'a typical English country house party'. As the *Japan Society Bulletin* (June 1953) later conveyed:

> The Crown Prince was to feel at home, and so fulfill the
> representative duties required of him from a background
> of ease and comfort reminiscent of those distant
> Victorian and Edwardian days when his country and ours
> were the closest friends and allies, and when many of her
> famous statesmen, ministers, admirals, and merchants
> stayed in this historic house.

Crown Prince Akihito spent eight days at *Cragside* in 1953
as the guest of Lord and Lady Armstrong
(The *Journal* and *Chronicle* Photo Library).

Even the setting was seen to be conducive to post-war reconciliation and the remembrance of things past.

The pursuit of the past should have taken the Crown Prince to Newcastle and the Vickers-Armstrong works during his stay in the North East. That the wounds of war had not yet healed was apparent from his thwarted pilgrimage. A mooted civic reception was strongly opposed by the city's Labour Party, the Newcastle and District branch of the Far East Prisoner of War Association and local trade union branches. While Lord Armstrong had recommended the Crown Prince's reception by the Lord Mayor of Newcastle on the grounds of 'the close association between Newcastle and Japan in the past', a Newcastle City Council vote on the invitation was only marginally in support of not withdrawing it.[29] Akihito's subsequent cancellation of his visit to Newcastle was hailed as a 'singular victory' by the deputation from the Far East POW Association who received the news from the Lord Mayor. Just a few hours after the cancellation was announced, five Japanese journalists who were to visit the region during his stay changed their plans, seemingly in response to the slight directed at a member of the Japanese Imperial family. The *Tokyo Evening News* responded to the controversy with indignation, stating that:

> It is a great pity this has happened for the sins of one generation should not be visited on another. Naturally there will continue to be bitterness expressed by those who were victims of the worst elements that disgraced the Japanese armies, but that bitterness should not be heaped on Crown Prince Akihito or his contemporaries.[30]

That there were differing local views on the Crown Prince's cancelled visit to Newcastle is suggested by one headline in the *Newcastle Journal* that same week which read – 'The North has acted below its traditions'.

Whatever the feelings for or against the visit, the arrival of the Japanese Crown Prince in Northumberland certainly generated much good will. As a council member of the Japan Society, Lady Armstrong welcomed him to Cragside and delighted in his response to the Armstrong family home: 'He thought the estate was just like Japan. Not the open moors and hills on top, but the pine trees, the lakes, and flowering shrubs.'[31] While Akihito's civic reception in Newcastle had not come to pass, the Lord Mayor of the city was invited to a private dinner party at Cragside during his stay. On that occasion, Lord Armstrong expressed the hope 'for a renewed Anglo-Japanese friendship "which might even surpass the friendship of the old days".'[32] The informal mood of the visit clearly pointed to such a possibility. This new spirit of friendship was to be symbolically registered in the cypress tree planted by the Crown Prince on the terrace overlooking the tennis-court at Cragside. Akihito planted the 'friendship tree' at a garden party held for more than two hundred local people on the Armstrong estate. The warmth of the occasion is still recalled today by the people of Rothbury.

The eight days spent at Cragside must have been a relaxing respite in a schedule otherwise filled with official engagements. Visits to the local tennis club and the Rothbury Bowling Club resulted in 'honorary memberships' of an unprecedented kind. Leisurely expeditions to Bamburgh Castle, the Farne Islands and an impromptu stop at Seahouses revealed some of the attractions of the Northumbrian coast. Lord and Lady Armstrong presented Akihito with an appropriate memento of his stay in the form of two paintings of Bamburgh Castle by the Japanese artist, Ogisu Takanori (1901–86). 'Oguiss', who lived in Paris, had spent part of the summer of 1952 at Cragside. His signature in the visitors' book is, in fact, accompanied

Crown Prince Akihito visiting Longstone Lighthouse on the Farne Islands, 11 May 1953. He was accompanied by (left to right) Matsumoto Shunichi (the Japanese Ambassador), Lady Armstrong, and Mitani Takanobu (the Grand Chamberlain) (The *Journal* and *Chronicle* Photo Libary).

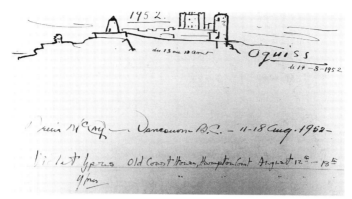

Oguiss signature and sketch of Bamburgh Castle in the *Cragside* Visitors' Book (Vickers Defence Systems).

by a quick sketch of Bamburgh Castle. During his stay at Cragside he also completed several views of the Armstrong family house which are still on display. What more appropriate token, therefore, of the Crown Prince's enjoyable stay in Northumberland! While the Oguiss paintings of Bamburgh are now part of the Imperial Household Collection in Tokyo, a similar view of the castle was acquired by Ambassador Matsumoto during the visit and was housed at Kensington Palace Gardens where it remains. The Armstrongs were given fitting keepsakes from Japan in the fine lacquer boxes and writing-set that the Crown Prince left in remembrance at Cragside.

Painting of Bamburgh Castle, Northumberland by Oguiss, 1952. Two similar views of Bamburgh were presented to the Crown Prince at the end of his stay at *Cragside* (M. Conte-Helm).

Signature of Crown Prince Akihito in
Cragside Visitors' Book, May 1953
(Vickers Defence Systems).

On his last evening, the Crown Prince joined his English friends in the
drawing-room of Cragside for a chorus of 'Auld Lang Syne'. General
Piggott's after-dinner speech summed up the warmth of feeling generated by
the visit and found a common ground through which to forget more
troubled times. In his toast. Piggott expressed the sentiments of all who had
gathered there to bid the future monarch farewell.

We would remember a youthful, boyish figure, moving
among us, easily and confidently; from whom emanated

The Mayor of Durham, Councillor Gordon
McIntyre, extended an official civic welcome
to the Japanese Crown Prince on 17 May
1953 (The *Journal* and *Chronicle* Photo
Library).

a spirit, not only of true and genuine friendliness, but
also of that typical Japanese quality (and one we like to
think that England still preserved), namely, dignity – a
dignity that had been inherited through 2000 years of
unbroken lineage. We appreciated and admired this so
much; for the Japanese and the English spoke the same
language – the language of ancient tradition, of valued
institutions of the past, and of reverence and love for the
Throne.[33]

Akihito represented a new generation, untainted by war. His presence in
the North East helped to recall a happier past and to re-establish relations
on a more equable footing.

The Crown Prince's journey to London was broken by a stop in Durham
where, under strict security, an official civic welcome to the North East was
at last extended. The city's Mayor, Councillor Gordon McIntyre, received
Akihito at the Town Hall where he signed the visitors' book and was
presented with further gifts. In his two-and-a-half-hour visit to Durham, he
toured the cathedral and castle before taking his leave of the region. No one
could pretend that the recent past had not left its scars, but the Crown
Prince's stay in the North East was a positive step in the direction of
reconciliation and friendship.

Japan's relationship with the North East survived its hardest test in the
aftermath of the Second World War. As North East shipbuilding contracted further and Japan continued on its path of post-war reconstruction,
earlier ties were openly acknowledged and the memory of the region's
historic associations with Japan restored.

6   The Japanization of the North East: NSK, Nissan, and Beyond

Japan's post-war recovery was stimulated first by American aid and then, from 1950, by procurement orders for the United Nations' forces in the Korean War. Industrial production rapidly rose to pre-war levels; indeed, it has been argued that by 1955 'recovery had ended and expansion had begun'.[1] The real growth rate of the Japanese economy leapt to 13.2 per cent in 1960 and a similar pace was maintained over the next ten years. Manufacturing industry contributed significantly to this advance although the war had altered the direction of industrial development. It was such 'advanced technology' fields as chemicals and engineering which, along with metals, doubled their share of the country's gross manufacturing production between 1930 and 1960. Over the same period, textile output and exports, which had been so central to Japan's economy in the pre-war period, declined in importance and changed character, with a growing shift to man-made fibres further enhancing the growth of the chemical industry.

There are many factors to which Japan's sustained growth over this period can be attributed. Certainly, between 1960 and 1970, her success as a trading nation became a measure of the state of her overall economic success. The scale of Japanese exports of ships, bearings, automobiles, cameras and man-made fibres may have resulted in accusations of flooding overseas markets and unfair competition but the dependence upon imported energy supplies was and remains the other side of Japan's 'economic miracle'. By 1965, Japan experienced its first trade surplus since the Second World War and this trend continued unabated until, in 1971, a currency crisis and international pressure led to a 16 per cent revaluation of the yen. From the late 1960s, cameras, bearings and steel had become particularly sensitive items in the international trading arena as had Japan's increasingly prominent role as a builder of world ships. Ships, steel and bearings remained 'problem sectors' well into the 1970s.[2]

It was the oil crisis of 1973 that most severely tested Japan's economic resilience. With over 90 per cent of her oil imported and a 70 per cent reliance on this form of energy to maintain the nation's growth, the 'house of cards' analogy seemed apt to some. In the wake of the 'oil shock' came high inflation and a balance of payments deficit, along with a sharp reduction in the value of the yen. Japanese economic growth, for the first time in ten years, slowed to a standstill in 1974. But in 1976 Japan would once again show a trade surplus. As the GNP climbed and the yen gained strength, the Japanese economy emerged from its latest crisis intact.

The rise in Japanese exports had aided a second post-war recovery but had also intensified existing trade frictions with western Europe and America. Against this backdrop of industrial growth and volatile foreign relations, Japanese overseas investment intensified. From the 1950s, Japan had sought commercial and then manufacturing bases abroad. The United States, Asia and Latin America were key investment areas, followed belatedly by Europe. As Britain came into the sphere of Japanese invest-ment, the North East of England witnessed the arrival of its first Japanese company.

In January 1974, NSK (Nippon Seiko Kaisha), Japan's leading ball-bearings manufacturer, announced its decision to establish a £7-million bearing factory in the UK. The announcement was made on the last day of a visit to Japan by Christopher Chataway, Britain's Minister for Industrial Development. Chataway's visit was dominated by discussions on the prospects for Japanese investment in the UK. He was accompanied by senior members of the UK bearing industry seeking assurances regarding the threat posed by Japanese competition. The joint communiqué signed in Tokyo promoted reciprocal investment in Britain and Japan and set down certain provisos on the implementation of the NSK project and investment in general. These included: the establishment of the plant in an 'assisted area', the export of at least one-half of the output, the addition of at least one-half of the value of the product in Britain (as opposed to a simple assembly operation) and 'considerable substitution' of current Japanese imports of bearings resulting from the investment.[3] Anticipating criticism of the Conservative government's stance on inward investment from Japan, Chataway pointed out that it was 'better for Britain that we should have investment in the UK serving the European market, rather than investment in Europe, from where the goods would be exported to Britain'.[4]

Despite the election of a Labour government in Britain later in 1974, NSK's plans for a UK plant proceeded. Some eighteen sites were considered within development areas in the North East of England, Scotland and Wales. Finally, in March 1974, NSK's managing director and Kawasaki

Toshiaki of the firm's international division expressed their preference for Peterlee in County Durham. This decision was based on a favourable factory site, the availability of skilled labour and a good communications network and local amenities. The initial £7-million investment was aimed at creating £2.6 million sales by 1977 with a work-force of 220 employees. But the presence of a major UK bearings plant just fifteen miles away at Annfield Plain in County Durham meant that NSK's establishment at Peterlee was not without controversy.

As soon as NSK's potential investment in Britain was publicized, the UK Ball and Roller Bearing Manufacturers' Association and the national firm of Ransome, Hoffman, and Pollard which employed some 1300 workers at its County Durham plant, criticized this new development, blaming the influx of cheap Japanese ball-bearings for recent cut-backs in the UK industry. Government grants and loans amounting to some £1.4 million further fuelled the fires of discontent. Local MPs and trade union leaders lobbied the Industry Minister, Tony Benn, but were told that proposals for the NSK ball-bearing plant were 'too far advanced' when the Labour government came to power.[5]

Local concern over the ramifications of Japanese investment in the North East inspired a succession of headlines like 'No Yen for the Japanese Factory', 'Land of Rising Hopes?' and 'Britain Needn't Fear Us, Say Japanese'. Suspicions of a future wages war, price-cutting, and redundancies in UK bearings firms were matched by rumours[6] of Japanese doubts over mounting such a project in a Labour-controlled Britain. Despite worries of industrial unrest, Britain, with its competitive wage levels, was still favoured by NSK as a base from which to trade freely with the European Community. It was also NSK's largest domestic market in Europe. The North East offered a further 'advantage' as an economically depressed area with tremendous potential for the rapid recruitment of a skilled work-force. Kawasaki Toshiaki who, for over ten years, was in charge of NSK's European operations, including the Peterlee factory, later confirmed that such factors and the anticipation of intensified global trade frictions brought NSK to its present site in the North East of England.[7]

Initial overtures had been made to NSK by a representative of the North of England Development Council (NEDC). This North East promotional body was established in 1962 and opened one of the first UK regional offices in Japan in 1975. In the move to attract Japanese investment to the North East, the NEDC, working closely with the Department of Trade and Industry and other local agencies, employed a long-term strategy. The story of NSK and the Japanese companies which eventually followed the ball-bearings firm to the area should be seen in the context of this planned regional effort, in direct competition with other parts of the UK, as well as that of the global economic factors which determined overall Japanese interest in investment overseas.

Some perspective on the state of the region in 1974 as NSK contemplated its investment potential can be gained from a glance at the post-war 'progress' of the North East's traditional industries. Shipbuilding and heavy engineering had suffered particular setbacks in the 1960s and early-1970s. As the post-war boom years drew to a close, North East yards received fewer and fewer orders. In 1962, William Gray & Company of West Hartlepool gave this as a reason for the firm's sad demise, adding 1400 workers to the growing regional employment statistics. Lack of orders led the Furness Company, one year later, to pay off 700 of its 1800 employees. In 1964, Short Brothers of Sunderland, an old family shipbuilding firm, was forced to close. While world merchant ship production went up by forty-two per cent between 1960 and 1965 with Japanese production increasing by 210 per cent, British output over this same period was reduced by nineteen per cent.[8]

An in-depth government investigation into the shipbuilding industry led, in 1967, to the publication of the Geddes Report, recommending certain changes and reorganization of yards which were soon implemented. The shortage of orders was an ongoing problem but increasing diversification helped some firms through the years of crisis. Nevertheless, the industry had already undergone a massive post-war decline. While some 84,000 men and women were employed in shipbuilding, repairing and marine engineering in the North East in 1945, representing over nine per cent of the working population, by 1959 that number had been reduced to 64,000 representing five per cent of the region's work-force. The drastic contraction of the industry in the following decade saw just over 44,000 people employed in shipbuilding and marine engineering in 1966, amounting to just 3 per cent of the regional work-force.

As an industry, shipbuilding was represented by some twenty-five separate trade unions. The 'high degree of union loyalty' and the 'fragmented structure of the union' have been partly blamed for the poor strike record of shipyard workers in the 1960s.[9] Industrial relations exacerbated the problems already central to an industry required to adapt to changing times. With British shipbuilding securing only 3 per cent of world orders in 1967 as opposed to Japan's 60 per cent, the time had come for reflection and for a reconsideration of Britain's role as a shipbuilding nation and the North East's position as a shipbuilding region.

Coal, steel, shipbuilding and heavy engineering represent the traditional industries of the North East that went the same route in the 1970s, leaving behind the scarred remains of an era of prosperity and regional pride. As

NSK Bearings (Europe) Ltd prepared to start production at Peterlee in the mid-1970s, a new day was dawning and a new phase in the industrial development of the region beginning. Despite the initial controversy over the establishment of NSK in the North East, the recruitment of the first British workers and contact with the local community started to turn the tide of opinion and to focus attention on the cultural differences and management style which characterized the Japanese way of work.

As puns about 'getting the ball rolling' were liberally dotted through the region's press, the Japanese were given an opportunity to counter earlier criticisms and to express their own point of view. The first six Japanese executives had moved into an office in Peterlee by March 1975. The Peterlee Development Corporation worked closely with the company they had helped to attract to County Durham throughout this settling-in period. Production at the new NSK plant began in April 1976 with thirty locally recruited workers and twenty Japanese. When questioned about the reputation of British workers for laziness, the Japanese quickly put the burden of responsibility on management whose job it was to inspire workers to identify with the company's success. This was to be an often-repeated theme in the philosophies of those Japanese firms which eventually followed NSK to the North East.

The British workers employed by NSK put such thinking to the test. By early 1976, the first section leaders and charge hands sent to Japan for three months' training had returned to Peterlee with a new outlook on production methods, quality control and the Japanese lifestyle. The importance of quality and communication ran through their assessments of the Japanese training experience. So did an equally foreseeable lack of enthusiasm for Japanese food; the blending of cultures produced some unwelcome sights at this stage in the Japanization process. Those employees trained in Japan passed on that training to new recruits at Peterlee. By the time NSK was working to full capacity with a labour force of 200, earlier prejudices had long been forgotten.

The Amalgamated Engineering Union (AEU) signed a single-union agreement with NSK early in 1976. In outlining the terms of the agreement, Personnel Manager, David Smith, later explained:

> It was suggested that this type of manufacturing process was fairly highly automated and traditional demarcation lines would not apply. Agreement was obtained on total job flexibility on the basis that anybody trained for a particular task could and would do that task irrespective of his or her job description.[10]

Flexible work practices as well as uniform terms and conditions of employment certainly distinguished this Japanese experiment from traditional industries in the North East. At NSK, in characteristically Japanese style, everyone wears the same navy-blue uniform, all staff clock on, and there is a single-status canteen. There is no company song but employee 'togetherness' is encouraged through shared social activities and a general 'family' atmosphere.

A true measure of NSK's successful transplantation in the North East has been its recent expansion which doubled the size of the plant and increased the work-force to 530, underlining the company's confidence in the region and its potential.

As the first Japanese company to invest in the North East, NSK came to represent, in some circles, a new kind of solution to the region's unemployment problems. Certainly, a flurry of activity followed the arrival of NSK, with NEDC representatives seeking further opportunities in Japan and Japanese companies making overtures to the region. Hitachi came close to establishing a colour television factory at Washington in the late 1970s. After first visiting the North East in October 1976, the Japanese television manufacturers had, within months, set investment plans in motion. After they had announced their intentions in April 1977, however, the UK television industry and trade unions rose up in protest. Although the northern region was generally supportive, a campaign was mounted against the firm which culminated in a Granada television documentary (31 October 1977) on Japanese investment in Britain and the Hitachi development in particular. The opening sequence showed the image of a Japanese

NSK Bearings Europe Ltd. established its factory at Peterlee, County Durham, in 1976. It was the first Japanese company to invest in the North East (The *Journal* and *Chronicle* Photo Library).

industrialist swinging a golf club fading into a samurai warrior wielding a sword.[11] It was a familiar allusion but, now set against the backdrop of Japanese overseas investment, had unfortunate repercussions for the region. The British government did little to reassure Hitachi and, in December 1977, the company, not surprisingly, withdrew. With them went the promise of further Japanese manufacturing investment in the North East for some time to come.

Talk of an 'invasion of Japanese industrialists' opening factories in the North East dates back to 1974 as does the regional 'wooing' of Japanese industry. Some Japanese sales and distribution outlets were set up in the region in the late 1970s and early 1980s, including the joint-venture company, Marubeni-Komatsu Ltd. (1979), and YKK Fasteners (UK) Ltd. (1981) at Washington. YKK Fasteners (UK) Ltd., with its centre of production at Runcorn, was the first large Japanese company to come to Britain in 1972. Dainippon Ink and Chemicals Inc. acquired the American-owned printing plate company, Polychrome (Berwick) in North Northumberland, in 1977. In the main, however, the hopes and fears of a wave of post-NSK Japanese investment were not realized until, with a Conservative government back in power from 1979, the Japanese car giant, Nissan, sought means of further internationalizing its operations. The search for a suitable European base had begun.

The high value of the Japanese yen and its impact on the domestic economy gave rise to an increasing trend towards internationalization from

NSK shares with other Japanese companies in the region (and elsewhere), a focus upon quality and communication (Ed Robson).

the mid-1970s onwards. As costs of wages and production rose and the threat of trade barriers loomed, Nissan joined other Japanese companies in deciding to extend its overseas production network. For the Japanese government, overseas investment was also seen as a way of reducing Japan's huge balance of payments surplus and was, therefore, actively encouraged. After much deliberation and detailed European studies, Nissan, like NSK, recognized in the UK a well-placed launching pad for exporting to Europe. With the UK representing its single biggest market in Europe (as it was NSK's), attention was turned to the establishment of a manufacturing base which could cater to both export demand and domestic consumption.

In January 1981, an announcement was made in the House of Commons that Nissan, Japan's second-largest car manufacturer, was seeking to build a major car production plant on a greenfield site in a development area of Britain. As Norman Tebbit, Minister of State for Industry, gave the government's blessing to the £200- to £300-million plant proposal, the race was on among local development agencies to secure the project. If this group responded with unqualified enthusiasm, there was a very different reaction from the British motor industry which expressed its immediate fears for the future of indigenous car production in the UK. Was a 'back door' being provided for the Japanese 'car invasion' or would a Nissan car plant offer 'a glittering employment prospect' to those areas of the country worst hit by the recession?[12]

By April 1981, it was revealed that three sites in the North East of England, two in South Humberside and three in Wales were on the Nissan short-list and would be incorporated into the feasibility study being conducted later that month. The announcement was made just after 600 northern trade unionists boarded a specially chartered London train at Newcastle as part of the region's contribution to a TUC week of action. The group marched through the city to the House of Commons, registering their protest over unemployment and the economically depressed state of the North East.

While the northern debate raged in the House of Commons, the Nissan team, led by managing director Kawai Isamu, began their progress through the country. All eight sites to be visited were in 'assisted areas', the two in the North East and one in Wales (at Shotton) qualifying for the very highest rate of grant available as 'special development areas' or SDAs. Investment in SDAs meant the automatic payment of 22 per cent on all new plant, buildings and permanent machinery.[13] The remaining five were also eligible for grant assistance but at a lower level.

During their two-day visit to the North East (23–24 April 1981), the ten-man delegation from Nissan closely inspected potential sites in what the

Northern Echo described as a 'magical mystery tour'. Trailed everywhere by the press, the Nissan team toured the region in a luxurious air-conditioned coach which usually served the Sunderland football team. At Teesside, they visited the once-thriving township of Ingleby Barwick followed by a second site in Eaglescliffe. Their trip to the Sunderland airport site was made memorable by the freak blizzard which confirmed all preconceptions about the unpredictability of the British weather and cast a carpet of clean, white snow over the northern landscape.

It was seen as significant that, along with the briefings arranged by local government bodies on the region's potential, the Nissan party paid a special visit to NSK's factory at Peterlee to observe its operation at first hand. Just prior to their arrival in the North East, three Japanese car union officials on a labour relations tour of Britain had included NSK on their itinerary. A private dinner held between the Nissan team and NSK management furnished a further opportunity to assess the real possibilities for exporting the Japanese style of management to the North East. As the only close involvement with Japanese industrialists resident in Britain during their tour, this was interpreted as a positive sign of the seriousness of Nissan's intent. With more than 22,000 unemployed engineering workers in the region, a choice greenfield site and the smaller but successful precedent of NSK set before them, the Nissan team concluded their feasibility study and returned to Japan to contemplate further.

While most regional hopes were set on Nissan, the company's highly public feasibility study sent ripples of concern through the UK motor industry. Fears of an assembly operation, using imported Japanese components, which would then undercut UK car prices were openly voiced. The managing director of Ford Britain, Sam Toy, predicted 'devastation' in some parts of the components industry and motor trade and raised a warning: 'the Rising Sun is getting a bit too hot for comfort'.[14] The Government's blunt dismissal of such scare-mongering took the form of Norman Tebbitt's inimitable rhetoric: 'Surely it is better for the British people to buy Japanese cars made by British workers than to buy German cars assembled by Turks.'[15] The sentiments echoed Christopher Chataway's remarks on the occasion of the NSK investment announcement. Such consistency on the part of Conservative government ministers would not have gone unnoticed by the Japanese.

Other responses to the Nissan visit came from local trade unions. Some three weeks after the event, a Stockton TUC meeting was called to debate the motion: 'This Trades Council calls upon the TUC to support British Leyland and British car workers and to resist attempts by Nissan Datsun to set up a car factory in the UK.'[16] A NALGO representative, Geoff Bulmer, complained of being 'steamrollered by high unemployment into a position where unions are having to promise there will be no trouble'. Tempers flared further as Okuma Masataka, executive vice-president of Nissan, expressed his concern over component sourcing in the UK. During a radio interview with Jimmy Young, he acknowledged a potential problem in maintaining Japanese standards of quality.[17]

While the image of Nissan as a 'Trojan horse' dominated some thinking, there was a parallel impatience over the winning of this much-prized investment project. As the initial June and then July deadlines passed, the regional headlines summed up the state of play again and again. From 'Nissan Keeps Us Guessing'[18] in July to 'Make Up Your Mind Nissan'[19] in September, the deadlines came and went. The promise of a major boost for the North East, however, kept the 'Nissan-watchers' tuned in.

In November, 1981, rumours were circulating that British Leyland's 'tea break strike' had raised doubts among Nissan's management over the tenor of labour relations and inter-union rivalry in Britain. Such doubts prompted another feasibility study and a return visit to the North East later that month. With a decision forecast for the New Year, UK industrial relations became a focus, some would say an 'excuse' for postponing the decision once again. Talks between Industry Secretary Patrick Jenkin and Nissan's Okuma Masataka in February 1981 revolved around components and government aid. The project seemed to be inching forward until, in July 1982, an indefinite postponement was announced. The 'world outlook for the car industry in general' was officially blamed for the disruption of plans but the industrial relations problem in Britain was later cited as a 'major influence' in Nissan's postponement of the project.[20] Following major rail and health service strikes, Okuma spoke of extending Nissan's feasibility study 'to take a closer look at the whole area of industrial relations in Britain and particularly into the possible effects of the Government's forthcoming revision of the Employment Acts'.[21] At this stage, the decision-making process was considerably slowed down by the need to satisfy Nissan's company union and senior management in Japan of the viability of successfully establishing a manufacturing base in the UK. Though the press reports focused on the problems within British industry, it was the failure to reach a consensus in Japan which, temporarily, prevented further action.

Margaret Thatcher's visit to Tokyo in September 1982 provided an opportunity to add direct government persuasion and assurances to the Nissan package. Later, in October, the Prime Minister and Patrick Jenkin met in London with Nissan president Ishihara Takashi to this same end. It was not until August 1983 that the rewards of such official efforts were reaped. Nissan had finally reached agreement that the UK project, albeit in a reduced form should go ahead. The build-up to 80 per cent local sourcing of components would be slower but the 100,000-car-a-year plant would nevertheless become a reality.

A further Nissan delegation arrived in the North East on 25 February 1984 and was met by a local consortium made up of senior officers of the North of England Development Council, the Department of Trade and Industry, Tyne and Wear County Council, Sunderland Borough Council and the Washington Development Corporation. A leading member of the team described Nissan as 'one of the last opportunities to revitalize the economic base of the region'.[22] The co-operation and co-ordination between the local agencies conducting the campaign certainly impressed the Japanese and has often been cited as one of the reasons for the North East's ultimate success in this lengthy 'poker game'. Lord Marsh, senior UK adviser to Nissan, strongly complimented the regional authorities on their unified effort which had clearly registered with the many Nissan executives who had passed through the North East. One final two-day visit began on 13 March and involved a tour of the Washington site and parts of the new town, as well as trips to the port of Tyne and Teesport.

The waiting game at last drew to a close when Nissan made its now-historic announcement in favour of Washington on 30 March 1984. Lord Marsh spoke in terms of giving 'a new lease of life to a part of the country which has had little to cheer it for a long time'.[23] Local exhilaration over the announcement was more graphically summed up with the comment:

Nissan executives survey the Sunderland airport site in February 1984. They are accompanied here by senior officers of Sunderland Borough Council, Washington Development Corporation, and Tyne & Wear County Council, Lord Marsh can be seen in the background. (NMUK).

'It's like winning the cup again'.[24] For the North East, Nissan meant employment opportunities but it also meant a shot in the arm to a region that had once known better days.

The Nissan development was geared to two phases. Company president Ishihara Takashi spoke from Tokyo of his expectation of UK workers 'to show flexibility in moving from job to job, a principle now frequently opposed by British trade unions. We want to negotiate with the unions on job mobility terms.'[25] Industrial relations remained an issue which would partly determine Nissan's progress through to 'phase two'. 'Phase one' was to involve the construction of a £50-million purpose-built factory of 900,000 square feet, assembling car kits imported from Japan with a voluntary 20 per cent level of local component sourcing set by the Japanese on arrival. Annual production of 24,000 Nissan Bluebirds would be accomplished with a staff of some 500 workers. A decision on the 'phase two' development was scheduled to be taken in 1987.

With a regional unemployment rate of 20 per cent, it was not surprising that there was a dramatic rush for jobs. The carefully worded advertisement – 'Working With Nissan Will Be Different' – attracted 3500 applicants for twenty-two supervisors' posts; 1000 applicants for forty team leader posts; and 11,500 applicants for 300 manufacturing staff posts.[26] At a celebratory reception earlier held for the Nissan delegation in Sunderland Civic Centre, the company's vice-chairman, Kanao Kaichi, had been presented with an inscribed brass figure of a miner. Perhaps no deeper symbolism was intended, but the image of the North East's dying industrial past was thus

The *Evening Chronicle* reported the welcome news of Nissan's decision to invest in the North East on 30 March 1984. (Ed Robson)

Continued jubilation at the groundbreaking ceremony on 20 July 1984. Mr. Tsuchiya, the future Managing Director of Nissan Motor Manufacturing (UK) Ltd. is shown holding a decanter (The *Journal* and *Chronicle* Photo Library).

poignantly present on this occasion marking the new shape of its industrial future.

The ground-breaking ceremony took place at the Sunderland airport site in July 1984 and work rapidly proceeded on the largest clearance and land reclamation scheme ever carried out by Tyne and Wear County Council. Of the overall 800-acre site, an initial 297 acres would be developed for the 'phase one' factory complex. By late 1985 the factory was completed and by spring 1986 fully fitted. The work-force in place, Nissan launched into production in July 1986. In just two years, the old Sunderland airport site had been converted into a sophisticated modern car plant. That Japanese decision-making can be slow and tortuous while implementation can be effected at great speed was borne out by this schedule. Even before the first Bluebirds rolled off the assembly line, the company had published a list of twenty-seven British car component suppliers who had won contracts with the Japanese firm. The established 20 per cent level of local sourcing was already being exceeded.

Much publicity was attached to Nissan's official opening in September 1986. The visit of the Prince and Princess of Wales to Japan during the previous May had included a tour of Nissan's car plant at Zama where the royal couple were presented with the keys to the first Nissan Bluebird scheduled for completion at Washington in July. This would later be auctioned and the proceeds presented to the Prince's Trust Community Venture scheme in Sunderland. Before leaving Zama, they painted in the eye of a good luck *Daruma* doll and received gifts of tiny car models for their sons. For the Japanese, such royal 'patronage' was a welcome pledge of British support for their enterprise in the North of England.

Back in Britain, as preparations for the Nissan opening continued, the debate was on as to its actual timing and the identity of the official dignitary who would preside over this important 'launch'. The regional news media were much perplexed when the first Bluebird came off the production line on 8 July. 'Nissan Hides Its Splash' wrote the *Journal* (9 July 1986) for the historic event was only to be witnessed by company employees and registered by an official photographer. The public fanfare would be saved for a later date.

Though the press was kept guessing until the last moment, the likelihood of Mrs Thatcher being present at the Nissan opening was increasingly apparent. As some local MPs and union leaders threatened to boycott the proceedings, the Newcastle and District Far East Prisoners of War Association added its voice to the criticism surrounding the approaching ceremony.

On 8 September 1986, Nissan Motor Manufacturing (UK) Ltd was officially opened by the Prime Minister. The voices of dissent were subdued following the unexpected announcement by company president Kume Yutaka that, one year ahead of all projections, Nissan would indeed move on to 'phase two'. A fleet of red, white and blue Bluebird saloons paraded by as the Newcastle Brown Ale Band played the Geordie anthem, 'Blaydon Races'. Mrs Thatcher carefully painted a second eye on the good luck *daruma* doll on which the Prince and Princess of Wales had invoked their

The first *Bluebird* leaves the production line of Nissan's Sunderland plant on 8 July 1986 (NMUK).

Nissan President Kume Yutaka looks on as the Prime Minister paints in the eye of the *Daruma* at the official Opening of the Sunderland car plant in September 1986 (The *Journal* and *Chronicle* Photo Library).

blessing for 'phase one'. It was a day for extravagant images and East meeting West. It was a day, too, for quelling the critics, for the expansion of production from 24,000 to 100,000 cars per year would entail a further £340-million investment and the employment of a total of 2700 workers. This represented the largest single investment every made by a Japanese company in Europe. The Sun had truly risen on the North East!

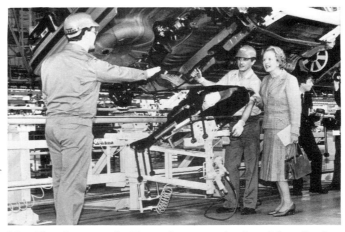

Mrs. Thatcher tours the Nissan factory on the day of the official Opening (The *Journal* and *Chronicle* Photo Library).

That the Japanese 'remembered' the historic links which added a depth of meaning to contemporary associations was underlined by the speech made by their Ambassador, Yamazaki Toshio, at the opening. He acknowledged 'that Nissan's was not the first successful collaboration between the North East and Japan. The region had provided Japan with know-how when it was industrialising ninety years ago.' The relationship between Japan and the North East had, it would seem, come full circle.

The bunting down and the guests gone home, Nissan set about the more serious business of making cars. The 'phase two' announcement had involved a pledge that the company would move to 80 per cent local content by 1991, the year that full production would be reached. With the opening of the plant, a single-union agreement was signed with the Amalgamated Engineering Union (AEU) and yet another hurdle was crossed. The Northern TUC had voted shortly after Nissan's investment decision was announced in support of the princple of single-union agreements. Co-operation from the regional trades union leadership and the effective implementation of this decision was another factor that contributed to the company's advancement of its own deadlines.

Like NSK, Nissan has adhered to 'common terms and conditions of employment' with the same blue uniform worn by all employees, a single car park for managers and workers alike and a shared canteen. Unlike NSK, there is no clocking-on for the responsibility for time-keeping falls to the supervisor who meets with his team at the start of each day. Nissan's director of personnel, Peter Wickens, is quick to emphasize in his book, *The Road to Nissan*, that the good elements of Japanese management practice are 'international' and that the Nissan approach evolved through a careful

Ikeda-Hoover Ltd., providing car seats and interior trim for Nissan, was established at Washington in 1985 (Mike Blenkinsop Studios).

Eguchi Yoshinori of Yamato Kogyo and
Councillor John Mawston, Mayor of
Sunderland, cut the first turf at the new site
of Nissan Yamato Engineering in April 1988
(The *Journal* and *Chronicle* Photo Library).

consideration of those elements which might be transferable to a UK environment. It was in this way that the Nissan tripod of 'flexibility, quality consciousness, and teamworking' was adopted.[27]

Following the introduction of a night shift one year ahead of schedule, Nissan, in December 1987, registered yet another vote of confidence in its work-force. An additional expansion plan was announced which would provide facilities by 1992 to produce a Nissan Micra-class passenger car at the Washington factory. This would be in addition to the 100,000 Nissan Bluebirds scheduled for annual production by that time. The investment of a further £216 million would bring Nissan's total commitment in the North East to more than £600 million with provision made for an additional 1000 jobs, taking the employment total to around 3500. Some 400 associated jobs would be introduced at the Sunderland site. With quality standards equalling and sometimes surpassing those in Japan, the workers at Nissan's Washington plant have collectively justified the faith placed in them and the North East by the Japanese car giant.

The Nissan success story, some would argue, has had a knock-on effect

The Dunlop factory at Washington, now part of S.P. Tyres UK Ltd., was one of three UK plants taken over by Sumitomo Rubber Industries in 1984 (The *Journal* and *Chronicle* Photo Library).

on regional ambitions to attract more Japanese firms. Certainly, interspersed with the reports of the company's landmarks, have been reports of an industrial renaissance in the North East and the growth of a 'honey-pot' syndrome bringing many other 'yen-laden bees' to the region.[28] Ikeda-Bussan's joint venture with the British company Hoover would seem to be a case in point. Providing car seats and interior trim for Nissan, Ikeda-Hoover Ltd, which was established at Washington in 1985, now employs some 250 workers. TI Nihon UK, another UK-Japanese joint-venture company, supplies components to Nissan in Amsterdam, and set up its operation for the assembly and distribution of automobile exhaust systems at Washington in March 1986.

In 1986, SMC Pneumatics (UK) Ltd, a subsidiary of Japan's SMC Corporation, opened a distribution outlet for the North East in Washington. As a supplier of components for Nissan's automatic assembly lines, SMC's expansion was directly related to the presence of one of its best customers in the locality. Then, in July of 1987, Nissan announced a joint venture between itself and Yamato Kogyo, to be known as Nissan Yamato Engineering Ltd, for the manufacture of steel pressings and associated subassemblies which were previously supplied from Japan. The £26.5-million development scheme would create 250 new jobs with a manufacturing plant built on land just adjacent to the factory. Such companies clearly came to the region in the wake of Nissan but other Japanese firms followed a different path to the North East.

SP Tyres UK Ltd represents a rather unusual case in the spectrum of Japanese companies in the North East. The car tyre manufacturing plant has been in production at its Washington site since 1970 but, along with two other factories in Birmingham and Manchester, was under the ownership of Dunlop Ltd. In 1984, as part of an £82-million deal, Dunlop's three UK plants were taken over by Sumitomo Rubber Industries. A total of £15

The Princess of Wales is welcomed Japanese-style to the Tabuchi
factory at Thornaby in March 1987 (The *Journal* and *Chronicle*
Photo Library). (pictured below)

million was invested in the existing factories to improve their quality and efficiency. Washington could claim another Japanese company overnight.

While the Sumitomo takeover was unrelated to the Nissan development, the Washington plant soon found itself supplying the contiguous car factory with 60 per cent of its tyres. This amounted to 5 per cent of the weekly output of 48,000 tyres produced by a staff of 480. As Nissan moved into 'phase two', the potential impact on sales and jobs at SP Tyres was evident. Today a work-force of approximately 500 produces some 9600 tyres per day.

Employees at Washington were introduced to a more open Japanese style of management and work practices and, within twenty-one months, the loss-making operation had been turned around. By 1987, SP Tyres was making a profit, with productivity highest at the Washington plant. Since Dunlop's British managers and its multi-union trade union structure were retained, the Japanization process could be seen at its purest. Improvements in machinery, the working environment, and communication have been credited for the dramatic transformation. An initial team of three Japanese advisers helped to encourage employee involvement, introducing, among other things, single-status clothing and dining facilities. The increase in production levels and reduction of waste with a lower staffing ratio has illustrated how narrowing the gap between management and workers and instilling a sense of company loyalty can produce Japanese-style results. The Dunlop experiment was all the more interesting for its absorption of Japanese methods into an existing British manufacturing framework.

Tabuchi Electric (UK) Ltd was established early in 1985 at Thornaby-on-Tees as the sole European headquarters for Tabuchi Electric Company Ltd of Osaka. The search for a European base for the manufacture and export of high-quality transformers and power supplies involved two years of feasibility studies and an investigation of twenty-seven sites in the UK alone. Tabuchi's investment in the North East was unrelated to Nissan's plans though some of the factors which led to their establishment in the region were inevitably similar. As they export some 32 per cent of their products to Europe, a good communications network to suppliers and continental markets was essential. The availability, through English Estates, of a pilot factory and a project management package for a custom-built factory were other important features.

Tabuchi's initial employment figure of fifty workers has leapt to 480, with temporary workers swelling the numbers to nearly 700 at busy points in the year. The work-force is 75 per cent female with an average age of twenty-two-and-a-half years. Producing 25,000 transformers per day during peak periods, the Tabuchi factory relies on a high level of automation to achieve those results as well as on the standard practices of human resource management central to Japanese industry. Thus, the 'team concept' of production prevails and the importance of communication between management and workers is stressed in aid of the common goal of quality. All staff wear the same dark brown Tabuchi uniform, share two single-status canteens and follow clocking-on procedures. Participation in company-arranged social activities is encouraged. Tabuchi, like so many other UK-based Japanese firms, has translated many features of Japanese management practice into the North East working environment.

Of the Japanese companies that have chosen to invest in the North East, Komatsu Ltd is another which has outlets worldwide and an international reputation. As a manufacturer of earth-moving equipment, Komatsu was able to tap into the region's existing supply of skilled labour and to move into a ready-built factory at Birtley near Gateshead which had previously been owned by the American Caterpillar Company. In an increasingly familiar cycle, the Americans withdrew and the Japanese breathed new life into a dying sector of industry.

Komatsu had been in touch with the regional promotion network for a number of years before negotiations over a specific site began in 1984. In December 1985, it was announced that the company would establish its

Komatsu UK's Company Brochure points to the regeneration of the region which is increasingly associated with Japanese investment in the North East.

The official Opening of Komatsu UK Ltd in July 1987. The Prince of Wales and the Japanese Ambassador at the time, Yamazaki Toshio, are on the platform (The *Journal* and *Chronicle* Photo Library).

fifth overseas plant at Birtley, investing £13 million on the 72,000-square-metre factory and fifty-acre site which would, by 1987, be transformed into a full production facility for wheel loaders and hydraulic excavators.

The theme of Komatsu UK's company brochure – 'A Bright New Dawn in the North' – was in keeping with the revitalization of the old Caterpillar factory and the new hope generated by the 270 jobs that would initially be created and the planned expansion to 370. With a core of twelve permanent and eighteen temporary Japanese staff and a British personnel manager appointed in March 1986, the company began its recruitment drive, taking into the fold some of the very workers made redundant by Caterpillar in 1984. It was on such recruits that the Japanese style of management would make the greatest impact for they had seen the plant as it was and watched it develop into a very different working environment. At Komatsu UK's official opening in July 1987, workers and management alike would be struck by the rhetoric of the Prince of Wales who did not shy away from direct comparisons: 'We in the United Kingdom have, I think, a considerable amount to learn from the Japanese way of doing things and looking after the work-force in their own organizations.' In congratulating the company on the part it was playing in the regeneration of the region, he spoke of 'the North East rising like a phoenix from the ashes of an older industrial past'. The analogy was both apt and poignant and would remain with workers as they returned to the production line.

Beyond the factory gates, however, not all responses to further Japanese investment were so positive. Lord Weinstock, head of GEC, later criticized the government for its subsidizing of Japanese industry and consequent disadvantaging of British industry. Referring to the international trading game, he complained, summoning up the most British of images, that 'we are playing Cricket while the Japanese have gone in for all-in wrestling'.[29]

At Komatsu UK, while the usual rules of Japanese management apply, an underlying company philosophy seeks 'to bring together the best of both worlds',[30] treating the views and suggestions of British and Japanese workers in tandem. This attitude has created some interesting cultural blends as when morning exercises, a common start to the Japanese working day, were introduced. Having recognized the benefits to health and safety of such a routine, the Birtley version sticks to the spirit if not the letter of the law. The concept may be Japanese but the Komatsu callisthenics were devised by the assistant director of *Starlight Express*.

As with several other North East Japanese companies, Komatsu signed a single-union agreement with the Amalgamated Engineering Union in September 1986. Built into the agreement were flexible work practices, effective consultation between work-force and management and an exhaustive negotiating and disputes procedure. The accent on flexibility, continuous improvement, co-operation and team effort has a familiar ring. So, too, do the single-status features of the factory recall the ambience of other Japanese firms in the region. Workers at Komatsu have embraced such concepts and the quality standards that seem possible when the barriers to communication are removed.

Now producing 120 excavators per month and exporting over 70 per cent of its output, Komatsu has reached a level of more than 60 per cent 'local' content in its products and is expected to meet an 80 per cent target before

Komatsu is the only Japanese company in the North East to adopt the Japanese practice of a morning exercise routine (The *Journal* and *Chronicle* Photo Library).

long. The expansion of its operations to include the manufacture of wheel loaders will bring the company's investment to £21 million.

The success of an enterprise like that at Birtley is based to a great extent on good supplier relations. Certainly, much planning has gone into building the Komatsu supplier network. Following the official opening of the company in July 1987, a 'Suppliers Day' brought 200 Komatsu suppliers together from all over Europe and the UK in aid of fostering the kind of 'long-term relationship' that characterizes the Japanese approach to component sourcing. In this as in many other areas, the North East is experiencing a number of firsts through the presence of Japanese firms. There is, too, a likely spin-off effect to be generated by companies like Komatsu which may, in due course, help to attract such UK and European suppliers into the region.

The list of Japanese companies in the North East has crept steadily upwards in the last few years. Early in 1986, Tokyo Yogyo Company, specializing in high-quality refractory bricks for iron and steel plants, announced that it was switching its European head office from London to Stockton-on-Tees and was contemplating establishing a small manufacturing works. It chose Stockton because of 'the importance to BSC and ourselves of the Redcar-Lackenby complex'.[31] A factory for the manufacture of specialist pipes for use in steel production has since been built on the Chilton industrial estate in County Durham.

In the same year, Koike Sanso Kigyo Company officially opened Koike UK Ltd on the Airport Industrial Estate in Newcastle. The company handles sales, service and distribution of Koike welding and cutting equipment for steel fabrication, shipbuilding, offshore oil and plant engineering industries.

By the end of 1987, with a fall in regional unemployment to below 200,000 for the first time since 1981, the state of the North East was being reassessed. Nissan's announcement of its factory expansion in December was quickly followed by news of two further investment deals from Japan. Mitsumi Electric Company was to set up its first European manufacturing base at the Bede Industrial Estate in Jarrow, producing tuners for colour television sets, modulators for video cassette recorders and integrated electric and electronic sub-assemblies for the consumer electronics industry. Some 280 workers would be employed in the 45,000-square-foot factory in South Tyneside, rising to 400 at full production. Another electronics company, SMK Corporation, also took the opportunity at this time to announce its plans for a British base, creating up to 200 jobs at Aycliffe Industrial Estate in County Durham. In a single month, more than 2000 jobs had been brought to the region by the Japanese. Christmas 1987 was to see the North East proudly toasting its accumulation of the largest concentration of Japanese engineering investment in Europe and widening investment prospects.

The pattern of investment from Japan in the North East has been an interesting one, starting with the ball-bearing industry, moving on to cars and construction equipment, and, more recently, centring on electronic components. In March 1988, Sanyo Electric Company Ltd, one of Japan's largest producers of electronic equipment, announced that it would be setting up three factories in the region to manufacture microwave ovens and microwave oven parts. The £11-million investment would bring a further 500 new jobs to the North East with two adjacent factories in Newton Aycliffe producing the microwave ovens and a third factory on the Teesside Industrial Estate at Thornaby producing magnetrons. An output goal of £20 million per year by 1989 was confidently predicted.

Sound economic factors have governed the scale of Japanese investment in the North East. In addition to manufacturing firms, a series of trading houses have set up their offices in the region including the well-known Marubeni Corporation, which is represented in Washington, and Mitsui & Company in Sunderland. Bansho Company Ltd has its office in Newcastle. The formalization of links between Japan and the North East has also led to the signing of economic co-operation agreements between the Northern Development Company and the Fuji Bank and Marubeni Corporation in May 1987, the Sanwa Bank Ltd in June 1987, and, more recently, the Industrial Bank of Japan and Kyowa Bank. Such agreements serve to promote a two-way information exchange in inward investment, joint ventures, licensing agreements, technology transfer and other means of increasing economic activity in the North.

In 1986, the North of England Development Council (NEDC) became absorbed into the newly formed Northern Development Company (NDC) in an attempt to provide a more unified promotion policy for the region. The Department of Trade and Industry, local councils, new town corporations and other agencies who had combined forces in the drive to bring Nissan, Komatsu and further Japanese firms to the region, all recognize the importance of presenting a co-ordinated front to the potential investor. Organizations like the North Eastern Electricity Board have lent their full support to the Japanese investment drive, adding to the impression increasingly gained by visiting firms of a strong regional identity in the North East and a co-operative framework for welcoming newcomers to the area.

Each day seems to hold new opportunities for the region to enhance its commercial links with Japan. A twenty-five-acre vehicle import centre built for Nissan UK, distributors for Nissan cars, at Teesport was opened in March 1988 by Transport Secretary Paul Channon. The £2-million terminal and parking compound has provided a delivery inspection facility and represents a major expansion in the company's British distribution

The Nissan *Executive*, top of the *Bluebird* range, 'launched' in 1988 and shown here at the Quayside in Newcastle (NMUK).

programme. The much-coveted contract to export cars built at Nissan's Sunderland plant was won by the port later in the year. Teesside, with the highest unemployment rate in the country, has thus secured its share of the Nissan cake. The temporary location of the Nissan European Technology Centre at Washington in 1988 has added a European design facility to the existing production network.

On 30 March 1988, the Washington Development Corporation ceased to exist, its role having been fulfilled in its lifespan of twenty-four years. It was appropriate that Mr Tsuchiya Toshiaki, managing director of Nissan Motor Manufacturing (UK) Ltd, should officially bury the time capsule marking the end of the Development Corporation and celebrating the new town's coming of age. Before Nissan, Washington, perhaps, would have been remembered as the ancestral home of the first American president. After Nissan, its future would remain inextricably linked to Japan's.

The North East is witnessing the regenerative effects of Japanese investment in its new towns as well as its old. It is also witnessing the start of a dialogue between the local community and the Japanese who have now become part of it. Global economic factors have guided Japan back to that region of Britain she once knew so well. As the Japanese presence in the North East grows, so too are the opportunities for social and cultural exchange renewed.

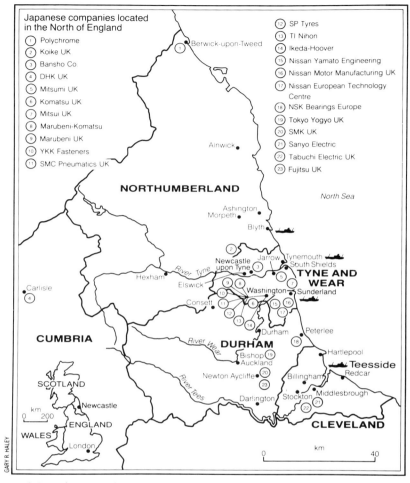

Map showing location of Japanese companies in the North of England (As of April 1989)

Japanese investment in the North of England began in County Durham when NSK Bearings Europe Ltd established its factory at Peterlee in 1976. The second major manufacturing investment from Japan came with the establishment of Nissan Motor Manufacturing (UK) Ltd at Washington in 1984. Washington, a new town in the Borough of Sunderland, has a large concentration of Japanese companies and is the home of the Japanese Saturday School. The wider spread of Japanese investment in recent years is reflected in the location of electronic component factories in the counties of Tyne and Wear, Durham and Cleveland. The map also indicates the major seaports and shipbuilding centres in the North East. That the region's old and new industries are in close proximity is readily apparent.

Japanese Companies Located in the North of England

Bansho Company Ltd., *Trading house*
The Granger Suite, Dobson House, Regent Centre,
Gosforth, Newcastle upon Tyne. Telephone (091)284–2213
Parent company Bansho Company Ltd, Osaka

DHK UK Ltd, *car seat belts, retractor springs*
Unit 12, Kingston Industrial Estate,
Carlisle, Cumbria. Telephone (0228) 26624
Parent company Daido Kogyo Company Ltd, Tokyo

Fujitsu UK, *semi-conductor manufacture*
St Cuthbert's House, St Cuthbert's Way, Newton Aycliffe, Co. Durham.
Telephone (0325) 300511
Parent company Fujitsu Ltd, Tokyo

Ikeda-Hoover Ltd, *seats and interior trim for motor cars*
Cherry Blossom Way,
Sunderland, Tyne & Wear. Telephone (091) 415–6000
Parent company Ikeda Bussan Company Ltd, Tokyo

Koike UK Ltd, *sales and distribution of gas cutting equipment*
Unit 3 A, Airport Industrial Estate, Kingston Park,
Newcastle upon Tyne, Telephone (091) 271–1616
Parent company Koike Sanso Kogyo Company Ltd, Tokyo.

Komatsu UK Ltd, *earth-moving equipment*
Durham Road,
Birtley, Co. Durham. Telephone (091) 410–3155
Parent company Komatsu Ltd, Tokyo

Marubeni-Komatsu Ltd, *sales of construction and earth-moving equipment*
13, Tilley Road, Crowther Industrial Estate,
Washington, Tyne & Wear. Telephone (091) 417–2899
Parent company Marubeni Corporation, Osaka

Marubeni UK plc, *trading house*
13, Tilley Road, Crowther Industrial Estate,
Washington, Tyne & Wear. Telephone (091) 416–7503
Parent company Marubeni Corporation, Osaka

Mitsui UK plc, *trading house*
Unit 2, Bridge House, Bridge Street,
Sunderland. Telephone (091) 510–8176
Parent company Mitsui & Co, Tokyo

Mitsumi UK Ltd, *electronic components*
Bede Industrial Estate,
Jarrow, Tyne & Wear. Telephone (091) 428–0333
Parent company Mitsumi Electric Co Ltd, Tokyo

NSK Bearings Europe Ltd, *ball bearings,*
South West Industrial Estate,
Peterlee, Co. Durham. Telephone (091) 586–6111
Parent company Nippon Seiko Kabushiki, Tokyo

Nissan European Technology Centre
Washington Road
Sunderland, Tyne & Wear. Telephone (091) 418–5155

Nissan Motor Manufacturing (UK) Ltd, *motor car manufacture*
Washington Road,
Sunderland, Tyne & Wear. Telephone (091) 415–0000
Parent company Nissan Motor Company Ltd, Tokyo

Nissan Yamato Engineering Ltd, *presswork and sub-assembly for the motor industry*
Washington Road,
Sunderland, Tyne & Wear. Telephone (091) 415–1282
Parent companies Nissan Motor Company Ltd and Yamato Kogyo Ltd, Tokyo

Polychrome Ltd, *printing plates*
East Ord Industrial Estate,
Berwick, Northumberland. Telephone (0289) 305455
Parent company Dainippon Ink, Tokyo

SMC Pneumatics UK Ltd, *pneumatics for the automotive industry*
Unit 65, Hutton Close, Crowther Industrial Estate,
Washington, Tyne & Wear. Telephone (091) 417–0043
Parent company Shoketsu Kinzoku Kogyo Company Ltd, Tokyo

Sanyo Electric Manufacturing UK Ltd, *microwave ovens at two factories in Newton Aycliffe and magnetrons at Thornaby, Cleveland*
Hilton Road, Aycliffe Industrial Estate,
Newton Aycliffe, Co. Durham. Telephone (0325) 300677
Parent company Sanyo Electric Co, Osaka

SMK UK Ltd, *electronic components and sub-assemblies*
Northfield Way, Aycliffe Industrial Estate,
Newton Aycliffe, Co. Durham. Telephone (0325) 300770
Parent company SMK Corporation, Tokyo

SP Tyres Ltd, *car radial tires*
Birtley Road, Wear, District 5,
Washington, Tyne & Wear. Telephone (091) 416–2515
Parent company Sumitomo Rubber Industries Ltd, Kobe

TI Nihon UK Ltd, *assembly and distribution of automobile exhaust systems*
Glover Industrial Estate, District 11,
Washington, Tyne & Wear. Telephone (091) 417–0084
Parent company Nihon Radiator Co, Tokyo

Tabuchi Electric UK Ltd, *high quality transformers and power supplies*
Tabuchi House, Teesside Industrial Estate, Thornaby,
Stockton-on-Tees, Cleveland. Telephone (0642) 750750
Parent company Tabuchi Electric Co, Osaka

Tokyo Yogyo UK Ltd, *sales and distribution of refractories and manufacture of pipes*
Chilton Way,
Chilton Industrial Estate, Ferry Hill, Co. Durham
Telephone (0388) 720210
Parent company Tokyo Yogyo Co. Ltd, Tokyo

YKK Fasteners UK Ltd, *zip fastener distribution*
24 Bridgewater Road, Hertburn Industrial Estate,
Washington, Tyne & Wear. Telephone (091) 417–6478
Parent company Yoshida Kogyo KK, Tokyo

7   East Meets North East: Japan in the Local Community

Responses to the Japanese presence in the North East have been many and diverse. At an Industrial Society conference in Durham in October 1987, the outspoken bishop of the diocese questioned the value of Nissan to the North and the likely impact of such Japanese firms on local unemployment. He asked sceptically: 'What is the subsidy per job and isn't it the case that most people who got employment there came from other employment?'[1] His conclusion did not offer any answers to these questions nor to the overall problems of the North East: 'I should think the way forward doesn't lie through trying to get more Nissans, but through something much more diverse and worked out on many fronts.' The audience could not have been blamed if they saw in this dismissal of the significance of Nissan, a somewhat unholy attempt to use the increasingly 'sexy' subject of Japanese investment to mount yet another attack on government policy. It was not the first time, nor would it be the last, that the matter of Japan's presence in the region would be invoked in aid of larger issues.

Those who have greeted the influx of Japanese companies in the North East as a positive phenomenon have generally done so in terms of the employment they generate. In addition to the direct creation of jobs, there is also the benefit to local firms supplying components to the Japanese. Curl Engineering Ltd of Washington illustrates the possible spin-offs derived from companies like Komatsu for whom they supply sheet metal products. Five years ago, Curl occupied a 20,000-square-foot factory and employed eighteen people; it has now doubled its factory space and employs eighty workers, thirty-five of whom are directly involved in producing components for its Japanese customer.[2] Opportunities for local firms to supply company plants in Japan have also arisen and resulted in a further expansion of jobs. Both Nissan and Komatsu subscribe to youth training schemes, guaranteeing employment to successful participants at the end of their training period. These are the less-publicized aspects of Japanese company-related employment.

Negative responses to Japanese investment in the region have been directed not so much at the firms themselves as at government policy which, some would argue, has not done enough to protect the North East's traditional industries like shipbuilding while providing heavy subsidies to attract outside firms. Certain sectors of industry, such as the automobile and ball-bearing manufacturing establishment, have seen particular forms of Japanese investment in the North East as representing an insidious threat to their British counterparts. Some trade unions have taken up the cudgels in defence of indigenous industries, just as others, like the Amalgamated Engineering Union (AEU) which operates in a number of Japanese companies, closely monitor any sign of grievance from within. In January 1987, representatives of the Sunderland District of the AEU passed a resolution roundly condemning the famous Saatchi and Saatchi Nissan television commercial which used as its central gimmick the North East-Japanese language divide. In the advertisement, as Japanese and local co-workers from the Sunderland factory are juxtaposed, an interpreter homes in on an 'inscrutable' North East accent to make the requisite points about Nissan cars. Complaints about the commercial centred on the negative impression of the region that it conveyed. Then, too, Sunderland people see their accent as distinct from other local varieties and Tim Healy's Geordie voice-over was clearly unacceptable. The sensitive nature of public relations in Japanese firms in the North East was highlighted by the response to the campaign. Despite a subsequent Nissan survey which suggested its overall success, it remained unpalatable to local taste.

Much media attention has been devoted to the North East's present-day links with Japan. There is, in this, an element of jobs being newsworthy in the North but, below the surface, lies the exotic fascination which Japan continues to exert upon the western mind. Newspaper headlines have made this apparent. So, too, have the television documentaries that have been born out of the relatively recent meeting of East and North East. In July 1986, Tyne Tees Television broadcast its aptly titled focus on the first Nissan workers to train in Japan – *Sayonara Pet*. Then, in July 1987, a series of three BBC television programmes looked at the first year in the life of Komatsu (UK). The documentary title – *Chopsticks, Bulldozers, and Newcastle Brown Ale* – overlooked the fact that bulldozers were not included in the Birtley factory's product range. Like *Sayonara Pet*, however, it directly reflected the juxtaposition of different cultures in its wording. Channel Four's 'Japan Season' in the autumn of 1987 featured many

Nissan's first group of supervisors set off for training in Japan in 1985. Tyne Tees Television focused on their experience in the documentary, *Sayonara Pet* (The *Journal* and *Chronicle* Photo Library).

Japanese-made programmes but only two British-made documentaries about Japan. One of these, *Turning Japanese*, was, more specifically, about Japan and the North East and the cultural contortions evolving out of two communities living in one. All three documentaries illustrated that the interest in Japan's association with the region has spread well beyond its boundaries.

There is news and then there is the newsworthy. Nissan is newsworthy. Shortly after it announced its joint venture with Yamato Kogyo in July 1987 and the expansion into land adjacent to the original Sunderland airport site, an article appeared in the *Journal* (6 August 1987) outlining the threat to local wildlife ensuing from the shrinking of the 'green belt' between Tyne and Wear. Making a case for the retention of a pond in the south-west corner of the complex as a bird migration centre, the author expressed his hopes that, 'next to the ranks of newly-produced Bluebird cars could be a good variety of birds of the feathered kind'.[3] Another 'environmental' issue involving Nissan arose in February 1988. Prominently featured in several local newspapers was the Nissan 'Ghostbusters' story. Here, the company was on view for the effect its new building was having on television screens in Pensher View, Sulgrave (Washington). The building was acting as a giant reflector, disrupting radio and TV signals reception in the area. Not major news but made more important by the source from which it came.

It seems that all eyes locally are fixed on Nissan and the other Japanese companies based in the North East. Responses to them range from the sublime to the ridiculous. There are, however, less publicized effects of the

Channel Four filmed this group of YTS
trainees mixing with local Japanese
schoolchildren at a course arranged
by Sunderland Polytechnic's Japanese Studies
Division in 1987 (Channel Four).

Japanese presence in the region. As Japanese investment in the North East
grows, so too do its social and cultural consequences. These reverberate on
the British and Japanese employees working side by side on the production
line, the families living in close proximity to one another and the children
attending the same schools. For them, 'Japanization' and 'internationalization' are not abstract concepts but ones which increasingly inform their
daily lives.

There are some 400 Japanese, including families, living and working in
the North East of England and also those who regularly visit the area
through their business connections with Japanese and other local firms. The
overall numbers are not large; in some ways, the attention focused on Japan
and the Japanese may seem disproportionate to such figures. Yet, there is a
widening consciousness of Japan in the North East. This is partly a
reflection of the experiences of those who deal directly with the Japanese
and are most affected by their lifestyle and attitudes to work. A significant
proportion of company employees, suppliers and individuals within the
service sector of industry, in working with the Japanese, take on board a
host of cultural values which differ markedly from their own.

For the employee of a Japanese firm in the North East, there are both
company policies and work practices which contrast with those to be found
in British industry. The emphasis on in-house training, for example, comes
to many as a pleasant surprise, reflecting the long-term commitment which
the company is making to their future. NSK, Nissan, Komatsu and Tabuchi
have all sent groups of staff to Japan for periods of training. While first-hand
observation of the factory environment there has aided the implementation
of company methods in the UK, it has also provided a context within which

to relate to Japanese co-workers and technical training which can be passed on to other production staff back home. Continuous on-the-job training emphasizes the flexibility and job mobility inherent in the structure of the lifetime employment system. One production line welder at Komatsu recently progressed to team leader and then to fabrication supervisor after just seventeen months, an upgrading which he felt would not have been likely in a British company.

The emphasis on consultation and dialogue in Japanese firms has also been well received by employees in the North East, although the actual process can by mystifying. Encouraging workers to make suggestions is not mere tokenism but is taken seriously. The philosophy is based on a common-sense assumption that those who are actually producing the bearings, cars or excavators are best placed to recommend changes in production technique. Increased employee involvement has a direct impact on quality standards which are never seen as static goals but always capable of being surpassed. When asked what he most liked about working for Nissan, a check and repair man at the Sunderland factory referred to 'the challenge of always striving to do better'.[4] The introduction of the Japanese notion of *kaizen* or 'continuous improvement' has, in many cases, led to increased job satisfaction.

If all this begins to have a utopian ring, there is another sometimes frustrating side to working for Japanese employers that stems from mutual preconceptions and expectations. Both the language barrier and different approaches to decision-making are at the root of misunderstanding. For the

Team Meeting Area at Nissan's Sunderland factory. The emphasis on consultation and dialogue has been well-received by employees in the North East (NMUK).

Japanese, a decision is often reached only after lengthy and seemingly indirect discussion, by which time something approximating a consensual view is determined. The new lifestyle of the Japanese meeting does not always sit well with British supervisors and managers who are accustomed to speedier – and apparently more decisive – courses of action.

There are other factors which contribute to the communication gap. While identification with one's company and its goal may be a way of life in Japan, the practices which reflect total company loyalty can be a cause of cross-cultural conflict in the UK. The Japanese work longer, if not harder, than the British and the implications for the employee of a UK-based Japanese firm are clear. While the local staff are asking their wives and husbands to be patient about late nights and overtime, the Japanese staff are surprising their families by the unusually early hours they keep. In Japan, this would be a real cause for concern; in the UK, it signifies the mutual adjustments necessitated by the respective demands of two cultures working together as one.

Companies supplying Japanese firms in the UK find themselves in a similar position to the actual employees with respect to the mechanics of inter-cultural communication. Relationships with suppliers in Japan are very often life-long and will affect the component manufacturers' planning and working methods as a whole. With a pre-determined 'local content' factor at stake, much hangs on the ability of UK and European manufacturers to respond flexibly to the requirements of Japanese customers. To firms in the North East, there is an immediate advantage to be gained from such adaptability.

Japanese quality standards are at the heart of the relationship with suppliers. At the very beginning of its first feasibility study in the North East, Nissan underlined the fact that the whole project could stand or fall on the supplier issue. Japan's economic success has been partly determined by the calibre of its work-force and the quality of the products which they manufacture. In the North East, there have already been murmurs that a high ratio of 'local content' and Japanese standards of quality may prove an unequal equation. Some, though not all, Japanese companies in the region subscribe to 'just-in-time' procedures of production and delivery. The demands placed upon component suppliers to adjust their production schedules for perhaps one customer have created difficulties. In 1986, the northern branch of the CBI addressed this issue with its Gateshead seminar on *Kanban* (just-in-time) manufacturing technique. North East industrialists were encouraged to adopt the Japanese approach in aid of reducing production lead times, cutting labour costs, eliminating excessive stock levels and improving quality. Regional CBI chairman Tom O'Connor raised the challenge: 'You either follow suit or go out of business, because more and more we are becoming part of a global market. We have to be able to compete with overseas companies on equal terms.' *Kanban* has been readily adopted by some British companies for its practical advantages and as an aid to competitiveness; it is also being put into practice by those suppliers who are faced with the more direct demands of Japanese industry in the region. The imported concept has reverberated on warehousing and haulage operators as well as component manufacturers, all of whom are finding that doing business with the Japanese demands nothing less than total commitment.

For the service sector, the side-effects of Japanese investment in the North East are considerable. Standards of service are extremely high in Japan. Hotels, restaurants and shops respond to the role of serving the customer with total dedication. This outlook informs the attitudes of desk clerks and component suppliers alike so that those Japanese who find themselves in the North East have certain expectations in this regard. Their code of entertaining – particularly business entertaining – outside the home is providing Japanese business opportunities for the regional service network. Restaurants, hotels and catering firms are finding a new market in arranging dinner meetings and company functions throughout the year. An increasing concern with Japanese taste in food, decor and etiquette is becoming apparent in a range of establishments. The dilemma of whether to serve raw fish or sirloin steak is made worse by an uneven pattern of westernization of Japanese eating habits. One local hotel chef has learned

Mr Honda Takami of Marubeni UK was awarded a bottle of champagne and a weekend in Paris as the 1,371,446th traveller to pass through Newcastle Airport in 1988 (The *Journal* and *Chronicle* Photo Library).

Japanese children from the English Language Unit of Usworth Comprehensive School are presented with a memento of their June 1987 visit to *Cragside* which was sponsored by the North Eastern Electricity Board (North Eastern Electricity Board).

to prepare *sushi* and other Japanese delicacies; his customers for this exotic fare, however, tend not to be Japanese.

The North East hotel trade is ever seeking new ways to respond to and encourage Japanese custom. In another hotel, the confusion generated by such misunderstood questions as 'Shall I turn down your bed now, sir?' has created a demand for Japanese language lessons and for chambermaids better versed in the ways of the East. At the George Washington Hotel, the expansion of services aimed at Japanese clientele even extends to the provision of religious literature. *The Teachings of the Buddha* can now be found in every bedroom along-side the more usual Gideon Bible. The North East spirit of welcome would seem to know no bounds.

On 9 March 1988, traveller number 1,371,446 passed through Newcastle Airport, beating its previous largest-ever annual passenger figure. A bottle of champagne and a weekend in Paris were awarded to North East resident, Mr Honda Takami of Marubeni UK. In the regional records, against all likely odds, yet another statistic on the Japanese presence has been registered.

The growing awareness of Japan in the North East is not confined to the world of business. Groups of Japanese women shopping at the Gateshead Metrocentre and Washington's Savacentre are no longer an unusual sight. Savacentre began stocking Japanese foodstuffs shortly after the arrival of Nissan and now does a booming trade in rice-crackers. There are different perspectives on Japan being offered by the wives and children of company workers living in the local community. Certain schools, like Usworth Comprehensive at Washington, have a small contingent of Japanese students. English language units, set up by Sunderland Borough Council, assist in their integration into the British education system. For local pupils, contact with members of their peer group from Japan offers valuable insights into the reality of a country which has always seemed totally different and very far away.

Japanese women and children living in the North East have, to varying degrees, entered into local life. School socials, sports days and other family-centred activities largely form the focus of their relationship with the community. Some schools have reaped the educational benefits of this association with origami, flower arranging and calligraphy experts identified among the new arrivals. In the main, however, the presence of Japanese families in places like Washington, Sunderland, Gateshead, Newcastle and Thornaby has produced no sudden 'awakening' or culture shock but, rather, the gradual realization that the Japanese live largely as we do, whether at home or abroad.

What, then, do the Japanese make of the North East? For those company workers and their families posted in the region, the prospect of coming to Britain, and the North East in particular, represents various levels of the unknown. The Japanese admire the British and things British; indeed, companies like Tabuchi have cited the identification with another island nation and historic culture as one reason for establishing their factory in the UK as opposed to on the Continent. The Japanese come with their preconceptions in tow, however, and the image of Buckingham Palace, beefeaters and Savile Row does not equate with the reality of the North East. Neither does the other common preconception of a densely populated northern industrial landscape with smoke belching out from every chimney.

A standard first response to the North East, then, is one of surprise at the green fields and countryside in close proximity to factories and housing. Compared with Japan, the sense of space is striking. The houses and gardens are far larger here and the golf courses offer a particular luxury. In Japan, such facilities would be non-existent or unaffordable; in their new habitat, they are plentiful, inexpensive and easily booked. The North East's Japanese community was quick to defend the region when, in June 1987, the Environment Minister, Nicholas Ridley, uttered his instantly regretted statement that it was not providing the right facilities, especially golf courses and decent executive housing, for incoming industrialists. An impromptu survey conducted for the *Guardian* at Komatsu proved the locally born Ridley wrong.

While housing and leisure facilities allow newly arrived Japanese what

Wives and children on a housing estate in
Washington. Japanese families are becoming
part of the wider North East community and
adjusting local perceptions of Japan
(The *Journal* and *Chronicle* Photo Library).

must seem an automatic change of status, there are other aspects of life
outside Japan to which adjustment is not so readily made. The Japanese
education system is highly competitive and places great pressure upon
students to gain admission to the right sequence of schools and, ultimately,
universities. Employment prospects are very much determined by educational success. Company managers and workers posted overseas must,
therefore, decide whether to leave their wives and children behind to cope
with the education treadmill or whether to brave the British education
system and find ways of readjusting later on. Many choose the latter route
though worries about schooling are ongoing during their residency abroad.

In 1985, representatives from the Washington Development Corporation,
Sunderland Borough Council and Nissan combined forces to bring about
the establishment of a Japanese Saturday School at Washington. There are
now eight such schools across the UK[5] providing top-up facilities for
Japanese youngsters attending local schools during the week. Some one
hundred children now attend the Washington Saturday School where the
focus is on Japanese language study. With a complex writing system which
requires considerable memorization and writing practice to maintain standards of literacy, such tuition is essential preparation for their eventual

The first official photograph of the Japanese Saturday School in the North East of England. Approximately one hundred students now attend the Washington school (Japanese Saturday School).

return to Japan. Three hours per week, however, will still leave these students lagging far behind their contemporaries in Japan. There is, too, a considerable gap in mathematics and science education to be resolved; in these subjects, the average fifteen-year-old in the West is doing the work of a twelve-year-old in Japan. The problem of returnee school children is finally beginning to be addressed in government and education circles in Japan. With official policy very much in support of internationalization, changes in the framework of education, which will accommodate the increasing numbers of children who have studied overseas, must follow. The present situation penalizes returnees rather than seeing their experience as advantageous to Japan's changing world perspective. One Sunderland-based Japanese schoolchild described her delight in having the opportunity to experience and compare education in Britain and Japan. Summing up her reactions in the *Sunderland Echo* (10 July 1987), she pointed to the greater teacher-pupil ratio in Britain as allowing for more individual attention. She also noted the friendlier classroom atmosphere with British teachers far less strict than the Japanese variety. Conversely, her negative reactions were related to lack of discipline and responsibility. She was surprised by school rules frequently being broken and people dropping their litter without thinking about 'who has to tidy it up'. In Japan, children have the shared responsibility for cleaning their schools on a daily basis. In later life, this has implications for the working environment. The orderliness and efficiency of Japanese factories, often remarked upon in the West, have their roots deep in the social discipline which is instilled in children both at home and at school. The experience of another culture may well highlight such differences and widen understanding but, for this Sunderland schoolgirl, like many other Japanese pupils in the region, the problems to be faced on re-entering the Japanese education system will be many.

The experience of living in an English-speaking country does offer certain kinds of advantages and compensations. Many Japanese companies look to Britain for investment opportunities because English is Japan's principal second language; it is universally studied and is also the language of international business. Japanese schoolchildren study English for six years from the start of junior high school at twelve years old to the end of senior high school at eighteen. There is, therefore, a great educational benefit to be derived from living in an English-speaking environment. For the children, attending local schools and forming friendships rapidly results in fluency. Their fathers will more gradually acquire a command of the language. Association with Japanese colleagues at work and the time lag between formal study and the practical use of English can slow the process down considerably. There is the additional stumbling block of local dialect; the ability to comprehend the Queen's English will not necessarily solve the problems of communication in a North East-based Japanese factory!

While the Japanese company employees and their children have a daily focus in their places of work and schools, it is the Japanese women, the wives and mothers, who must find some way of fitting into both a new country and a new way of life without any set framework in which to operate. The husband's firm does provide some kind of support system. It is usual, for example, for friendships to be formed with other company wives. In Japan, the company-orientated lifestyle affects the family as a whole. Japanese wives in the North East, as in Japan, will describe themselves as Mrs So-and-So of NSK, Tabuchi or Mitsumi. They see their own position in relation to that of their husband. Not all Japanese companies in the locality are large, however. In some cases, only one or two Japanese families from a particular firm have come to the region. Friendships may then be established with other company wives or with British neighbours. The language barrier does inevitably hinder close involvement with community life.

One family in Sunderland has come to the North East complete with grandmother. This is an unusual phenomenon and was linked to their personal circumstances rather than any company policy. In this way, another level was added to the acclimatization process. 'Grandmother' has no understanding of English and has never lived abroad. When neighbours invite her in to tea, it is her sixteen-year-old grandson who acts as interpreter. He is the only Japanese pupil at his Sunderland school and has acquired a good command of English. Communicating through a third party, however, does not make for close friendships. The garden of their family home on a housing estate in the area is his grandmother's preserve. As in Japan, she spends her spare time growing vegetables and, as in Japan, it is *udon* (radishes) along with other native specimens that she tends. The seed packets are another unique import from Japan.

Japanese households are traditional in the sense that wives do not generally go out to work, at least until the children are older. For the North East Japanese wives, their domestic situation raises particular challenges. Access to Japanese rice and other foodstuffs is a major concern. While western food of every sort is available and popular in Japan, most families prefer to eat Japanese-style at home. The growing market for Japanese food supplies has led to some interesting developments in the region. In 1984, an enterprising Japanese grocer based in London, Mori Akihiko, turned the attention of his small family-run business, Setsu Japan, to the food needs of the Japanese community scattered across Britain. He initiated a delivery service on the third Friday of each month to Japanese companies and households in the North East. Not only cooking ingredients but, during the New Year season, festive *o-bento* (lunch boxes) and other delicacies would be delivered to customers in the region. Of all the staples most missed by Japanese living abroad, the native, sticky short-grained rice is the most important. The Bakufu mission who visited Newcastle in 1862 had left Japan with their rice on board. Some years later, Middlesbrough's Japanese community similarly found a way of importing this commodity into the area. As the monthly sacks were lifted off the back of his van, Mr Mori more recently decided that his thriving trade in the North East warranted the expansion of his empire. Late in 1987, he opened a Setsu Japan shop on Heaton Road in Newcastle, stocking Japanese food and goods of every

Nissan has brought three generations of the Suzuki family to Sunderland (M. Conte-Helm).

description. Among the other services on offer are a Japanese take-away (on weekends only) and a Japanese video library, the first in the North East.

In addition to Mr Mori's emporium, a Japanese restaurant is planned to open in Newcastle. Here, again, is a facility generated out of the Japanese presence in the North East but one which will add a new dimension to the city and to the character of business entertaining in the area.

While the North East Japanese wives generally purchase their Japanese cooking supplies from Mr Mori, the bulk of their shopping is done in local supermarkets and in the neighborhoods in which they live. There is, too, such a demand for fresh fish that group expeditions to North Shields fish quay are a regular feature of life. During their stay in the region, many wives have attempted to penetrate the secrets of British and North East cooking. Apart from 'stotty cakes', local people would find the latter difficult to define. There is, nevertheless, an almost universal interest in roast beef and Yorkshire pudding along with the ritual of the English afternoon tea.

Spare-time pursuits are similarly Anglo-Japanese in nature. As at home, Japanese women attend classes in different handicraft skills at local community centres. They meet with friends, have outings with younger children and go shopping. While their children attend the Japanese Saturday School at Oxclose in Washington, a number of the women participate in the English conversation classes organized at the same venue by the local education authority. In Japan, they would be the moving force behind their children's education; in the UK, such a role is difficult to

Mr and Mrs Mori Akihiko with the Manager (centre) of their new enterprise, *Setsu Japan*, the first Japanese food shop to open in the North East (M. Conte-Helm).

Learning the essentials at an English
language class for Japanese wives (The
Journal and *Chronicle* Photo Library).

assume given the differences in the system and initial problems of communication. Japanese parents do take an active part in the conduct of the
Saturday School, however. Both mothers and fathers are involved in its
organization and preparation for annual events.

The same kind of internal co-operation applies to the running of the
North East Association of Japanese Women. This acts as a more formal
framework for information exchange and for the co-ordination of an annual
charity event. In June 1987, the Association organized a successful 'Charity
Hoedown' and barbecue supper at the Riding School for the Disabled in

NORTH-EAST ASSOCIATION OF JAPANESE WOMEN

CHARITY
HOEDOWN

WITH LIVE BAND
'CROSS COUNTRY'

AT RIDING CENTRE STEPHENSON WASHINGTON

ON SATURDAY 6TH JUNE '87   6:00 - 11:00 P.M.

TICKET £2.50 ADULT & OVER 13 YRS.

INCLUDING BARBEQUE SUPPER

TICKET NO. 572

A Charity 'Hoedown' organised by the North
East Association of Japanese Women in June
1987. (M. Conte-Helm).

Washington. A 'Country and Western Dinner Dance' followed in 1988. In addition to the overall planning of these events, the Japanese women have applied their handicraft skills to the decoration of stalls and production of 'prizes', bringing yet another manifestation of Japan to the North East.

While the tendency to operate in groups seems innate to the Japanese, some women have found themselves living in relative isolation in various parts of the region and this has contributed to changing perspectives. One Japanese company wife does regular volunteer work at her local hospital. She welcomed the opportunity to improve her English and to make some contribution to the local community at the same time. In cases like her own, as language ability grows, so too do the possibilities for deeper relationships.

The Japanese living in the North East have established their own social networks whether at work, school, at home, or in the wider community. They also take part in company-organized social activities which involve the family as a whole. Nissan has an annual sports' day each September to commemorate its opening. Komatsu similarly arranges periodic family days with organized events and factory tours. A Komatsu-sponsored fun run in May 1987 at Usworth Comprehensive School saw the Japanese contingent far out-numbering the local staff. Here was a community event to which a Japanese company responded with financial support and direct participation.

If the Japanese presence is welcomed in the North East, it is also given the full official support of local government authorities and municipal agencies. When Nissan was negotiating over the Sunderland airport site, a new approach road and full services were a standard part of the package. Assistance with housing, schools and other amenities were also provided to ease the process of settling in. Komatsu has similarly found a good support

Komiya Torio, Managing Director of Komatsu UK, reflects on Japan's earlier associations with the North East at an exhibition to mark the Opening of the Birtley factory. (M. Conte-Helm).

The British weather does not affect company spirit at a Komatsu-sponsored Fun Run in May 1987. (M. Conte-Helm).

network in the region, existing on many levels. Traffic lights were installed, without delay, at the entrance to their Birtley factory when the company notified the local council of the difficult access due to heavy traffic on an adjacent road. Civic agencies are anxious to facilitate the arrival of Japanese firms and, once here, to ensure their smooth integration into the community. Northumbria Police have a Race Relations Unit which aims to circumvent cross-cultural misunderstandings and to assist in explaining aspects of British law to North East residents from abroad. Staff have undergone training to provide assistance to the Japanese, among other local groups.

Late in 1985, Sunderland Borough Council announced its support for a major Japanese festival in the Sunderland-Washington area. It was to be a five-week celebration of Japan and the largest British focus on Japanese art and culture ever to take place outside London. The Washington Arts Centre initiated and co-ordinated this grand-scale project. In addition to Sunderland Borough Council's, grants from Tyne and Wear County Council, Washington Development Corporation and Northern Arts were to make the festival plan a reality. Further support came from the Japanese Embassy, Japan Foundation, Japan National Tourist Organisation, Great Britain-Sasakawa Foundation, the Visiting Arts Office and the National Association of Arts Centres. Commercial sponsors included Price Water-house, the North Eastern Electricity Board, Nissan, Komatsu and SP Tyres – all of whom received awards under the Business Sponsorship Incentive Scheme for first-time sponsorship of the arts. With the backing of these and other organizations, an ambitious programme was set in motion which would bring to the North East Japanese art, crafts, gardens, theatre, film,

Japanese Festival Brochure (Washington Arts Centre).

music and dance. The culture of Japanese investment was being officially embraced, while, in the process, an interesting experiment in intercultural education was being realized.

From the early stages of planning, the educational significance of the Japanese presence in the region was highlighted within the Festival and reinforced by a range of events aimed at children in local schools. Two leading kite-makers from Japan, Ohashi Eiji and Nishibayashi Takeshi, arrived in the North East in June 1986. Over the next three months, they held kite-making workshops and demonstrations in thirty-five schools in the Borough of Sunderland. The enthusiasm which their contact with local schools engendered was reflected in the overwhelming success of the Japanese Festival's opening event, the 'Festival of the Air'. Britain's largest-ever kite festival was held in Washington on 14 September 1986 with an estimated attendance of 28,000. Ohashi summed up the spirit of the day, and of the Festival as a whole, when he reflected: 'It is very far from England to Japan but it is the same sky.'

The 'Festival of the Air' launched a five-week focus on Japan that involved members of the North East and Japanese community throughout. A 'Japan Week', sponsored by the Embassy of Japan, brought Ambassador and Madame Yamazaki to the region for a three-day visit. They toured the festival exhibitions and watched a schools' performance by the Himawari Theatre Group which would, at the end of the five weeks, have been seen by 7000 children in the Sunderland area. On the last day of the Ambassador's visit, a *judo* demonstration by the Olympic Gold Medallist

The 'Festival of the Air' which opened the 1986 Japanese Festival
has become an annual event in Washington
(Washington Arts Centre).

Nishibayashi Takeshi conducts a kitemaking
Workshop in Washington during the 1986
Japanese Festival (Washington Arts Centre).

Yamashita Yasuhiro provided the opportunity to witness one of Japan's greatest 'heroes' in action. It was, however, heroes of the past who occupied the Ambassador's attention on the final afternoon of his stay in the North East. A visit to Cragside in Northumberland, the home of the first Lord Armstrong, completed the cycle of celebrating Japanese links with industry in the North East.

Exhibitions and events during the five weeks of the Festival were wide-ranging and took place in museums, galleries, theatres and public buildings in all parts of the Borough of Sunderland. At the Washington Arts Centre, an exhibition of traditional kimono and costume accessories featured the crowd-pulling kimono presented to the Princess of Wales during her visit to Japan in May 1986. Exhibitions of traditional packaging, Japanese swords, *noh* masks and historical photographs illustrating Japan's links with the North East could be seen at this central festival venue. A specially constructed traditional Japanese room was the setting for daily demonstrations of *kumihimo* (braid-making), *ikebana* (flower arranging), *origami* (paper folding) and the wearing of kimono. The Sunderland Museum and Art

The 100-metre long 'Friendship Kite' made at the Washington Arts Centre in 1986 bears many signatures, including those of the Prince of Wales, Ambassador Yamazaki, and the present Japanese Ambassador to Britain, His Excellency, Mr Chiba Kazuo.
(M. Conte-Helm).

Gallery organized a major exhibition of 'Japanese Art from North East Collections' and the Northern Centre for Contemporary Art in Sunderland another on 'Japonisme: Japanese Influence on Western Art'. Additional exhibitions and displays could be seen at Sunderland Polytechnic's Backhouse Gallery, the Sunderland Civic Centre, Crowtree Leisure Centre, Sunderland Central Library, Savacentre and other local venues.

Throughout the Festival, exhibitions and schools' programmes were interspersed with daily demonstrations and workshops which covered a wide variety of traditional arts. Musical performances ranged from recitals of *koto* (Japanese harp) to the antics of the punk rock duo, 'Frank Chickens'. In all, an estimated 160,000 visits were made to events within the Festival and a tremendous impact was exerted upon local schools which pursued their interest in Japan through follow-up projects of various kinds. So successful were the residencies of the kite-makers that they would be invited back to the region in the summers of 1987 and 1988 for a wider programme of schools' visits and the co-ordination of what has become in the North East an annual 'Anglo-Japanese Festival of the Air'.

For the North East Japanese community, such a celebration of Japanese culture came as something of a curiosity and a surprise. Japanese company wives contributed to demonstrations of traditional arts and crafts, made items for exhibitions, and dressed large numbers of visitors in kimono. Japanese children sat side by side with local children, mesmerized by the magic of the Himawari Theatre Group. Families participated in the 'Festival of the Air' and it was a Komatsu company team that won the kite-fighting competition.

Yamashita Yasuhiro, judo champion, instructs students
at Biddick School in September 1986
(The *Journal* and *Chronicle* Photo Library).

The Japanese Festival opened just one week after the official opening of Nissan Motor Manufacturing (UK) Ltd. Connections were readily drawn between the Japanese companies in the North East and the need for broader cultural understanding. As with reactions to the companies themselves, however, the response to a Japanese Festival in the region was not universally positive. When the Tyne and Wear Museum's Committee voted to back the Sunderland Museum and Art Gallery's Japanese exhibition in April 1986, a Labour Councillor on the Committee registered his vote against the display. As an ex-serviceman and member of Gateshead's war pensioners' committee, Councillor Reg Strong made his personal protest and expressed feelings which, though understandable, were not voiced by many at this time of Anglo-Japanese détente.

While the Nissan opening and the Japanese Festival highlighted the region's more recent associations with Japan, these events also brought to the surface an 'underworld' of Japan enthusiasts who had been quietly pursuing their interests long before such developments were contemplated. *Ikebana*, *kendo* and *bonsai* associations have been operating in the North East for many years. A new demand has been created for Japanese-style flower arrangements in those hotels and restaurants which cater to the Japanese. Official openings and other organized events provide further vehicles for Japanese displays. The first North East Kendo Club was started some twenty years ago by a miner at Blyth. There are now *dojo* all over the region. Many other martial arts organizations are similarly represented in the North East. The individuals who subscribe to such pastimes have

Demonstrating the art of wearing kimono to schoolchildren at the Washington Arts Centre during the 1986 Japanese Festival (M. Conte-Helm).

become initiated into the particular vocabulary of the sport or art form. In this way, Japan may be first perceived as a backdrop to a particular activity but the heightened local profile of Japanese investment is both intensifying existing interests and drawing attention to societies with a longer history in the area.

For many reasons, from curiosity to pragmatism, the desire to learn about Japan is increasing in the North East. No survey has yet been conducted to pinpoint numbers, but more and more people, including company employees, are now studying the Japanese language and other aspects of culture in direct response to the presence of Japanese firms and families in the region.

As the Japanese seek to master English and the North East community takes on things Japanese, certain questions must be asked about the interplay of cultures and the real potential for communicating across the East-West divide. Attempts at mutual understanding abound. When a Japanese couple in Newcastle invited some British acquaintances around for the evening, expectations of exotic *sushi* tastings and other glimpses of the 'real Japan' ran high. The serving of cocktail

The red-and-white 'Celebration Arrangement' done by local *ikebana* expert, May Hyam, to mark the Nissan 'announcement' in March 1984 (*Sunderland Echo*).

Growing numbers of people in the North East, including employees of Japanese firms, are studying the language and culture of Japan (M. Conte-Helm).

sausages, scotch eggs, and other local delicacies produced a general disorientation. The British often expect the Japanese to behave quintessentially so, just as the Japanese hope that their stay in the North East will provide insights into the 'traditional' British way of life. Sunderland-based Vaux Breweries experimented with the depths of cross-cultural fascination when, in June 1987, they test-marketed Japan's oldest lager, 'Sapporo', in twenty-two of their pubs. The resident Japanese, meanwhile, are developing a taste for Newcastle Brown Ale. There is, for both groups, an inherent meeting ground in the culture of the North East pub which, like Japan's after-hours drinking establishments, is largely a male preserve.

The Japanese living in the North East are experiencing some customs and facets of life which the North-South divide would render 'foreign' in Surrey, let alone Tokyo or Osaka. While New Year is Japan's biggest national festival, marked by visits to friends and family throughout the season, the local practice of 'first-footing' on New Year's Eve is viewed with a mixture of bewilderment and interest.

'To place oneself in another's shoes' is an expression gaining currency in North East-Japanese circles. If those shoes are shed at the entrance to one house, however, and left firmly on at the entrance to another, the scope for empathy is limited. Local people visiting Japanese homes are learning to cope with the practice of going shoeless therein – the origins of which lie in cleanliness and common sense. According to one Japanese housewife, the only guests allowed to breach this rule of etiquette are the region's meter men who remain swift of foot and a law unto themselves. With exposure to such customs, another layer of 'difference' is peeled away.

North East businessmen listen to the experiences of a local firm
successfully exporting to Japan at a weekend briefing arranged
by Sunderland Polytechnic's Japanese Studies Division
(M. Conte-Helm).

A toast to the future. Sarada Osamu of
Sapporo Breweries and Frank Nicholson of
Vaux Breweries celebrate the first shipment
of Sapporo lager to arrive in the North East
from Japan (The *Journal* and *Chronicle*
Photo Library).

The current wave of Japanese investment in the North East of England has been positively assessed as a counterweight to regional unemployment and negatively viewed as a threat to indigenous industries. The phenomenon which brings increasing numbers of Japanese people to the area has another dimension, however, and that is the opening of minds and the growth of awareness which may or may not result in mutual understanding.

Conclusion: A Relationship Reversed?

Japan's first contact with the North East of England in 1862 witnessed a nation on the brink of modernization and industrial development turning to a region enjoying its 'finest hour' of industrial growth and economic ascendancy. The present-day relationship is of a different tenor. On the threshold of world economic leadership, Japan is 're-investing' in a North East of England which has suffered the ravages of industrial decline and high unemployment but now seems headed towards recovery.

A relationship reversed? The irony and poignancy of this altered perspective can be illustrated on a number of levels. As Japanese industrialists arrive in the North East seeking investment opportunities, they, like the earliest Japanese visitors to the region, enter into a world in which two cultures stand enquiringly face to face. Whereas Victorian technology and values once served as a model, in today's encounter, the teacher and the pupil have exchanged positions and the lessons are geared to a new phase of history. Japan's record of post-war economic success has established a trade surplus and a high-value yen as motives for the internationalization of her industries and, in particular, the establishment of manufacturing bases in Europe. With the approach of 1992 and the abandonment of trade restrictions within the European Community, Britain has re-entered the sphere of Japanese interest and the North East has regained its share in a partnership that was formerly based on coal, ships and guns.

If 'eastern ethics, western science' first determined the relationship between Bakumatsu Japan and Victorian Britain, current debate centres on the Japanization of British industry and the impact of the Japanese style of management and work practices on employees throughout the land. For the Japanese, the state of regional industrial relations and the 'flexibility' of the local work-force are of major importance to the investment process. The transferability of Japanese styles of management has been put to the test in the North East and in other parts of the UK and has thus far proved successful. Beyond Japanese subsidiaries, however, the issue of 'Japanization' within British industry has remained a sensitive one. When Ford sought to introduce flexible 'Japanese-style' work practices in its British plants from October 1987 to February 1988, workers responded with a three-week strike. The banners brandished on the picket line – 'We're Brits, Not Nips' – summed up the strength of feeling generated by the call of British management for its work-force to imitate the methods of Japanese industry.

In Meiji Japan, ironically, the westernization debate once raged with no less intensity and some violence. The Iwakura mission returned home from their tour of Europe and America in 1871–2 much impressed by what they had seen of western industry and technology and certain that change was a necessary condition of progress. The question of imitation and trans-plantation of western work practices was much discussed and, beyond these, the deeper value systems of the West which Japan could never hope to fully penetrate. Catching up with the West remained the clear-cut goal but the demands of westernization were variously interpreted.

In viewing the past from the perspective of the present, it is easy to forget the realities which once governed lifestyles and working relationships. The journal of the Iwakura mission serves as a reminder of the early impressions of Britain and the North East which were formed by the Japanese. It also highlights some aspects of western industry that were not, after all, so very different from those which have since come to be associated with Japan. Great stress was placed, in the chronicle of this important fact-finding tour, on the western capacity for 'cooperation and large-scale coordination of efforts' as well as the 'careful forethought and meticulous planning' with which any task, large or small, was approached.[1] Conversely, while present-day Japanese companies advocate the advantages of non-specialization and flexible work practices, the opposite tendencies in British factory life excited much admiration in 1872: 'Artists make the drawings, wheelwrights make the wheels. Dyers dye, painters paint. There is a fine division of labour and the benefits are numerous. The various talents become increasingly specialized.'[2] Another facet of western industry which gave rise to comment in Kume Kunitake's account was its inherent paternalism:

It is the general practice for factory owners to give protection and assistance to the worker. Accordingly, the government establishes ways of encouraging and relieving the laboring commoner; and it has the responsibility of providing him protection. This protection is an all-important duty with respect to the

wealth and poverty of a nation. Its main purpose is to
encourage and patronize the labor and enterprise of
every man.[3]

In the factories of such leading North East industrialists as Sir William
Armstrong and Bolckow & Vaughan, workers in late-nineteenth-century
England could look forward, if not to lifetime employment, at least to the
strong possibility of regular employment within a single firm for life and a
degree of company paternalism. For the skilled worker, as with today's
Japanese, the long-term commitment of the company to his future was
ultimately determined by the overall success of the enterprise. The
apprenticeship system assumed a long-term relationship with a firm and,
like the Japanese view of training, it provided workers with an education
directly linked to the practices of a particular trade and a particular
company. As the present-day strengths of Japanese industry attract more
and more scrutiny, the memory of such traditional British practices seems to
fade. They should not, however, in the Japanization debate, be forgotten!

Japan's historical links with the North East encompass both technological exchange and cultural assimilation. If Tyneside-built ships helped
Japan to win the Russo-Japanese War and Middlesbrough once served as a
key port for NYK's European Line, such developments were effected by
people, both those who ordered and built the ships and those port
authorities and seamen who handled the traffic. The Japanese industrialists
who come to the North East today can find parallels in the naval and
industrial missions which came to the region so long ago. The lavish
entertaining that once took place at Cragside is now echoed in the dinners
and celebrations surrounding the inward investment process. Feasibility
studies may include tours of factory sites but they also include pilgrimages
into the past. The Nissan party who were taken on a river tour past the old
Elswick shipyard in March 1984 were following in the wake of the Iwakura
mission (1872) and Admiral Togo (1911) who had sailed down the Tyne
before them. They were also ensuring their own place in history. While
earlier visitors had thus observed the main artery through which the
lifeblood of the region flowed, for these latter-day ambassadors from Japan
the river held a different significance.

Each of the region's rivers has its own tale to tell in the story of the North
East's changing relationship with Japan. From naval shipbuilding on the
Tyne to merchant shipbuilding on the Wear, the contact and intercourse
remained steady into the twentieth century. Middlesbrough's links with
Japan were of a special character, given the role played by this northern
port town in NYK's European Line service and the integration of Japanese
seamen into the local community. Able seaman Furihata's instructions to

his family that his ashes be eventually scattered in the Tees symbolizes the intense identification with their adopted homeland which these early residents must have felt. The last of Middlesbrough's seagoing Japanese community, Akiyama Taichi, died in 1986, exactly ninety years after NYK established its connections with the city. It was not known then that Teesport was to win the lucrative contract to export the Nissan cars being built at Sunderland.

There is a sense of coming full circle in these developments. The North East aided Japan's progress towards modernization in the late-nineteenth and early-twentieth centuries. Today, Japanese investment is contributing to the revitalization of a region that followed a very different course in the post-war period. Many of the old shipyards no longer stand but are the sites for new industrial enterprises more in keeping with the times. The Armstrong works and shipyard at Elswick have been razed to make way for a comprehensive business park, the Armstrong Centre, which will incorporate factory units and exhibition and office space – all in the spirit of the great age of the Tyne. Work has already begun on the site of the Walker naval yard at Wallsend. This will be transformed into an Offshore Technology Park. Meanwhile, the old Smith's Dock, the last yard to build ships on the river Tees, has been reincarnated as the Tees Offshore Base, which aims to become the world's leading centre for sub-ocean technology. Another timely riverside scheme will see the old Hylton Colliery yard on the Wear turned into a business park. Initiatives such as these are being carried out under the auspices of two new urban development corporations for Tyne and Wear and Teesside, established in 1987 to inject the region's old and decaying industrial sites with new life. That Japan should be investing heavily in the North East at this stage in the region's industrial history is a sign of renewed faith in its future.

The early associations with North East shipyards have been well recalled since Japan emerged from post-war devastation to assume a leading role in world shipbuilding. It is easy to read irony into the slow collapse of this same industry in the North East. But, Japan, too, now faces a crisis in her heavy industries as shipbuilding and steel production suffer from competition with Korea and Taiwan. 'A relationship reversed?' is too simple an epithet to place on a changing world economy and the changing structure of heavy industry which has had a mutual impact on Japan and the region of Britain to which she once turned for ships.

More than any sense of a shared history, the need to export to survive has brought Japan back to the North East. A deeper irony lies, perhaps, in the circumstances which have brought the automotive industry, via Japan, back into the region that once gave birth to the 'Armstrong car'. Had

Armstrong-Siddeley not retreated to Coventry after the First World War, Nissan might have found a competitor in the subsidiary of its former leading business associate on the Tyne.

The announcement in April 1989 that Fujitsu, the Japanese electronics giant, would be building a £400 million semiconductor plant in County Durham has consolidated Japan's position in the North East. The Fujitsu project represents, next to Nissan's, one of the largest Japanese manufacturing investments in the UK. It brings with it 1500 jobs and the promise of high technology training at a time when the Region is re-evaluating its industrial base.

As old images fade into new, the past offers a perspective on a relationship which has not so much reversed as changed gear. To launch a ship is to complete one phase and embark upon another. Likewise, the future success of Japanese investment in the North East depends upon our mutual willingness to learn from experience and adapt to changing times.

Notes

Chapter 1

1 J.W. Murray quoted in Felix Beato, *Photograhic Views of Old Japan* (1868).
2 W.G. Beasley, *The Modern History of Japan* (1981 edn), p.48.
3 Norman McCord, *North East England, The Region's Development 1760–1960* (1979), pp.41–2.
4 R.W. Johnson, *The Making of the Tyne, A Record of Fifty Years' Progress* (1895), p.235.
5 Nikolaus Pevsner, *The Buildings of England: Northumberland* (1974 edn), p.223.
6 *Newcastle Daily Chronicle and Northern Counties Advertiser*, 27 May 1862
7 The *Times*, 8 May 1862
8 J. MacDonald, 'From Yeddo to London with the Japanese Ambassadors', *Cornhill*, 7 (1863), p.620.
9 Sir Ernest Satow, *A Diplomat in Japan* (1921), p.110.
10 *Illustrated London News*, 19 November 1864.
11 Satow, op.cit., p. 119.
12 Beasley, op.cit., p.112.
13 Sugiyama Shinya, 'Glover & Co.: A British Merchant in Nagasaki, 1861–1870', in Ian Nish (ed.), *Bakumatsu and Meiji Studies in Japan's Economic and Social History* (1982), p.7.
14 Ibid. This was certainly the case with his sales of ships to the Japanese between 1864 and 1867; out of a total of twenty sold during this period, three were supplied to the Bakufu and the rest to Satsuma, Higo and various other domains.
15 Eugene Soviak, 'On the Nature of Western Progress: the Journal of the Iwakura Mission', in D.H. Shively (ed.), *Tradition and Modernization in Japanese Culture* (1971), p.13.
16 *Newcastle Daily Chronicle*, 24 October 1872.
17 Kume Kunitake, *Tokumei Zenken Taishi Bei-O Kairan Jikki* (1878), (1978 edn), pp.252–82.
18 Letter from Armstrong to Stuart Rendel, 27 November 1872, *Rendel Papers*, Tyne and Wear Archives Services (TWAS) 31/1425.
19 Makino Nobuaki, *Kaiso Roku* (1948), quoted in Soviak, op.cit., p.8.
20 Beasley, op.cit., p.147.
21 All statistics relating to *yatoi* taken from H.J. Jones, *Live Machines: Hired Foreigners in Meiji Japan* (1980).
22 Ibid., p.7.

23 Ishizuki Minoru, 'Overseas Study by Japanese in Early Meiji', in A.W. Burks (ed.), *The Modernizers: Overseas Students, Foreign Employees, and Meiji Japan* (1985), p.169

24 Jones, op.cit., p.153.

25 Beasley, op.cit., p.137.

Chapter 2

1 Peter McKenzie, *W.G. Armstrong, A Biography* (1983), p.100.

2 F.T. Jane, *The Imperial Japanese Navy* (1904), p.22.

3 Letter from Major Bridgford to Ordnance Dept., Armstrong Works, 17 July 1882, *Rendel Papers*, TWAS 31/4190.

4 Conway's *All the World's Fighting Ships 1860–1905* (1979), p.216.

5 Minutes of Board Meeting, 4 April 1883, *Armstrong Papers*, TWAS 130/1264.

6 David Dougan, *The Great Gun-Maker* (1970), p.138.

7 Letter from Bridgford to Rendel, 4 December 1883, *Rendel Papers*, TWAS 31/2591.

8 Minutes of Board Meetings, 24 April 1884 and 2 November 1884, *Armstrong Papers*, TWAS 130/1264.

9 Seki Shigetada, *Yushuu*, pp.99–100, and *Newcastle Daily Chronicle*, 19 March 1885.

10 Minutes of Board Meeting, 16 July 1884, *Armstrong Papers*, TWAS 130/1264.

11 Ibid., 30 January 1884 and 4 June 1885. The minutes for 30 January 1884 indicate that, in addition to his usual 2 per cent commission, Bridgford received a further payment, in the case of the Japanese cruisers, to a total of £4000.

12 Conway, op.cit.

1e The *Onlooker*, 2 January 1901, quoted in M. Girouard, *The Victorian Country House* (1971), p.146.

14 Yamanouchi Masuji, *Kaikoroku* (Memories of the Past) (1914).

15 Minutes of Directors' Meeting, 14 September 1893, *Armstrong Papers*, TWAS 130/1265.

16 Ibid., 27 September 1894.

17 Conway, op.cit., p.217.   ·

18 Minutes of Directors' Meeting, 23 May 1895, *Armstrong Papers*, TWAS 130/1265. Noble received his knighthood in 1893.

19 *Evening Chronicle*, 28 February 1896. Armstrong was raised to the peerage in 1886.

20 Minutes of Directors' Meeting, 16 September 1897, *Armstrong Papers*, TWAS 130/1266.

21 Ibid., 25 July 1900.

22 *Newcastle Daily Chronicle*, 28 June 1898, and all other quotes relating to *Hatsuse* launch.

23 Details of Japanese construction engineers and Hawthorn Leslie trainees from Professor Nakagawa Keiichiro, Aoyama Gakuin University.

24 In Science Museum collection, Blandford House, Newcastle upon Tyne, 29–4–1986.

25 Minutes of Managing Committee Meeting, 19 September 1887, *Armstrong Papers*, TWAS 130/1264.

26 J.F. Clarke, *A Century of Service to Engineering and Shipbuilding, A Centenary History of the North East Coast Institution of Engineers and Shipbuilders* (1984), p.5.

27 Details of Japanese members from North East Coast Institution of Engineers and Shipbuilders *Minute Books*, TWAS 1376/2–3.

28 Kita Masami, *Kokusai Nihon o hiraita hitobito: Nihon to Scotland no kizuna* (Links between Japan and Scotland) (1984), p.304, Barr & Stroud became famous for their invention of the range-finder for battleship and field artillery use in 1898.

29 Clarke, op.cit., p.91.

30 Fukasaku Yukiko, 'Technology Imports and R & D at Mitsubishi Nagasaki Shipyard in the Pre-War Period', *Bonner Zeitschrift Für Japanologie*, 8 (1986), p.82.
31 Li Hung-Chang's signature appears in the visitors' book from Andrew Noble's Jesmond Dene House according to Sir Humphrey Noble, *Life in Noble Houses* (1967), p.40.
32 Richard Storry, *A History of Modern Japan* (1975 edn), p.127
33 Conway, op.cit.
34 David Dougan, *The History of North East Shipbuilding* (1968), pp.89–90.
35 quoted in Storry, op.cit., p.139.
36 Japan's military expenditure had risen from the level of 10 million US dollars in 1893 to 65 million dollars in 1900, an increase spent mainly on major additions to the Navy. Noel Busch, *The Emperor's Sword: Japan vs. Russia in the Battle of Tsushima* (1969), p.60.
37 *Newcastle Weekly Chronicle*, 28 April 1906.
38 Busch, op.cit., p.141.
39 Letter from Henry Gladstone to Ordnance Department, Elswick, 19 January 1905, *Rendel Papers*, TWAS 31/3686.
40 All Amie Noble references taken from her unpublished *Memoirs* (1955) with thanks to Mrs Laila Spence.
41 Noble, ibid. Prince Fushimi was later a guest of the Nobles at Jesmond Dene House where his signature appears in the visitors' book. He also stayed with the family at Chillingham Castle according to Lady M.D. Noble, *A Long Life* (1925), p.86.
42 Storry, op.cit., p.142.
43 Letter from Saxton Noble to Lord Rendel, 5 March 1905, *Rendel Papers*, TWAS 31/6975.
44 *Newcastle Weekly Chronicle*, 28 April 1906.
45 Confidential memo by Douglas Vickers, 5 June 1909, *Rendel Papers*, TWAS 31/7773.
46 J.D. Scott, *Vickers, A History* (1962), p.85.
47 R.V.C. Bodley, *Admiral Togo, The Authorized Life* (1935), pp.62–3.
48 Bush, op.cit., p.35.
49 As Captain of the *Naniwa*, he sailed to Hawaii in 1893 to represent Japan's interests during a political crisis which, it was thought, might affect the 20,000 Japanese living in the islands, Bodley, op.cit., p.76.
50 *Newcastle Daily Chronicle*, 20 July 1911.
51 Log Book, HMS *Calliope*, TWAS 1577/2.
52 *Newcastle Daily Chronicle*, 20 July 1911.
53 Ibid., 21 July 1911

Chapter 3
1 *Newcastle Daily Journal*, 27 May 1862.
2 Ibid., Letter to the Editor.
3 *Newcastle Daily Chronicle*, 2 June 1862.
4 McKenzie, W.G. *Armstrong, A Biography*, p.28.
5 *Newcastle Courant*, 24 December 1852.
6 *Illustrated London News*, 20 September 1862.
7 *Newcastle Courant*, 25 October 1872.
8 Ibid.
9 Ibid.
10 *Newcastle Daily Journal*, 27 May 1862.

11 Ibid., 26 October 1872.

12 Ibid., 9 November 1878.

13 Lord Redesdale, *Tales of Old Japan* (1910 edn), pp.283–4.

14 Dougan, *The Great Gun-Maker*, p.165.

15 The *Times*, 6 February 1904, quoted in Jean-Pierre Lehmann, *The Image of Japan: From Feudal Isolation to World Power 1850–1905* (1978), p.149.

16 *Newcastle Weekly Chronicle*, 28 April 1906.

17 Jane, *The Imperial Japanese Navy*, p.178.

18 Wilfred Wilson Gibson, 'A Lyric of Japan', *The English Illustrated Magazine*, 15 (1896), p.385.

19 Kurata Yoshihiro, *1885 Nen London Nihonjin Mura* (1983), pp.24–65.

20 *Newcastle Daily Chronicle*, 18 January 1886 and 1 February 1886.

21 *Programme of Variety Entertainment* in Local Studies Collection, Newcastle City Libraries.

22 Now housed in the Laing Art Gallery, Newcastle upon Tyne.

23 F.T. Jane (ed.), *1905–1906 Jane's Fighting Ships* (1970 edn), p.391.

24 W. Petrie Watson, *The Future of Japan* (1907), p.178.

25 All Quotations from Canon Tristram, *Rambles in Japan: the Land of the Rising Sun* (1895).

26 See Chapter 2, Note 40.

27 Lady M.D. Noble, *A Long Life*, p.95.

28 Interview with M. Rutter, grandson of W. Rutter, October 1986.

29 Petrie Watson, op.cit., p.179.

30 H.G. Wells, *A New Utopia* (1906), p.660.

31 A movement advocating a more disciplined and organized approach to society which would enable Britain to compete in the harsh world of the twentieth century.

Chapter 4

1 Yui Tsunehiko, 'Introduction', in Yui T. and Nakagawa K. (eds), *Business History of Shipping: Strategy and Structure* (1985), p.xv.

2 *Voyage of a Century: Photo Collection of NYK Ships* (1985), p.22.

3 For NYK's history during this period and the establishment of the European Line, I have drawn heavily on the following definitive study: William D. Wray, *Mitsubishi and the NYK 1870–1914* (1984), pp.306–36.

4 Nakagawa K., 'Japanese Shipping in the Nineteenth and Twentieth Centuries: Strategy and Organization', in Yui and Nakagawa (eds), op.cit., p.6.

5 *Voyage of a Century.* p.21.

6 Yui, op.cit., p.xviii.

7 Storry, *A History of Modern Japan*, p.123.

8 Malcolm Trevor, *Japanese Industrial Knowledge: Can it Help British Industry?* (1985), p.2.

9 Nakagawa K., op.cit., p.9.

10 McCord, *North East England, The Region's Development 1760–1960*, p.113.

11 Dougan, *The History of North East Shipbuilding*, p.44.

12 McCord, op.cit., p.53.

13 Ibid., pp.121–2.

14 J.W. House and B. Fullerton, *Tees-side at Mid-Century: An Industrial and Economic Survey* (1960)), p.170.

15 McCord, op.cit., p.128.

16 See Olive Checkland, Kita Masami, 'A.R. Brown (1839–1913): Servant of Japan', *BAJS Proceedings*, 9 (1984), pp.58–61.

17 The *Sharyo Maru* (1862) had orignally been built by Oswald & Co.; the *Shinagawa Maru* (1872) by J. Blumer & Co.; the *Toyoshima Maru* (1873) by Doxfords; and the *Tamaura Maru* (1874) by James Laing.

18 General information and statistics on NYK ship purchases are primarily taken from Kizu Shigetoshi, *A 100 Years' History of the Ships of Nippon Yusen Kaisha* (1985).

19 Wray, op.cit., p.177.

20 *Voyage of a Century*, pp. 15 and 37.

21 These include the *Matsuyama Maru* (1885) and *Yamaguchi Maru* (1890) by J.L. Thompson of Sunderland; *Otaru Maru* (1886) and *Ryojun Maru* (1892) by R.W. Hawthorn Leslie of Newcastle; *Kokura Maru* (1887) and *Kinshu Maru* (1891) by Sir Raylton Dixon of Middlesbrough; *Himeji Maru* (1888) by Palmer's of Jarrow and *Kagoshima Maru* (1891) by William Dobson & Co. of Newcastle.

22 Wray, op.cit., p.374

23 These included the *Jinsen Maru* (1895) and *Kitsurin Maru* (1895) built by Sir Raylton Dixon of Middlesbrough; the *Colombo Maru* (1901) built by R. Craggs & Son of Middlesbrough; the *Tiensin Maru* (1894) by James Laing, *Mikawa Maru* (1894) by Bartram Haswell & Co. and *Totomi Maru* (1901) by S.P. Austin & Sons, all Sunderland yards; and the *Urajio Maru* (1890) by Schlesinger Davies of Newcastle.

24 These included the *Saishu Maru* (1897) (previously the *Rossija*) built by J. Priestman & Co. of Sunderland; the *Eboshi Maru* (1901) built by William Gray & Co. of Hartlepool; and the *Moyori Maru* (1902) built by Craig Taylor & Co. of Stockton.

25 *Sunderland Herald*, 5 November 1896

26 *Sunderland Daily Echo*, 5 June 1897.

27 *Sunderland Herald*, 25 April 1898.

28 Ibid., 8 July 1898.

29 Ibid., 3 December 1888.

30 Sugiyama Shinya, 'Glover & Co.: A British Merchant in Nagasaki, 1861–1870', in Ian Nish (ed.), *Bakumatsu and Meiji Studies in Japan's Economic and Social History*, p.12.

31 As documented in the Parsons' Marine Steam Turbine Company Data Sheets, TWAS 1361/7.

32 Fukasaku Yukiko, 'Technology Imports and R & D at Mitsubishi Nagasaki Shipyard in the Pre-War Period', *Bonner Zeitschrift Für Japanologie*, p.82.

33 For statistics on Japan's industrial growth during the First World War, see Beasley, *The Modern History of Japan*, pp.215–16.

Chapter 5

1 Quoted in Dougan, *The History of North East Shipbuilding*, p.132.

2 Ibid., p.136.

3 McCord, *North East England, The Region's Development 1760–1960*, p.218.

4 Beasley, *The Modern History of Japan*, p.229.

5 Ian H. Nish, *The Anglo-Japanese Alliance: The Diplomacy of Two Island Empires 1894–1907* (1985 edn), p.2.

6 Minutes of Directors' Meeting, 25 May 1911, *Armstrong Papers*, TWAS 130/1268.

7 TWAS 2001/3/2.

8 Minutes of Directors' Meeting, 20 February 1913, *Armstrong Papers*, TWAS 130/1269.

9 Ibid., 15 February 1912.
10 Scott, *Vickers, A History*, p.146.
11 Minutes of North East Coast Institution of Engineers and Shipbuilders, 1918–33, TWAS 1376/4–5.
12 See Elswick Shipyard visitors' book, 1920–4, TWAS 130/1578.
13 As reported in the Tokyo *Asahi Shimbun*, 18 January 1922.
14 Agawa Hiroyuki, *The Reluctant Admiral: Yamamoto and the Imperial Japanese Navy* (1986 edn), p.75.
15 McCord, op.cit., p.221.
16 NYK Company Records.
17 Oral History Records, Cleveland County Archives, Accession Number 104, and *North Eastern Daily Gazette*, 28 December 1906.
18 Details of Middlesbrough's Japanese community have been primarily gathered from family papers and interviews with Tommy Doi, Tamako Akiyama, Roy Betsho, Diane Furihata, Francis and Robert Ikeshita, Peggy Lancaster and Taichi Akiyama, the last of Middlesbrough's Japanese.
19 Alan T. Moriyama, *Imingaisha: Japanese Emigration Companies and Hawaii 1894–1908* (1985), p.13.
20 *Northern Echo*, 20 May 1932.
21 Cleveland Products *Company Newsletter*.
22 Connery Chappell, *Island of Barbed Wire: Internment on the Isle of Man in World War II* (1984), pp.142–3.
23 *Newcastle Journal and Northern Mail*, 9 December 1941.
24 Ibid., 11 March 1942.
25 *Evening Chronicle*, 8 October 1945.
26 Ibid., 18 November 1945.
27 Dougan, *The History of North East Shipbuilding*, p.192.
28 quoted in ibid., p.197.
29 *Newcastle Journal*, 1 May 1953.
30 quoted in *Evening Chronicle*, 4 May 1953.
31 *Newcastle Journal*, 11 May 1953.
32 Ibid., 12 May 1953.
33 *Japan Society Bulletin*, June 1953, p.12.

Chapter 6

1 Beasley, *The Modern History of Japan*, pp.304–5. Statistics and general interpretation of Japanese trade developments from this period are reliant on this same source.
2 Endymion Wilkinson, *Japan Versus Europe: A History of Misunderstanding* (1983), p.170.
3 Financial Times, 24 January 1974.
4 Ibid.
5 *Evening Chronicle*, 6 June 1974.
6 Robert Whymant, 'Japan Fears Put Big North East Factory Plan in Jeopardy', The *Guardian*, 28 April 1974.
7 Northern Development Company (NDC) Seminar at Keidanren headquarters, Tokyo, October 1987. In 1986, the NEDC was absorbed into the NDC.
8 Dougan, *The History of North East Shipbuilding*, pp.205–11, for general statistics on post-war decline of shipbuilding.

9 Ibid.
10 The *Times*, 30 July 1982.
11 Stephen Holly, *Washington: Quicker by Quango. The History of Washington New Town 1964–1983* (1983), pp.49–50.
12 The *Daily Telegraph*, 30 January 1981.
13 The *Financial Times*, 8 April 1981.
14 The *Journal*, 25 April 1981.
15 The *Financial Times*, 21 April 1981.
16 *Evening Gazette*, 14 May 1981.
17 The *Financial Times*, 29 May 1981.
18 *Northern Echo*, 17 July 1981.
19 *Hartlepool Mail*, 18 September 1981.
20 The *Daily Telegraph*, 21 August 1982.
21 Ibid.
22 *Sunderland Echo*, 27 February 1984.
23 Ibid., 2 April 1984.
24 Ibid.
25 The *Financial Times*, 31 March 1984.
26 Peter Wickens, *The Road to Nissan: Flexibility Quality Teamwork* (1987), pp.175–6.
27 Ibid.
28 M. Halsall, 'Far East Hope for the North East', The *Guardian*, 23 October 1985.
29 The *Journal*, 18 July 1987.
30 Dr Clive Morton, Director of Personnel and Administration at Komatsu UK.
31 Higaki Osamu, quoted in the *Journal*, 23 April 1986.

Chapter 7
1 quoted in the *Journal*, 23 October 1987.
2 *Sunderland Echo*, 16 March 1988.
3 Brian Unwin, 'Jobs and the Call of the Wild', the *Journal*, 6 August 1987.
4 *Sunderland Echo*, 21 December 1987.
5 Three of these are in London.

Conclusion
1 Soviak, 'On the Nature of Western Progress: the Journal of the Iwakura Mission', in D.H. Shively (ed.), *Tradition and Modernization in Japanese Culture*, pp.20–21.
2 Ibid.
3 Ibid. p.22.

Select Bibliography

Anthony, D.W. and Healey, G.H., *The Itinerary of the Iwakura Mission*, University of Sheffield Centre for Japanese Studies, Occasional Papers 1 (1987).

Armstrong Papers, Tyne and Wear Archives Service.

Beasley, W.G., *The Modern History of Japan* (1981 edn).

Boxall, Michael (ed.), *Warships of the Imperial Japanese Navy* (1986 edn).

Clarke, J.F., *Power on Land and Sea: 160 Years of Industrial Enterprise on Tyneside* (1980).

Dougan, David, *The History of North East Shipbuilding* (1968).

Dougan, David, *The Great Gun-Maker* (1970).

House, J.W. and Fullerton, B., *Tees-side at Mid-Century: An Industrial and Economic Survey* (1960).

House, J.W., *The North East* (1969).

Jane, F.T., *The Imperial Japanese Navy* (1904).

Jones, H.J., *Live Machines: Hired Foreigners in Meiji Japan* (1980).

Lehmann, Jean-Pierre, *The Image of Japan: From Feudal Isolation to World Power 1850–1905* (1978).

McKenzie, Peter, *W.G. Armstrong, A Biography* (1983).

McCord, Norman, *North East England, The Region's Development 1760–1960* (1979).

Nish, Ian (ed.), *Bakumatsu and Meiji: Studies in Japan's Economic and Social History* (1982).

NYK, *A 100 Years' History of the Ships of Nippon Yusen Kaisha* (1985).

Rendel Papers, Tyne and Wear Archives Service.

Scott, J.D., *Vickers, A History* (1962).

Storry, Richard, *A History of Modern Japan* (1975 edn).

Trevor, Malcolm, *Japanese Industrial Knowledge: Can It Help British Industry?* (1985).

Walder, David, *The Short Victorious War, The Russo-Japanese Conflict 1904–05* (1973).

Wickens, Peter, *The Road to Nissan: Flexibility and Quality Teamwork* (1987).

Wilkinson, Endymion, *Japan Versus Europe: A History of Misunderstanding* (1983).

Wray, William D., *Mitsubishi and the NYK 1870–1914* (1984).

Yui, T. and Nakagawa, K. (eds), *Business History of Shipping: Strategy and Structure* (1985).

Many North East and national newspapers contain coverage of Japanese visits, ship launches, and investment in the North East. These are fully referred to in the Notes.

Index